Mother Rabbit

Mother Rabbit

by

Tekla Dennison Miller

Oak Tree Press Hanford, CA

Oak Tree Press
Publishers Since 1998

For information, address Oak Tree Press, 1820 W. Lacey Boulevard, Suite 220, Hanford, CA 93230.

Oak Tree Press books may be purchased for educational, business, or sales promotional purposes. Contact Publisher for quantity discounts.

First Edition, July 2014

ISBN 978-1-61009-091-9
LCCN 2014937566

For my sister Alyce Bonura

Acknowledgments

Foremost I want to thank my husband Chet who has always supported my adventures and endeavors no matter how crazy they are.

I would never have been a published writer without the instruction and encouragement from three dear friends and writers with whom I have been meeting for 15 years. Thank you, Elizabeth, Joan and Joyce.

I am also delighted to work with the helpful and congenial staff at OTP.

August 1967

The afternoon thunderstorm that swept through Miami left no
relief from the humidity which clung to my body like a wet bathing
suit. A limousine had dropped my older sister Alyce, a Playboy
Bunny Mother, and me, a U.C.L.A. senior, at the terminal moments
before the summer downpour. As she and I waited at the airport for
the Playmate of the Year, the heavy air laden with a pungent mixture
of ozone, sweat and diesel fuel, wafted across the tarmac. It wasn't
exactly the scent I'd imagined for my college vacation in the subtrop-
ics.

A mass of eager reporters and photographers teemed around
Alyce, nearly pushing her aside as they rushed to the waiting area.
The all-male media appeared hungrier for a peek into a Playmate's
lifestyle than for an interview with the one who managed the Bunnies. Did they wonder as I had whether Miss January would wear a
conservative traveling suit or a cleavage-exposing mini-dress in the
latest 1960's style?

The plane carrying the beauty taxied to the gate. A hush fell over
the audience. As the stairs were rolled in place, the photographers
made last minute checks of their equipment. The plane's door was
flung wide. Cameras were raised. Pencils poised over note pads.

Suddenly a tall, willowy, auburn-haired woman filled the doorway. She paused, giving everyone ample time to appreciate her entire form. Flashbulbs popped from every part of the waiting area. The Playmate of the Year descended the stairs with as much pomp and dignity as an ambassador from another country. To my amazement her ensemble didn't reveal her true mission. She wore a deep rose-colored, tailored silk suit with a silk shell beneath. The long, fitted jacket was held closed by a single pearl button at her waist and cleaved to every curve. Each graceful step exposed her slender legs. The Playmate walked without toppling forward in her three-inch heel, pointed-toe shoes. I wondered whether the photographers were disappointed because she looked more like a Vogue model than a titillating center-fold.

"Oh my," Alyce whispered.

"She's that impressive?" I asked.

"No. Her breasts have grown."

I covered my mouth to muffle a laugh. "What?" I asked through my fingers.

Alyce leaned closer to me. "When her picture was taken for the Playboy centerfold, she had to lie on her stomach because her breasts were too small for the image the magazine wants. But Hef was so captivated by her overall good looks he forfeited the large breasts."

"So what are you saying?"

"She's had implants. Her breasts have more than tripled in size."

So this is what Playboy calls natural beauty, I wondered to myself. Poking fun at this unrealistic world felt good.

"Not exactly the girl next door, I'm afraid," Alyce added.

We both laughed, then Alyce composed herself so she could fulfill the rest of her duties. The Playmate strutted through the door into the waiting area. Cameras again flashed. Alyce advanced to welcome Miss January and handed her a dozen long-stem American Beauty roses, petals drooping from the heat.

As I looked at the two of them standing together, I decided that Alyce, ever graceful and demure, truly represented the American beauty. Her classic, elegantly understated royal blue suit hugged her body in a feminine, not provocative way. Her natural red hair radiated health and flowed freely from under her ever-present hat, while the Playmate's locks were glued together in heavily lacquered mass of auburn straw forced into a French twist and further confused by a fashionable hairpiece.

While reporters interviewed the Playmate, a photographer cozied up to Alyce.

"Are you the runner-up?" he asked.

"No." Alyce shook her head. "The boss."

She led the Playmate of the Year away to make the rounds of luncheons, dinners and cocktail parties.

The reporter gazed after them. Did he think the same as I? Alyce was special because there was only one Bunny Mother and so many Bunnies? It's human nature to want to conquer what appears to be out of reach. The boss would be a fine catch.

That evening, as Alyce and I sat overlooking the ocean and sipping wine, my sister began telling me about her time with Playboy, Inc.

Chapter One

Moving Up

Ever since urban men of good taste first recognized PLAYBOY as a magazine with a point of view like their own, the PLAYBOY CLUB became a natural to project the plush and romantic mood of the nation's most sophisticated publication. Playboy Club Bunny Manual/1963

I folded the last of my blouses and patted it into the suitcase that once had belonged to my mother. It had been a fast and often distressing 10 years since Mom committed suicide in 1956. I had just turned twenty-three then. Three years later this suitcase became the only item I could retrieve when I escaped a tumultuous marriage early one steamy July morning. I fled from upstate New York with my two sons and Tekkie, my fifteen-year-old sister and ward. We finally settled in Los Angeles. Now again in July, I was headed for yet another city to start over for the second time.

The sun crested the horizon as I loaded my two suitcases into the old station wagon that had made my first escape possible.

"I guess that's it."

Despite my need to be strong for my children, I couldn't hold back a noticeable quiver in my voice. I gained enough composure to tightly hug my sons, Carl, age 14, and Greg, age 11.

"I'll see you in Chicago."

I forced a smile but my eyes moistened. The boys only sniffled in reply. My smile changed to a half frown, half grin as I turned to my sister.

"Well, Tekkie, it's time to head to the airport."

I walked slowly to the car and compelled myself to slide into the passenger seat. I didn't think I had the emotional strength to drive.

As we drove away from the house, one of five homes we'd lived in during the past seven years, I questioned my reasons for leaving. Not only had I given up a good job as an office manager of a prosperous company, I was once again uprooting my sons. I was also running from a man just as I had with my first move across country, but not because of overt abuse this time. My current man had been the love of my life, my soul mate for the last four years, but Clark Greenberg had stayed married. Though he claimed to love me, he didn't seem to have plans to leave his wife and only child. Clark's refusal felt like another form of abuse, but I shuttered that thought refusing to think of Angelo.

I swiped a tear from my cheek before Tekkie took note. I was determined not to dwell on the situation with Clark, but rather look forward to my next stop on life's challenging road. As the Bunny Mother of the Chicago Playboy Club, at Playboy, Inc. headquarters, I could easily move up the corporate career ladder. After my interviews, I received a letter from Barry Fleishman, Chicago Playboy Club's General Manager, which offered me the job and practically promised me the Bunny Director's position if I performed as well as he expected. After all, hadn't I already managed the Roaring Twenties Club? I'd worked at both the club and as an office manager simultaneously to get the monthly bills paid. How hard could this new job be?

Tekkie parked the car at the loading zone. I turned to her. "I can't stay here long because I'm afraid I'll change my mind and not go at all, no matter how convincing I know that my own arguments have been."

We both got out of the car. I hugged Tekkie. "I miss you and the boys already. I wish Carl and Greg were going with me."

But I would have too much to do my first days in Chicago to take Carl and Greg along. First I had to find a rental that took children and a German shepherd and for only a small deposit. Nearly broke, lack of money gave me the major reason to take the job at Playboy. The pay and benefits were good, especially if a promotion appeared already in the works. Yet that familiar starting over reminded me of a similar undertaking years earlier when I had reached L.A. with only $60.00. I didn't have much more than that now and I was tired of living from paycheck to paycheck.

When I released Tekkie, I gave her final instructions about Carl and Greg and hurried into the airport terminal. As the lobby door closed, I called out, "Love you. See you at Christmas."

I waved with as much grace as I could manage, and then laid my hand on my mouth. Tekkie and I held each other's gaze for several moments, then I turned and joined the crowd sweeping along the concourse to the gates.

Once checked in, I headed to the ladies' room where I examined myself in the bathroom mirror. I hoped the special attention I had given to my appearance that morning would pay off. So far, so good. My hair, a deep natural red, flipped just at the perfect spot near my shoulders in the latest style. I'd purposely chosen a professional-looking emerald green suit with a matching hat, which accented my coloring and enhanced my hazel eyes. Wondering if I picked the right shoes and purse, I shrugged. Too late, if not.

When I heard my plane announced, I slid my gloves back on and glanced once again in the mirror. I had to look better than ever when Barry Fleishman met my plane. Image was the most important characteristic in the Playboy world. But my nose. What would Mr. Fleishman think of my nose? Frankly it was too big, after all, and I doubted it met the "Bunny Image." Fleishman hadn't interviewed me; Shar Young, the Bunny Director, had and in Los Angeles, not in Chicago. Though others never mentioned my nose as a detriment, Angelo had made nasty comments about its size all throughout our turbulent marriage. Those remarks stuck with me and fueled my self-consciousness. And Shar had warned me about Fleishman's high expectations. Would he see what Angelo had?

"Oh well. Can't switch anything now, can I?"

Once buckled into my seat, a great weight seemed to press me down. Was I feeling guilty or depressed or a little of both? What kind of mother was I, to leave my sons like this? Sure, it was only for a short time. Sure, Tekkie was reliable. But doubts clamored for attention.

What about my motives? I was heading to work in an environment where the most important aspects of a young woman were her weight, the size of her breasts and the shape of her legs. That flew in the face of Betty Friedan's fight for equal rights for women, especially the right not to be treated as sexual objects. My own sister had no problem sharing her concern about my taking a job in Hugh Hefner's frivolous, male-dominated domain while men were dying in Viet Nam. How could I indeed?

The captain announced the plane's take off. I squeezed the arms of my seat so hard my knuckles turned white. The plane bumped down the tarmac faster and faster until soon it was aloft. After an hour, finally lulled by the constant hum of the engines, I loosened my grip. I had almost given into the idea that I absolutely did the right thing to move to Chicago when a momentary turbulence caused a sudden drop in altitude, which brought the contents of my stomach straight up to my throat. As I gulped it back down, I grasped the seat arms again and recalled the sullen faces of my two sons huddled together in front of our rented white stucco house on Plymouth Blvd. What did I hope for in this move? What did I want? My desire seemed simple enough. Happiness and stability for the boys, Tekkie and me. I hoped Chicago held all this for our future.

To be honest, I had to admit the glamour connected with Playboy also seduced me. Yet the one thing I'd learned over the past years crept into my thoughts and dispelled any fantasy I had about my future. Life's experiences seemed to tumble round and round like clothes in a washing machine only to end in the same jumbled pile I started with.

And Clark Greenburg? How had he managed to slip into that confused mess? I loved Clark, married or not. In fact, I most likely loved him too much—I already missed him almost as much as my own sons. Certainly there could never be another man to take his place.

I had met Clark five years ago. To pay the monthly bills, I was working a second job as a cocktail waitress at Kelly's Steak House in West Hollywood. He and his best friend, Bruce, frequented the bar, but rarely the restaurant.

I couldn't imagine why Clark attracted my attention from the start. On the short side— my height exactly, 5'9"—he was no Mr. America. In fact, he could lose weight. Yet he was bright, charming, soft-spoken and a lawyer. Besides the ever-present smile that lit his eyes, and besides his well-timed compliments, he always had an ear to hear about all of my many ordeals, as I managed my life as a single mother in a married world.

At first I hired Clark as my attorney to help clean up loose ends in my divorce and custody issues with Angelo, whom I then still feared. It took little time for our relationship to deepen. Soon it seemed we were destined for a torrid love affair. Unlike Angelo, Clark only saw my good points and encouraged me to be whatever I wanted. "You sound like my mother," I once told him. Clark chuckled and said, "I know a good thing when I see it and you're too smart to spend your life waiting tables or typing."

By the time Clark decided to tell me about his wife and child, I was entrenched in the relationship. Until then I had been sure we'd get married. I had after all given up a couple of years to the man. When he finally broke the stinging news, I still stuck out the affair thinking Clark would take the leap and leave his wife about whom he said, "She doesn't understand me and she lost any desire for sex after our son's birth."

Looking back, had Clark ever really promised to leave his wife? Few men do part from their wives to be with their mistresses. Why should they when they have the best of both worlds? Against all rational argument, the affair continued another three years. Then one night as I debated taking the Playboy job, Clark once again tried to justify his position. He said he loved both his wife and me. I was the only romantic love of his life while his wife, also his high school sweetheart, was the mother of his child. How could he dump her now after so many years, especially when she had no way to support herself? I fumed. I imagined the heat burning my face to the same deep red as my hair.

"You mean to tell me she can't type for a living? I have."

When he attempted a response, I held up my hand to stop him and said, "I understand."

Clark's face brightened.

"Your wife's your wife and she's Jewish like you and unemployed and I'm not. I bring excitement into your life. You want both."

Clark actually nodded in agreement.

"What about my life?" I asked.

Clark tried to weasel his way out of the problem by professing his love for me. We were soul mates, he said, made for each other.

My answer? "I'm moving to Chicago."

So why was Clark furious when I reminded him that my decision to leave fulfilled that dream he had encouraged me to snag? A dream I hoped would lead to a management career and enough time and money to go back to college. Clearly Clark couldn't have the two women and their diverse worlds if I settled in another state.

First Angelo, then Clark. I always seemed to get myself into negative relationships. But things were going to be different. I was taking the first step at this moment. "Men."

"What?" the man seated to my right asked.

I had forgotten about the other passengers. Had I said other things out loud?

"Oh, nothing. I was just. . .nothing."

It was a relief when the stewardess announced the plane's descent into O'Hare. I had been so deep in thought the flight went much faster than I had expected. I hardly had a chance to finish my coffee and snack. And I didn't have to talk with my seat partner. Now I only had to get through my first encounter with the General Manager of the Chicago Playboy Club. I should have had a drink.

I stayed in my seat until most of the passengers had disembarked, then I inhaled one last deep breath before gathering the courage to face the inevitable. Could I meet Barry Fleishman's standards? I'd know soon.

I walked from the plane through heat that could melt the soles of my shoes and gratefully entered the frigid air of the terminal's waiting area. The contrast between the two climates made me think about my own life's discrepancies. In the mid 1950's I had fled from an unhappy and threatening marriage in a time when my Catholic upbringing and town forbad such an independent move. In those days, a woman was supposed to know her place. Soon I'd enter a male-dominated world where men were gratified by the women who supposedly accepted their roles as sexual objects, the very role which I thought I had escaped by leaving Angelo.

I quickly shoved those thoughts aside and scanned the crowd for any clue as to who might be Barry Fleishman. Someone shouted, "Alyce." A woman was shaking a pink hanky in the air. I blinked. Then, I recognized Shar Young.

"So good to see you," Shar said once she made it through the throng. She brushed her lips lightly against both my cheeks like a French woman or a Hollywood starlet.

The scent of Shar's White Shoulders stung my nose and made it twitch. I made a note not to wear my favorite fragrance anymore. "I thought –"

Shar interrupted, "Barry sent me. He had other commitments. He'll see you at the Club tomorrow."

Chattering nonstop, she ushered me to the baggage area.

"The Bunnies really liked Coco Loveland. You know, the girl you're replacing. But between you and me, Coco gave into their every whim. They got away with murder. That won't make your job easier. Anyway she's out of the picture for a while, though the girls do have her home phone number."

Shar stopped her prattle just long enough to push the door open to the baggage claim area and take a deep breath. She turned to me.

"Baggage isn't here yet."

Without missing a beat went on with her monolog.

"You do know, Coco is having a baby, her third, or maybe fourth. Oh, don't be startled." Shar shook her head. She leaned closer and whispered, "She terminated the others. This time she said she had enough of the boys, especially married ones, who kiss and run. She's keeping this baby, single mom or not."

I felt as though I had been hit over the head. I had already been aware that most newly hired Bunny Mothers worked at smaller Clubs. "We train 'em or I should say the Bunny Mother trains 'em, then we ship 'em," Shar had announced when we met at the interview, then she'd gone on to explain that my hire for Chicago was an exception because of my administrative and restaurant experience. But maybe I might just be the hurried replacement for Coco. Hurried, and temporary?

The luggage carousel hummed to life.

Already the woman's manic conversation exhausted me. How could Shar give up all this information about Coco as if it were everyday news? Shar was puzzling to me. Her fast New York-accented clip seemed to belie her painstaking imitation of Jackie Kennedy, right down to the pill-box hat. Yet Shar's extra flair would make the former First Lady look drab. The question of manners aside, I did envy

Shar's impeccably sculpted face, high cheekbones and huge lapis colored eyes, but I especially admired her cute nose. Had she had it fixed? I raised my gloved hand to my own nose. Though nearly the same age, I suddenly felt like Shar's mother.

I grabbed my two bags and followed behind Shar who made no offer to help. Struggling to keep up, I caught the continued rendition of life with Coco Loveland.

"Coco," Shar said as she pointed toward the exit we were to take, "is a sweet girl, but messed up."

I nodded but asked, "How could she let herself get into such a mess?"

"Oh, that's nothing," Shar laughed heartily. "Most Bunnies are either pregnant or getting it fixed. Get used to it. You'll fill your days with their tales of woe."

Shar laid the back of her hand against her forehead for dramatic emphasis. I acknowledged her theatrical pose with a weak smile. As Shar opened the door to the parking lot, she confided, "No one is supposed to know that there are such goings-on, but everyone does. It's daily gossip who's dating who, who got knocked up and who's getting an abortion. Welcome to the world of Playboy."

I stood on the curb, barely able to hang onto my heavy bags any longer. What was I getting into? I started to step off the walk and head to the parking lot when a limousine pulled up. A chauffeur hopped out, took my luggage and opened the door. Why hadn't he helped carry the damn things from the carousel?

I plopped into the back seat as Shar glided into the car. Once inside, Shar confined her comments to pointing out Chicago landmarks.

Despite my frustration with this chatty woman, I couldn't help but admire Shar. Not a beautiful woman, Shar still had a knack at playing up her assets right down to her model-thin body. From conversations with employees at the L.A. Club, I knew, though, that Shar had been married twice before. Each divorce had left her with enough money to maintain her expensive wardrobe and lakeshore apartment. Yet Shar's impeccable bearing and folksy conversation seemed incongruent to the back-stabbing bitch from the other side of the tracks I had heard about from the Bunnies at the L.A. Club. Shar still hunted for Mr. Right, preferably wealthy and without children. During my brief encounter with her in L.A. she made it clear that her employment with Playboy provided the best way to fulfill her plan. She wouldn't stand for anything getting in her way and had little care about the people she bulldozed to get there. So I had to be sure to stay on her good side and well out of her reach.

The limousine parked in front of the Sheraton Hotel. Playboy, Inc. had agreed to pay one month's hotel costs to allow me time to find a place to live. The chauffeur jumped out, opened my door and helped the bell hop retrieve my luggage. As I climbed onto the sidewalk and into the steamy air of downtown, Shar rolled down her window and gestured toward the building with a cheerful, "Home for the next few weeks. You're on your own until tomorrow morning."

The chauffeur returned to the driver's seat.

Shar waved, "See ya."

Suddenly I was alone. I followed the bellhop to the reservation desk through a huge throng of lively teenagers, most of whom were overly made-up girls. When I checked in, I discovered the popular Dave Clark Five band was also staying at the hotel. The groupies probably were hoping for a glimpse, perhaps autographs and maybe even a one-night stand.

If sharing the hotel with hundreds of hyper-active teens weren't bad enough, the imaginative desk clerk seemed to be carefully scrutinizing me. He had noted my reservation card said Playboy and seemed confused by my "single room" request. Through the clerk's careful questioning I discovered a gentleman with a last name similar to mine had checked in earlier asking about another man with whom he was to room. The clerk apparently made the assumption that a Playmate had been sent and the male roommate had been a ploy.

Once I straightened out the mistake, I thankfully locked myself in the quiet of my room. I sat in the only chair and opened the unsealed telegram from Clark the clerk had given me, which also had probably fueled the clerk's fantasy. "Remember you are not alone," Clark wrote. "My love and thoughts are with you." I didn't want his thoughts with me. I'd rather have him.

Chapter Two

First Day

A Bunny Mother is stationed at every Playboy Club to coordinate and supervise the work of the Bunnies. She will schedule your hours and assign your stations. Her position is similar to that of a college advisor and you will find her a trusted and unofficial confidante.
Playboy Club Bunny Manual/1963

In the morning I walked the four blocks from the hotel to the Playboy Club. I needed to conserve every nickel until my first pay-check. I had little hope child support payments would catch up with my move, if they ever did. Angelo, my ex-husband hadn't been all that dependable in the past and if he discovered my new job, he might not pay ever again.

Despite these thoughts, I enjoyed the early morning coolness, knowing that by noon temperatures would reach the 90's with humidity to match. My pleasure dissolved all too soon when I caught a glimpse of my reflection in the passing windows, which reminded me of the reality of my new life. My administrative abilities would not be enough. I needed money for more than shelter and food for my sons and me. In order to survive as a Playboy manager I had to keep my appearance perfect. My clothes, hair and make-up would have to be as in-style and up-to-date as Shar's. Tough demands, given my immediate finances.

Mulling over my situation, I turned the corner onto East Walton Street. If the Playboy's rabbit logo hadn't been etched in the awning over the entrance, no one would have guessed the narrow five-story modern concrete building housed the infamous Playboy Club.

"Well, here I am, ready or not."

I pulled the heavy wooden door open and entered an empty and windowless lobby. A panel of television screens replaced the windows, giving a glimpse of the activities inside the Chicago Club as well as other Clubs in distant cities.

I took the elevator to the fifth floor, which housed the office and also the Playroom, one of five lounges in the Club. As the elevator passed each floor, a button lit identifying what lay behind the doors: second floor—Living Room, third floor—V.I.P. (Very Important Playboy) Room, the fourth floor—Penthouse and finally the Playroom. When I left the secure confines of the elevator I came face to face with a voluptuous young woman who asked, "Are you a new Bunny?"

Before I could respond, Shar appeared and answered, "Oh no, doll, this is your new boss."

The girl's eyebrows rose. "Oh, wow."

I interpreted her surprise as a compliment and felt my self-assurance strengthen. Then I got a good look at Shar who was dressed in the latest pearl-colored chemise with hose and shoes to match. She had set off the entire ensemble with a brilliant red floral scarf. When she studied me from my now humidity-frizzed hair to my dated shoes, Shar tisked without shame. I immediately felt as stylish as Betty Crocker.

"That shirtwaist dress has got to go," Shar announced. "We'll have to work on your image. Ya know, image is everything here at Playboy." Shar's hands, nails manicured in the newest pink, moved about with every word, but not for emphasis. Apparently Shar wanted to be sure her three large diamond rings would not be missed. Remnants from her marriages perhaps.

The image was spoiled, though, by Shar's gravelly voice and her course demeanor. Something told me she was no stranger to alcohol, and I wondered if she would light her next cigarette off the end of the last one. Shar must have forgotten that the image she referred to also included a positive attitude and proper articulation.

"Well, kiddo, here's your office." Shar shoved a door wide and exposed a small cluttered space furnished with what could be kind to describe as furniture for a bag lady. As with most restaurants and similar establishments, the decorating money was not wasted on employees in the back rooms. The glamour would only be found in the key holder's entertainment areas.

I fingered some sample yardage for Bunny costumes as I passed by a hunter green loveseat stained dark with oily head-sized patches. When I approached the undersized desk badly in need of a new finish my mood went from the normal first-day anxiety to questioning why I had taken the job at all. I shoved away someone's lipstick-smudged makeup bag left near what I assumed would be my typewriter. My forceful gesture caused the bag's contents to spill to the floor. Unable to hide my disillusionment, I kicked the mess aside and flopped into the desk chair, which nearly toppled me backward. I grabbed the desk to steady myself. The chair's back spring had sprung.

I could feel tears welling up as I recalled the far more elegant office I had left behind at the L.A. manufacturing company. I had expected my new office would at least be as nice as the Bunny Mother's at the L.A. Club.

I almost lost the battle to my tears when I opened the drapes behind my desk. Instead of the Chicago skyline I had hoped to see, I looked at the brick wall of the building next door and then to the trash-strewn alley below. California blue skies and palm trees flashed into my memory. "Can you ever see the sun?"

"Soon you'll be too busy to notice the bad parts," Shar lit a cigarette. "And we can try to squeeze some money from the budget or rather, from Barry to get some upgrading."

She blew smoke in perfect little rings.

"Speaking of Barry, let's give you the tour of the place and introduce you to what staff that's on duty now. A full meeting will take place later today and you'll meet the majority of the Hutch employees then."

"Hutch?"

"Yeah. That's what we call our little home—the Hutch."

Shar's smile was proud. She headed for the door, but turned to face me. "Don't let the Bunnies scare you off. They want Coco back and to them no one can take her place. You got big shoes to fill, kiddo, and the Bunnies won't make that easy. Besides you're an outsider, aren't you?"

Did I detect a slight smirk?

"Is Coco coming back?" My voice cracked.

That would mean I'd only be Bunny Mother for a few months

while Coco was on maternity leave. And since Shar seemed confident in her position as Bunny Director, where would I go?

"Probably, in some capacity. Coco doesn't want to give up working just yet." Shar crushed out her cigarette in the ashtray on the table near the door.

Though my confidence was diminished, I remained determined to make the best of my new job. I honestly didn't think Playboy would go through all the expense to hire and train me as Bunny Mother for just a temporary position. The management could have had someone local fill in until Coco returned. Maybe management planned to ship me off to another Club, which I didn't want because it would be less pay or, in the case of New York, a higher cost of living. I certainly couldn't afford that.

I took a deep breath, stood as erect as I could to hide my disillusionment and prepared for my Club tour. We headed for the Hutch an awkward pair with me trying to shorten my long stride to match Shar's surprisingly graceless and choppy steps. I decided to wait and see what the next few weeks brought before I jumped to any conclusions. Once in the hallway, I pointed to the rabbit logo on the wall and asked, "How did Mr. Hefner come up with this idea?"

"It really wasn't Hef who got the brainstorm, although he had to approve it as he does everything. He's very hands-on, ya know." Shar looked at me as though expecting a comment.

I knew Shar would never address Hugh Hefner to his face as Hef and had to be careful who heard her. "But the rabbit head?" I asked again.

"That was Art Paul's creation. He's the magazine's art director." Shar started down the hall. "We call it the Big Bunny, by the way."

I stayed put. "But you still haven't told me why he used such a logo."

Shar frowned at me as though I was a pesky child asking too many questions. "Mr. Paul once said he selected a rabbit as the symbol for the magazine because of the humorous sexual connotation and because the rabbit offered an image that was frisky and playful. He dressed him in a tuxedo to add the idea of sophistication and charm. The rest is history, as they say."

She shrugged and then motioned to me. "Let's get this tour over so we can get down to the real work of training you. I can use the help."

We descended the stairs to the main level. "Might as well start at the entrance." As Shar pointed out a large board to the right, headed *At the Club Tonight,* she explained, "The key holder's names are stamped in white on black oblongs and listed there. Celebrities and special guests are listed at the top."

Shar turned to me. "At 11:30 am this lobby will be filled with eager keyholders—all of them men, you know. Often the line of waiting members and their guests snakes clear out the door." She swept her hand toward the entrance. "Chicago is the busiest Club in the world. And you must make sure one of the best looking Bunnies is the Door Bunny to whet the patron's imagination of what lays ahead, if ya know what I mean?"

From there we took a few steps down to the Playmate Bar, a darkened den decorated with back-lit transparencies of Playmate photos. My face heated and I quickly looked away from the nearly naked portraits toward several small tables. Shar followed my eyes, but thankfully didn't mention my uneasiness. "Guests can request a plug-in telephone and a scratch pad at those tables."

Another few steps up from the Playmate Bar led us to the Living Room, which featured a nook in the back decorated with the originals of Playboy cartoons and called the Cartoon Corner. I now relaxed in the midst of this clever artwork. Shar pointed out where a trio would play at the piano bar while guests feasted. In here the buffet included breakfast since the Club stayed open until four in the morning. From midnight on, the Living Room served ham and eggs, hot rolls and jelly, a slice of pizza and coffee for $1.50. But that price was typical in every room, except the V.I.P. Room, for all food and all liquor of any kind. On the other hand, in the V.I.P. Room one consumed a lavish gourmet dinner for either $8.50 or $12.50.

Shar introduced me to the Room Director arriving for his shift. "Chris Malloy, meet Alyce, the new Bunny Mother."

A tall man with the physique of a body builder faced us.

"Pleased to meet you." Chris's iridescent eyes cruised over me. I noted he wore the standard tuxedo and Big Bunny cuff links.

Suddenly I recalled Shar's earlier words about how I dressed. Had Chris seen the same un-Playboy image?

"So, were you a Bunny before this?" Chris asked.

"No, but I have waited tables and did manage a large Club in Los Angeles."

I sounded almost apologetic since I knew Bunnies had been promoted to Bunny Mothers at other Clubs. It was the normal progression for many Bunnies fired for not conforming to the Bunny Image, especially when the Bunny had become too old to meet the Playboy fantasy.

"Umm," Chris replied. He lifted his square jaw enough to look down at me through narrowed eyes. His black hair glowed like patent leather even in the dim light. Though not a strand was out of place the sheen appeared natural and not from hair oil.

Shar jumped into the conversation. "Room Directors keep the lid on the place—no hanky panky."

"Hanky panky?" I asked.

"Well, think about it." Chris didn't try to hide his condescension. "When we've got a club which, unlike the typical show club, doesn't cut its liquor—in fact we serve a good ounce and a half of a very good grade of alcohol—and attractive girls in abbreviated costumes as waitresses, there is the chance of a problem." His almost-black eyes glowed.

"And what kind of problems have you had?" I pressed.

"My guess is that we have had fewer in the Playboy Club than other supper clubs." Chris smiled, full and toothy, as he nodded his head at the empty room and continued in a haughty tone, "The Room Directors keep an eye out like a watchdog whose motto is 'look, but don't touch'. We have been known to ask a guest to leave if he gets out of hand. But it's up to the Bunny Mother to hire proper girls."

Shar nudged me toward the exit as she said, "Thanks, Chris. But we gotta go. We've got a lot to cover today."

"See you," Chris called out.

I nodded at the man who looked more like a brute than a gentleman, however impeccably groomed. Yet he probably had no difficulty attracting a woman's attention.

I now followed Shar, this time more like a pup than a manager. We continued up several flights of stairs to the V.I.P Room, Penthouse and Playroom. The last two were showrooms that featured high caliber entertainment and dinner for a reasonable price, considering the quantity and quality of the food and drinks offered.

"Where's the elevator?" I asked slightly out of breath.

"No elevator, unless you're going to the Playroom on the top floor like you did this morning."

I bit my lower lip, a habit I reminded myself I needed to break. I may have processed the information, but still it didn't make sense. "So how do the keyholders get around the Club?"

"Easy," Shar said as we sat in the Penthouse. She lit her first cigarette since we'd left my office.

"Can't carry a lit cigarette around." She took a long drag and puffed out those same little rings. "Rules say we must take a puff and then place the cigarette into an ashtray." Shar demonstrated. "Same with the Bunnies when they smoke, but only at the service bar unless they are a Door or Gift Bunny. They can smoke at their stations using the ashtray rule." Shar demonstrated again. "But then you don't smoke, do you?"

"Do they use the stairs?" I was becoming more impatient with Shar's babble, which left out answers to my questions. Would this be how her entire training would go?

"Oh, yeah. You want to know how the key holders move around. Clever really," Shar chuckled and took another drag from her cigarette. "The Club is set up so other than the elevator that goes straight to the top, keyholders must go up and down by stairs even when they return from the Playroom."

"But the elevator."

"It only goes one-way. Up." Shar flipped her thumb in that direction. "For guests, that is. Guests have to pass all other rooms on foot to exit, hopefully when another show is about to start which will lure them to stay longer and spend more. The Club does get big names to perform here. Ya know —like Mel Tormé, Barbra Streisand, and that kid, what's her name?" She squinted. "Oh, yeah, the kid wonder, Aretha Franklin. Good shows stay on the Playboy Circuit for 46 weeks and can really make the entertainer." Shar snuffed out her cigarette and stood. "Did they tell you that you don't get paid for training?" Then she turned on her heels and left without so much as a word more.

I again followed quickly to keep up while inside, the bottom had fallen out of my stomach. I had so little money. How would I ever survive without being paid for these two weeks? I felt so betrayed. No one had mentioned I wouldn't be paid during training.

Shortly after Shar and I returned to my office, Barry Fleishman raced through the door so fast he reminded me of the Road Runner. Shar snuggled into the sofa and lit another cigarette.

"Meet the boss," she announced.

I sensed both sarcasm and hostility in her voice. How did Shar get away with such disrespect?

I walked straight to him, offered my hand and said, "Good to meet you."

Barry hesitated. He stared at my hand as though it held poison, but shook it. Then he quickly let it drop.

"We have a lot to get done in the next two weeks. I hope you're up to the pace."

"The question should be, are you ready for me? Because I'm not only capable of keeping up but I can outrun you."

The words slipped from my mouth before I realized the possible implication that I considered myself better than the current Playboy management. Would I regret my boldness before Barry had a chance to know the real me?

As I waited to be dressed down for my behavior, Barry teetered slightly back on his heels. Was he shaken by my apparent cockiness? After all, he was a small man, slender and a couple inches shorter than me, and none too attractive. Although he was only in his mid-thirties, his rather average brown hair had begun to recede, leaving a half moon-shape glare above his forehead. What hair he still had gleamed from a generous application of Brill Cream. Was he unsure of himself or did I overact? Time would tell. I tucked the thought away for the moment.

The right corner of his mouth twitched upward and Barry finally answered, "I apologize. I've had a tough morning and it's only Monday. We're five Bunnies short, the girls want to unionize and my wife hates my long hours." His mouth twisted upward again. "Besides, your resumé clearly shows you are more than capable."

Unsure how else to respond, I simply smiled and decided not to add anything. It could make our first meeting even worse.

Shar walked to the door. "I have a ton of work to do. I'll let you two get to know each other a little before we meet the rest of the

Hutch." She looked at her watch. "Which by the way, is half an hour from now." She gave us a mock salute.

Barry and I said nothing as we each took facing chairs, mine behind the desk. My chair creaked and tilted a little to the right but I knew not to lean too far back this time. The squeak broke the silence. I had nothing else to lose so I said, "This may not be the time to bring up a concern of mine, but. . ."

"No, no, go right ahead. That's what I'm here for—to settle problems. And lead, of course."

My demure nod seemed to relax Barry. "It was my understanding that I would get paid for training. Now I've discovered I do not." My foot fidgeted with the makeup bag I'd knocked to the floor earlier. "I'm not sure I will be able to make ends meet without some kind of compensation for the next two weeks."

"Who told you that?" Barry's voice went up an octave and increased by a hundred decibels.

At his shout, I pressed back into the chair, forgetting its unsteadiness. I grabbed the desk. In only minutes I had managed to have agitated him twice. His forehead even radiated red into his bald patch. What could his blood pressure be like?

"Oh, oh, never mind. I know who," he said as the tips of his ears turned red to match. "Well, it's not true. There's a misunderstanding. I'll handle it."

"Thank you." Had Shar deliberately misinformed me? Could she be that evil?

"On to why I'm here," Barry rushed his words as he stood. "You'll find the Bunny Mother's job is demanding, frustrating and fun. You'll not only report to the Bunny Director, but to me." He paused and said in a quieter, more thoughtful tone, "Though I have the final say it's not easy to have two bosses." Then as though an afterthought, he added, "But that shouldn't be for long."

I raised my eyebrows in question. Before I could ask him to explain, Barry moved close to me and almost whispered, "I don't want this to go any further than this room."

"Whatever you say will remain confidential." What would this funny little man say next?

"I'm positive you'll be the next Bunny Director, and soon." With that, he stood back and motioned me to the door. "Let's get you introduced."

As I gingerly extracted myself from the treacherous chair, I caught Barry checking me out. He might as well have been sizing up a new car. Did I detect disapproval even after that carrot he dangled? I had so many impressions to process.

Nearly 100 people pressed into the smoke-filled conference room. I desperately wanted to put a handkerchief over my nose to block the odor. It seemed everyone smoked, but me. A hush fell over the room as Barry and I entered. All eyes were on me. I began to perspire, something I rarely did. What were they thinking? Perhaps I wasn't pretty enough or maybe I needed a whole make-over, hair, makeup, clothes. I was an outsider. Did any of them approve?

Barry swaggered to the head of the room and announced, "This is our new Bunny Mother, Alyce Bonura. As most of you know from the First Page, Alyce comes to us from L.A." Barry half-bowed to me. "I'm sure you'll give her a warm welcome and help her get settled." Barry started to sit, but halted halfway. Without rising to a full standing position he asked, "Oh, Alyce, would you like to say anything before the meeting gets started?"

"Yes, I would."

Was that my tiny voice I heard? I hesitated as I gathered my confidence and thoughts. I also made a note to find out what the First Page was. A few cleared their throats and shifted in their seats. Others stared at the ceiling or played with their cigarettes, clearly bored. "I'm delighted to be here," I began, "and I know our future together will be productive and fun. I look forward to getting to know each of you." While making my brief remarks all I could really think was what a bunch of crap. How many in the audience felt the same way? I wasn't yet sure I had made the right decision. But I smiled and sat.

Barry began with introductions followed by issues. I tuned in and out of the meeting. I was more interested in the employees gathered. Except for the girls dressed in their costumes ready to go to work, I couldn't identify other Bunnies unless they were introduced that way. In street clothes and everyday makeup, the girls looked unexceptional although some were certainly pretty. Having prepared myself by thumbing through both *Playboy* and *V.I.P.* magazines, I expected glamour rather than ordinariness from those chosen to be

Bunnies. I now understood there was a definite before and after Bunny effect, which added up to image. The makeup, hairpieces, and particularly the figure-enhancing costume individually sewn for each Bunny to enhance her figure created a Las Vegas showgirl-perfect appearance. If my assessment of the girls gathered and introduced was correct, even Bunnies less endowed could be made to look voluptuous in Playboy's ensemble.

When the meeting ended, each Bunny welcomed me, some half-heartedly, as everyone else shuffled from the room. Though overwhelmed for the moment I was sure I'd get to know every employee soon, including other management and business office personnel. From my past experience, I understood a large club's demands. Along with the daily work routine, a place like this would likely be a hot bed of rumors, jealousy—fueled by competition and unending excuses for why a task hadn't been met. That is—if the employee showed up for work at all.

Left alone in the empty meeting room, I wondered what I should do next. Had they forgotten me? I watched the clock's second hand as several minutes ticked loudly away.

"Hey!" I bolted up as Shar burst into the room. "What're ya still doing here?"

"I had no idea where I was supposed to go unless it's back to my office to sit alone there."

I must have sounded snippy, but I didn't care.

"Well, we need to talk about your training schedule." Shar slid into a nearby chair and placed a pad and pen on the table. "Let's see. You'll go through an abbreviated Bunny training so you'll understand what is expected of them. We'll have you work a schedule with me. You'll do a Bunny inspection in your office and on the floor, consulting with the Room Directors." Shar paused and studied me. "But first thing tomorrow you'll get a make-over."

My eyes stung. Management or maybe just Shar didn't think I was pretty enough. I had to fight hard to ward off tears. "Why?"

"Barry's unhappy with your hair, your makeup and your clothes." Shar shrugged.

"But he likes my brains, right?" I quipped to hide my defensiveness. But my earlier observation of his scrutiny was right on target.

"Huh?" Shar flapped her hand. "Never mind. We all have to go through this sooner or later. It's how Barry shows who's boss." Then Shar giggled, "Someone should give him an overhaul."

The mood lightened and I chuckled, but quietly. If I had a better understanding of her motives and standing in the corporation, I might have agreed with her out loud. Meanwhile, I would forgo any chumminess for the time being.

Chapter Three

Training

As a Bunny, you have joined a company of girls who, with good reason, are both respected and admired. You are more than a waitress. You are very much involved in an activity that comes closer to being in show business than anything else. You are holding the top job in the country for a young girl. Playboy Bunny Manual/1963

The next morning in the hotel elevator, a handsome Englishman introduced himself and invited me to join him for breakfast. My first thought was to politely decline, but then where would I eat?

Over breakfast I found out his name was Ethan and he was in Chicago for business, as he was several times a year. Ethan seemed somewhat aloof, but charming. I agreed to have dinner with him that evening.

With my mood buoyed by Ethan's attention I almost skipped out the hotel door and down the first three blocks to Playboy. In the block before the Club I heard pounding steps racing up behind. Then came a sudden strong tug at my purse. I resisted. The force pulled me around. I faced a wild-eyed teenage boy gripping the strap. Whether it was my morning's confidence or a split second reaction, I kicked the kid in the groin and screamed, "What's wrong with you get a job!"

The assailant doubled over and howled like a coyote before collapsing in a dark heap on the sidewalk. I sprinted the rest of the way to the front door of the Club and tripped over the threshold. I caught my balance just in time to prevent myself from sprawling at Barry's feet.

"Good morning," Barry greeted, without a hint of cheer. "Is this how you normally start your day?"

Breathing heavily I answered, "Kid." Breath. "Purse." Another breath. I raised my handbag to his face. "Theft."

"Some kid tried to steal your purse?" Barry shouted. "Call the police."

I collapsed against the coat check door. I shook my head. "I can't identify him." My breathing now slowed. "It all happened too fast." I straightened away from the door and tugged my jacket into place, then brushed strands of damp hair away from my face. So much for making a good impression before I got a make-over.

Barry's eyes narrowed. "Weren't you warned about this neighborhood?"

"Warned?"

"Last week's news said the crime rate in this area is up by 39%." He might as well have been scolding an unruly child.

I clutched my purse to my chest. "How else will I get to work? It'll cost too much to take a cab those few blocks. Is there a bus?" My desperate response almost took my breath away again.

Barry held his hand up like a traffic cop and said, "Cool it, babe. We'll figure something out 'til you find your own apartment. Speaking of which, there's a vacancy coming up in the complex where my wife and I live." He pushed his eyeglasses to the top of his head, which magnified the pink-blotched bare space. "At any rate, I hope the make-over helps your attitude."

I wanted to slug the little twerp, but he was the boss. "What attitude?"

"You're wound up tighter than that red hair of yours." He smirked and pointed to my unmanageable head of curls.

I smirked right back. "L.A. has its problems but I was never afraid to go to work."

"Oh, never mind." He flapped his hand in dismissal. "Get to your make-over."

I pivoted and slowly walked away, determined not to show either my anger or my wounded ego. When the elevator doors shut out Barry's beady-eyed scrutiny, I patted my hair and sneered, "At least I have hair."

Once I locked my purse in my desk drawer, I made a final check of myself in the mirror, and then reported to Shar. As expected she sat behind her desk shrouded in cigarette smoke. I sneezed. The mixture of White Shoulders and smoke was too much. I sneezed five more times before I could get out a stuff-nosed, "Good morning."

Shar waved the hand holding the lit cigarette. "Be with ya in just a sec. Need to finish the schedule changes."

I blew my nose and wiped my weepy eyes. "Do you usually have many?"

"Always. But you'll soon learn with these girls nothing is ever for certain." Shar doused her cigarette and stood. She flipped through the schedule and said, "Most of this really should have been done Friday, but Babs, the acting Bunny Mother and your assistant," she said as though accusing me, "didn't get around to it. God knows what she does with her time." Shar walked to the door shaking her head. "Hopefully you'll be more punctual with your reports." She motioned me to follow. "Let's get you done over. Then you can check-in at Bunny training."

I only had time for a brief talk with Babs Balboni when I met with the entire staff. A former New York Bunny, Babs was in her late twenties, although it was hard to tell. With her heavy makeup, stiff hair pieces, mini-dress and boots, she could have been any age. She had offered little at the meeting so it was hard to assess her. I now hoped Babs would be more responsive to my inclusive managerial style than she apparently was to Shar's more caustic, do-as-I-say one.

Shar marched me into the on-site hair salon. "Here she is," she announced to a man in too-tight glossy olive green pants who was leaning over a sink.

"You're late as usual, Shar, darling. You know I have a busy schedule today with all those new Bunnies coming on board." He shook his head and offered his limp hand to me. "Can't keep a full staff in this place to save our souls," he continued as he withdrew his hand and flitted around me picking at my hair. "Hmmm."

"I've got work to do, as always." Shar said leaving me alone with the hairdresser.

I sized up the man who circled me one more time with one hand on his hip, the other at his chin. If this were Hollywood, he'd have been perfectly cast.

"What is your name?" I asked the man since no one bothered to introduce us properly. I doubted any fiber of his permed hair would stray from its lacquered crown.

"Tobie with an i e, not y. Sit over there." He pointed to the first chair in a line of four facing floor-to-ceiling mirrors. Had I detected a lisp?

I sat. Tobie shook out a green plastic cloth as though preparing to fight a bull. He swung it around me and fastened it at my neck. I waited to hear him shout, "Ole!!"

He brushed my hair with such vigor I gasped. "Too many curls," he announced, like an archeologist facing a difficult dig. "Pay attention to what I do today and we should have this," he raised a handful of curls in the air and dropped it, "under control, sweetheart. You're lucky. At least it's natural." Tobie patted his own locks. A large diamond ring glowed from his pinky.

Within an hour, and with the help of a great cut and lots of spray, my hair had been persuaded into a fashionable flip. The bangs Tobie carved out gave me a youthful, but modern look that reminded me of Marlo Thomas, star of the brave new TV hit show, *That Girl*. "Oh my!" I cocked my head from side to side and studied the back with a hand-held mirror. "I look like a movie star."

"Not until the makeup. Lucinda here," Tobie pointed to a girl barely twenty years old, "will do you." Lucinda had entered the salon without detection. How long had she been sitting in the corner thumbing through *Glamour*?

"Come over to the stool," Lucinda directed. No one seemed to think I was important enough to address by name.

I slid from one chair and hopped into the higher one. Like Tobie's station, the lights surrounding the mirror cast a heartless glare on every flaw.

"Hmm," Lucinda echoed Tobie as she studied my face. "Freckles. You have so many freckles." Her gum snapped.

"God's gift, I'm afraid," I answered, feeling like a specimen under a microscope.

"I've handled them before." Lucinda sounded more like a tough cop than someone involved with creating beauty.

"Thank God," I responded, disappointed my sarcasm went unnoticed.

Lucinda flipped open a suitcase brimming with a rainbow of lipsticks, blush and eye shadow. Along with these, foundations to cover anyone's skin and its imperfections lined the case's outer edge.

My eyes settled on a specific item that looked like a large spider nestled in the corner. I touched them. "Do I have to wear these?"

"Yep. All the Playboy girls wear false eyelashes."

I had wondered about Shar's own overabundant application which took that cosmetic aid to new heights. One almost couldn't see Shar's eyes for the feathery forest on her lids.

"Are there different sizes?" I asked. "I mean I don't want them to look too fake."

"We'll try a couple and see which you like the best. For now, here's some makeup remover. You need to get everything off before I get started." Lucinda said all this without missing a chomp on her gum.

I applied the citrus smelling liquid over my face. Using several tissues I then removed all the work I had done that morning before breakfast. My face was pale, freckled and highlighted by sparse strawberry blond brows and lashes.

"Not much left without the makeup," Lucinda giggled.

I cringed. I supposed Lucinda meant no harm, but then girls could be so catty. As for myself, I could see only my nose. I lifted my hand toward my face, but stopped.

"Don't worry," Lucinda said. "I'll take care of that for now. Maybe you should think about having it fixed to fit your face."

I could feel a lump crawl to the top of my throat. I couldn't cry, not now, not ever in front of anyone at Playboy. Until this moment I hadn't seriously thought anyone else minded my nose as much as I. After all, it hadn't bothered Clark, had it? And that Ethan guy had wasted no time asking me to join him for breakfast and dinner.

Lucinda went on, "I didn't mean your nose is bad. You just looked like it bothers you." Lucinda removed the plastic cloth Tobie had wrapped around me and gave me a pink cotton robe to wear. "And my motto is if it bothers you, do something about it." She didn't miss a beat. "Take off your top and put this on. We don't want to cover your clothes in makeup, just your face." She giggled again.

The makeup session took twice as long as the hair. At first glance the eyelashes looked overwhelming. After a closer examination, I actually liked them. My eyes became enormous. The shadow brushed onto my lids brought out my unusual hazel color eyes. Stunned by the overall effect I screeched, "Lucinda! You created a miracle! Will I ever be able to duplicate it?" Even my nose seemed to have grown smaller.

"Sure, with a little practice. Any time you need some tips, just stop by. Most Bunnies can do this as well as me. So I'm sure they can help you too."

"Thanks," I practically shouted.

Could this beauty reflected in the mirror really be the same woman I'd spied in the storefront glass earlier today? Other women may have gotten make-overs like this, but I never dreamed it could happen to me.

Tobie handed me a bill.

"$40?" I gasped. Tobie was no Prince Charming. With this brief gesture he ruined a perfectly good moment.

"I'll have payroll deduct it from your check," Tobie said. "You can arrange how much at a time."

"But I thought this would be free as part of training." Panic now noticeable in my tone as I calculated what little funds I had and how I depended on a full paycheck.

"Nothing's free around here, sweetheart." Tobie patted my hand like an affable father. "And now I'm running late. So shoo." He checked his watch. "You're due down the hall."

That afternoon I watched as the newly hired Bunnies were fitted into their two costumes of different colors, each one chosen to enhance the Bunny's coloring. For purposes of training I also was fitted in a forest green one by Catalina, the talented but no-nonsense seamstress.

"Stand here," Catalina shouted like a drill sergeant as she pointed to a small stage the size of a table for two. She prodded and shoved until all parts of my body had an appropriate place in the corset. Catalina kept a good number of pins in her mouth as she altered the costume, her hands moving so fast from mouth to my body, they appeared like a blur. I held my breath, sure I would be wounded as Catalina tucked and pinned. Through all of it, Catalina made loud grunting commands that oddly enough I mostly understood. Grunt. I

moved right. A harsh grunt, grunt meant I misunderstood the direction. Once Catalina's mouth held fewer pins, she became quite clear
despite a heavy accent.

"Stand still. I don't want you back in here complaining the costume doesn't fit. I don't have the time for foolishness."

Catalina volunteered some personal history. Was it her way to let
me know she wasn't kidding about her lack of tolerance? "I emi-
grated from Colombia." She paused to remove a pin, "With my two
daughters after my worthless husband ran off with a teenager." She
stopped to yank me in another direction and pulled a couple more
pins from her mouth. "Married twenty years." How many more pins
could she have in there?

Catalina slurred the remainder of the short version of her reasons
for being in the United States making Bunny costumes. "Me and my
daughters are allowed to stay in the United States because my government gave the girls scholarships. Any American college of their
choice. They go to the University of Miami."

I still didn't have a clear picture of how Catalina ended in Chicago,
but I decided not to pursue that part of her life just yet. I both admired her and felt slightly intimidated by her. I would need to figure
a way to get on Catalina's best side once training had been completed. A good seamstress would mean a happy Hutch.

The Bunny Mother had to pick up where the seamstress left off.
Not only did the color of the Bunny costume have to complement the
girl wearing it, I would have to make sure when I prepared the schedule no Bunnies wore the same color while working together in the
same room. That could be complicated when the Bunny Mother fac-
tored in the last minute absences and that each Bunny only had two
of the patented costumes.

At my brief introduction when Shar interviewed me at the L.A.
Club, I had already discovered the secrets of the rich satin costume
which had characteristics similar to a corset. Yet once wearing my
own costume, I better understood its ability to ensure a perfect body
for almost anyone. In order to get into the Bunny suit I had to bend
slightly at the hips, keep my torso straight, suck in my stomach and
hold the one-piece corset in place so another girl could zip it. Zipped
tightly in, I could hardly take a breath as my waist became smaller
than it had been since before puberty. My breasts sat high on a shelf

and teased over the cup. Though I didn't need the help, this special feature made even the smallest cup size seem full and inviting. The costume snugged the body so well, it never rode up the way an ill-fitted bathing suit would.

"No Bunny wants to eat before she puts the corset on," Catalina warned.

"Why?" I checked myself in the mirror. Amazing.

"Once zipped in, the Bunny will know just how little she can eat before the corset gets unbearably uncomfortable. You'll see."

I rolled my eyes, but turned my attention back to my reflection. I admired how the high cut of the corset's thigh, the black Bunny hose and three-inch dyed-to-match heels gave my legs a long, sleek look. As I turned in front of the mirror to take in the costume's full effect, Shar stopped by.

"Even with this help," Shar said, "legs cannot be made to look much better than they are. Basically it's what you see. When hiring, of course we want the prettiest girls, but we can work around most flaws. Not the legs." She stopped and checked me. "Look at you, for instance. So hire the best legs."

My face heated. I knew my freckles had become a deep red. They always gave me away. I held my tongue and faced the mirror, pretending I wanted to see the results of the fitting. I would rather have given Shar a piece of my Irish temper. It hadn't been just my hair that had once earned me the nickname, Flame. Fortunately, Shar left as fast she arrived with little time for me to put my foot in my mouth. Yet, Shar did dampen the moment.

With the help of the wardrobe mistress, Catalina's other job, I put on the final signature touches: the white bunny tail, white cuffs held closed with the Big Bunny cufflinks, a white collar with black bow tie, name plate rosette, and the famed ears. A flashlight and Playboy lighter in the same color as the costume would go on my serving tray. I then took a few test steps in heels I was not accustomed to wearing.

How would I balance a heavy service tray while performing a model's walk? What if the worst happened? I pictured myself in training in front of my subordinates, toppling head first onto a table and spilling drinks every-which-way all the while trying to remain tucked into the ever-so-revealing Bunny costume. Mentally tottering in that image, I felt renewed respect for seasoned Bunnies.

And besides, here was a more pressing question: how would I, or any Bunny go to the bathroom in this ensemble?

It was a relief to shed the costume and get back into my everyday clothes. I could breathe, walk and sit like a normal female once again. I vowed to enjoy it while I could because such a break would only come while the newly-hired girls and I learned the other tricks of the trade—serving drinks.

Since I had experience as a cocktail waitress, I wouldn't have to memorize how to setup using the correct glass and call drinks in the proper sequence. Several girls had difficulty mastering the two typed pages of beverage texts, which meant knowing the brand names. For instance, Scotch whisky brands included J&B, Ballantine's and White Horse, among others. But each girl also had to commit to memory several more pages with the 11 different beverage categories, each having no fewer than 6 brands. Along with these she had to know by heart the one page garnish index to stage a drink, such as the lime wedge for a Bloody Mary, or a sprinkle of nutmeg for the Brandy Alexander. As if this weren't enough, the Bunny had to write her service check according to the code set forth in the Popular Drink Index. A scotch and soda would become S-S while a Black Russian would be B/R.

Then there were the tools of service layered in a specific order for the properly equipped serving tray. The order was: pens, Playboy lighter, tax chart under the tip tray, tip tray, Playboy matches on the tip tray, clean ash trays on the tip tray, bar rag or sponge under the napkins, the napkins with Playboy Logo, and on top the bar checks. After that the girls learned the proper tray set-up for the drinks in order to ease the bartender's pouring.

Finally, the girls learned how to use the Addressograph machine for charges, and how to tell the difference among the 10 Playboy Club Keys: regular initial key on which a member could charge, green admission when a keyholder must pay in cash, rose (temporary), green (celebrity–cash only), yellow (celebrity–can charge), permanent cash, private party, buffet, and food service.

All the new Bunnies would take a written test at the end of the training period (as would I), but their personal appearance and movements were tested every day. The true exam would come when they had to order, serve, and cash-out while in costume.

I marveled that somehow, even though some time had passed, I had not forgotten how to serve drinks. Juggling the loaded ten-pound tray was another story. The lucky customers rarely understood the complexities involved. All they knew was a pretty girl in a skimpy outfit would bring them exactly what they had ordered.

By the end of this session, my newly styled hair had returned to its natural curl and my now red eyes itched from the false eyelashes. When Shar popped into the training, she scrunched her face at the sight of me wiping my eyes with great ferocity. "We'll have to find a different lash," Shar said as she picked up the one that had slid from my lid to the floor. "But what can we do about this hair?"

Shar quickly turned her attention to the others. "Day one is complete, girls. Anyone want to give up yet?"

The girls lowered their eyes and stood statue-still in silence. The group stayed like this until I piped up. "I think we all did quite well for our first day. We'll be perfect by the end of the second week, if not sooner."

The Bunnies lifted their heads and smiled. One shouted, "We sure will. You'll see. Won't she, girls?" The others chimed in their agreement.

"See you tomorrow then," I said. "Get a good night's rest. Tomorrow I think we tackle the Bunny Dip." Several girls groaned and then giggled as they mimicked what they thought might be the Dip.

I hurried to the bathroom as the others fled. I needed to freshen up before I went back to the hotel to meet Ethan for dinner. As I entered the hall, minus false eyelashes, and with restored mascara, I bumped into Barry.

"Just the person I wanted to find," Barry greeted me.

"Oh?" What could he want?

"Yes." Barry grasped my elbow and led me away. "You and I are having dinner in the V.I.P. room so you can literally get a taste of Playboy's cuisine and watch the Bunnies in action."

So much for dinner with Ethan. "I have to make a telephone call first. I'll meet you there." I slipped to my office, called the hotel and left a message for Ethan.

Our dinner included Cherries Jubilee that rivaled any in a fine restaurant. We were joined by Shar and Brian, Shar's wealthy, handsome boyfriend of the moment. Brian also happened to be the owner of the Detroit Playboy Club, one of a handful of franchise clubs. Barry explained that when Hefner came up with the Playboy Club idea, money was tight so he allowed a few to be franchised to help the cash flow.

Bunny rumors abounded about that Club when a Bunny named Rose transferred to Chicago from Miami rather than go to Detroit even though she came from Grand Rapids, Michigan. Rose claimed the Detroit Club was run by organized crime.

If it hadn't been for the delicious food, the evening would have been spoiled by Shar's presence. I had a difficult time pairing Shar with Brian, or perhaps it was really envy. Why did she deserve such a dish and not me? Even the two notes delivered to Barry from other key holders asking to meet me did nothing to ease my resentment. I suspected those members would turn out to be married anyway. Never mind, I thought taking another quick glance at Brian, who wanted to be involved with the mafia, anyway?

To separate myself from watching while Shar continued to snuggle with and coo over Brain, I concentrated on the Bunnies. To my eyes, their routines seemed flawless and as fluid as a choreographed dance.

Barry leaned toward me and said in a low voice, "No mishaps, yet." He nodded at the three Bunnies nearby moving about the room. "Better than most evenings."

"What do you mean?"

"You'll see soon enough." He shrugged. "Just a hint, though. Often a Bunny will get into it with the bartender because she screwed up the order, or the Room Director because he criticized her appearance."

"Oh!" I could think of nothing else to say before Barry stood and reached to pull my chair away from the table, which meant our evening was over.

Barry drove me to the hotel. "Ciao," he said as I left the car. "See you tomorrow."

I waved back and pushed through the revolving door. It was nearly midnight when I entered the elevator. Before the doors closed, a man and woman slipped in. Ethan and a girl, ten years younger than me. "I see you got my message," I snipped.

Ethan smiled but gave no hint of embarrassment. "Yes, thank you."

End of the conversation, and the end of Ethan.

A telephone message from Clark waited for me. He said he was blue and missed me. He also wondered where I could be at 11 pm when he called.

"You have no right to ask," I told the operator who had recited the message.

"Pardon?" the operator asked.

"Nothing. Thank you for the information." I hung up. "Men!" I got ready for bed. Then I lay there for a long time crying.

Chapter Four

Dipping for Playboy

The Bunny is so much a glorification of the American girl, in the tradition of the famous Ziegfeld Girl, that the word "Bunny" has become recognized throughout the country, and indeed internationally, as being associated with the Playboy Clubs and the beautiful and glamorous young ladies they employ. Playboy Bunny Manual/1963

I held my hand over my mouth to stop a laugh from bursting out as I watched a new Bunny, Ellie, teeter backwards to the floor. On only my third day in training, I realized I shouldn't feel so smug. My turn would come next and I didn't think I could perform the Bunny Dip any better.

Carlie, the Training Bunny, offered a hand to Ellie. The two placed everything back on the serving tray in the proper order. "This may not be easy, but wait until you have a full order. The tray weighs about 10 pounds then," Carlie softly admonished. "Balancing, dipping and serving can be quite tricky. So take your time and try it again."

Ellie straightened her costume, took a deep breath and dipped. Though unsteady this time, Ellie didn't find herself sprawled on the floor among napkins, ashtrays, matches, checks and bar rags.

Just eighteen years old, Ellie had a fresh off the farm wholesome beauty. On the other hand, though only a few years older than Ellie, Carlie had the extraordinary classic looks that could stop anyone in his tracks. In three-inch heels she had to be nearly 6 feet tall—an Amazon stunner.

As Ellie made a few more improved attempts at Dipping, I reviewed the manual with headings that read *Bunny Dip, Bunny Stance, Perching*. Each had a brief explanation with an accompanying picture. At the moment the Bunny Dip held everyone's attention. I read under my breath to prepare myself for my turn.

When a Bunny sets napkins or drinks on the far end of a table, she does not awkwardly reach across the table—she does the Bunny Dip. I mumbled to myself, "And that's not awkward?" I continued reading. *This keeps her tray away from the patrons and enables her to give graceful, stylized service.* They hadn't seen Ellie's graceful but stylized service, had they?

I read the remainder quickly. *The Bunny Dip is performed by arching the back as much as possible, then bending the knees to whatever degree is necessary. Raise the left heel as you bend.*

"Whew. A lot to expect from a girl trapped in a corset, carrying a ten-pound tray and balanced on three-inch heels," I blurted when my turn came. Then I chuckled. "You girls come for the glamour and instead get back aches." Everyone chuckled too.

"Here it goes." Dressed in my costume, I lifted my tray and attempted the Dip. Within seconds I was chest down in the middle of the table of new Bunnies I was supposed to serve. The items on my tray flew about the room like missiles. All in the line of fire dove for cover.

I popped up, Bunny ears hanging to the side of my head, and announced, "Not bad." That did everyone in. They all laughed until tears washed mascara down their cheeks. It reminded me of a scene from a Lucille Ball show. But after several more attempts, I could deliver drinks, dipping as instructed. So what if my legs shook a little?

Carlie pulled me to a standing position and announced, "Class is finished for today. Tomorrow you'll learn the Perch and Stance."

"How can we wait?" I didn't hide my sarcasm. "Sorry, Carlie, but we need a little levity if we all plan to get through this."

Carlie smiled, "See you tomorrow then." She left as the others sauntered off to the dressing room to change. In no time a collective sigh of relief filled the room. The Bunnies in training and I had freed our bodies and feet.

Later I inspected the Club with Shar and the on-duty Room Directors, who I discovered all had degrees in hotel management. They considered the Playboy Club good training for their planned ascent into larger chains. After a quick dinner in the V.I.P. Room, a most welcomed perk, I checked my messages.

One call came from my sister. Greg had stepped on a four-prong screen nail and had to go to the emergency hospital. Guilt again etched my every nerve. I needed to be with my sons. I made a call to Tekkie. Greg was fine, especially after a hot fudge sundae. I spoke with him for a few minutes and he soothed my guilt with his ever-present humor as he explained, "I chased Fraulein up the driveway after she snuck down to the corner to poop on that old guy's lawn again. Good thing we're moving because we told the old coot our dog never leaves the yard. Fraulein doesn't like him any more than we do. She knows he's mean." He never mentioned any pain and no whining. What a kid!

Back at the hotel, I wrote down the name of each Bunny I had met so far, including those in training. Alongside each name I listed characteristics I had observed or heard about in my short time with Playboy. The girls were so willing to share their stories, and to my surprise, the majority didn't fit the negative profile Shar had described. Immaturity and poor judgment were often counter-balanced by grit and determination.

For instance, most either attended college or were single mothers like me. Mona, nineteen, had at fifteen eloped with her high school teacher sixteen years her senior. Yet her story turned out well. Still married and now a pre-med student, she also juggled her Playboy job and housework. Many other Bunnies were hoping for movie or acting careers and did local theater or modeled, and worked hard at those endeavors much of their time off, especially during the slow summer months at the Club when they needed to supplement their wages. Others though, too many of course, chased the dream of catching Mr. Right. The wealthier the better. Instead, many sadly found themselves pregnant like Coco. The father usually was a married man who encouraged an illegal abortion, which he didn't offer to fund. Often the father fled the scene leaving the girl to fend for herself. As the girl's lover skipped out on his obligation, he inevitably claimed he never promised her anything but a good time.

Several girls like Toti, who had been a Bunny for a year, lived with

and supported unemployed partners because they had been social-
ized to believe a girl had to have a man. In him she at least hoped for
a good lover.

The single mothers and girls working their way through college
tugged at my heart the most. Those girls took the job at Playboy because they could make more money here than in the more usual jobs
for young women such as in sales and the typing pool. My ambition
was not much different. For all of them, the glamour had been enticing, but the deeper I became entrenched in the daily routine here, the
more it became that Playboy was more about hard work than glitz.

I set the list aside, stretched and yawned. My body still stung from
where it had been pinched by the Bunny costume stays. I had already
been told many girls quit during training because the work was too
tough. Better they did that than walk off the floor.

As I reached to set the clock, my hand instead went for the phone
as if it had a will of its own. Should I call Clark? I desperately wanted
to hear his voice telling me out loud how much he missed and loved
me as he had written in his almost daily letters. But what good would
that do? I was clinging to Clark exactly like the girls who pursued an
unattainable dream of finding a rich man to take care of them. Those
girls and I only found ourselves as frustrated as a dog chasing his
own tail.

When I closed my eyes, I saw myself sprawled across the table as I
had been that afternoon. "Tomorrow, I'll learn to perch and to do a
stance—Perch? Stance? What was I doing here? I turned out the
light, glad to let the darkness enshroud me.

I managed to walk near a group of businessmen who left the hotel
with me and were headed in the same direction. Though they turned
off before I reached Playboy, I felt less of a target for a purse
snatcher. So concerned about being attacked again, I hadn't noticed
the dark clouds which produced a sudden downpour just as I reached
the entrance. No summer rains like this in L. A. I made a mental note
to buy an umbrella when I got paid. I touched my hair. An umbrella
would do nothing to protect my hair against the dampness. I wondered what Shar would say today about these curls tightening like
wire springs around my head.

I didn't have to wait long. When I entered Shar's office I found her on the telephone, back to the door and circles of smoke coming from her head as though she were a spewing chimney. I caught the tail end of the conversation. Shar was talking to someone from the corporation that I didn't know. "Your evaluation is the same as mine," Shar was saying. "Alyce needs some work."

From the way my stomach churned at that moment, I regretted eating breakfast. I wasn't chic enough and Shar was knifing me in the back. A double blow.

Shar turned in her chair and faced me. "Gotta go," she said and hung up. "Hey, your hair looks like you stuck your finger in an electrical outlet." If Shar was concerned about the possibility of me overhearing her phone conversation, she didn't let on.

I couldn't quite bring up a smile. Instead I avoided responding to Shar's remark and instead asked, "Should I go straight to training? The Bunnies and I are working on our dips, stances and perches."

"Yes, but on Friday I want you to do the schedule with me. What did you think of Brian?" Shar's sudden leap from one subject to another had become no surprise to me.

"Isn't he a dreamboat?" Shar mock-swooned.

"He's groovy." If Shar noticed that my answer could etch glass she didn't show it.

"Yeah, he sure is. I must be doing something right to catch a guy like that, right?"

"Right." I sensed Shar loved rubbing in her good fortune. "I'll see you later then. Maybe for lunch and quick rounds of the Club."

"Sure, sure. I'll check with you later." Shar started to thumb through papers on her desk. I assumed our session was over. I now truly looked forward to sharing the morning with the Bunnies who seemed more down to earth.

"Oh, by the way," I said. "I thought you should know I checked with Barry. He said I am paid for training."

Shar simply shrugged without even lifting her head.

By the time I reached the dressing room, the Bunnies had already begun their makeup and hair rituals. "Must practice, you know, so we get it right by the time we hit the floor," one told me.

"I'll need more than practice," I said as I brushed my kinky hair.

Several Bunnies came to my rescue. With the help of a hairpiece and their expert attention to sprucing up my makeup, I emerged model perfect. Even the eyelashes stayed on without irritation because Ellie had a hypo-allergenic adhesive she shared. Shar hadn't bothered to tell me about the glue which appeared common knowledge in the Bunny dressing room. "Many of us have that same problem," the generous Bunny related when she handed me the tube. "I'm surprised no one told you about it."

I shot evil thoughts to Shar and then brushed them aside to pose in front of the mirror, dipping and turning. "I think I'll pass." I giggled as I inventoried myself in the mirror. "Thanks for coming to my aid. Now let's get to today's tasks—the perch and stance."

Carlie wasted no time working through the next session. After she said her good morning and reviewed the Dip from the day before, she started right in with the Bunny Stance. "When you are in view of patrons, you must always stand in a slightly exaggerated model's stance. That is, your legs are together, back arched with hips tucked well under."

Each Bunny and I tried that pose. "Not comfortable now," Carlie said to the chorus of groans coming from the girls. "But you'll get used to it. A time will come when this stance will be second nature. You'll see."

Once each girl passed the stance test, Carlie moved on to the Perch. "A Bunny is never allowed to sit down while working on the floor. She may, however, Perch."

"Like a bird on a wire?" I asked. I couldn't resist the silliness of this absurdity.

That time Carlie noted my sarcasm. "If you weren't the boss," she scolded, but in a quiet, controlled voice, "I'd have to grade you down for your attitude." Carlie quickly turned her attention to the Perch.

I knew my freckles went a shade deeper as a line of heat streaked across my forehead. Carlie was right of course, but she should have told me in private. "To the Perch then," I said with a slight smile. I also decided to let Carlie know she would address her concerns to me in private in the future.

"To sit," Carlie said more firmly, "you must Perch." She eyed me. "On the back of a chair, sofa, or on a railing while waiting to be of service. Never Perch too close to where a patron is seated." Carlie demonstrated by resting the edge of her buttocks on the rim of a chair back, with one hand draped next to it while the other held her tray to the side. Her legs were slightly bent at the knees, her thighs well away from the chair back so as not to exaggerate their size. One foot lifted off the floor with toes pointed downward. As with the other positions, she performed the Perch with fluid ease, poise and grace.

Irresistible chatter ran through my mind, but I didn't utter one word aloud: *This is supposed to be comfortable? Do I look normal to you?* In fact, Carlie did look natural—as though she had been born to Perch.

"I want each of you to try all the positions you have learned." Carlie's enthusiasm was encouraging rather than demanding. "So we'll have four of you sit at the table as the others serve you and then we'll change roles."

Soon my classmates and I graduated, some having learned the Bunny skills better than others. A few graduates I doubted would make it through the seven-month average stay at Playboy. The short-lived fantasy would be transformed by reality—the work was grueling, and the man of their dreams would be elusive. And of course, those who failed to maintain the Bunny Image would be terminated.

That evening I was surprised when both the new and regular Bunnies celebrated my graduation at a surprise party. Carlie spearheaded the event and said, "It's our way to give you a proper welcome."

The following morning back in my own office, I examined each new Bunny's photograph and tried to determine who among them would get to wear the coveted black costume reserved for the top Bunnies and who would be fired. Certainly I would be fooled. So often the girl one suspected to be the best would be the worst and vice versa.

Shar burst through the door and demanded, "Let me see the schedule you did for the week."

"Good morning to you, too," I said as I shuffled through the pile of papers on my desk and gave Shar the hand-written schedule. "I haven't had the time to type it yet and the first page is just an outline."

Shar grabbed the pages. "Had too much fun at the party the Bunnies gave you to get it done?" Unfair. I had been back at the Sheraton by nine.

Shar thumbed through the pages as she forced each word through pressed lips. "So far so good. When do you plan to complete it?"

"It will be typed and copied by tomorrow morning when it is due," I snipped back. "And to answer your question, the party was great. Nearly every Bunny came and all the office staff." I retrieved a name plaque from my desk. It read *Mother Rabbit*. "They gave me this."

Shar barely acknowledged it.

"We missed you," I said with a noticeable nastiness in my voice. I had already heard Shar hadn't planned to go because she thought no one would show up.

I suspected something else besides the schedule and my party bothered Shar and braced myself to receive her fury. If Barry told the truth, Shar would be gone soon. Perhaps she already knew she was history. I could hang on until then.

"Toti can't go on the door. Keith doesn't think she's pretty enough and needs a nose job." Shar ran her finger down the names. "Switch her with Renee," she ordered.

"Sure," I nodded. As Keith Hefner's current fling, Renee got her choice of positions. It didn't matter whether she had enough experience or was better looking than Toti, whose nose suited her face just fine.

I made the correction as Shar watched like a teacher. "Remember the Bunny hierarchy," Shar snapped. "From top down: door, pool table, camera, showroom, etc." The favored girls, or sometimes even those who deserved it, would get one of the first three top positions where they could make good money with a lot less work.

We were interrupted by Mona—the first of several Bunnies fully outfitted for work. After Mona's inspection, I watched as the other Bunnies paraded before me. With Shar observing, I examined every inch of each girl—makeup, hair, nails, costume, weight. Before I could comment on Bunny Toti's shoes, Shar pointed to them. "They need to be cleaned. And be careful they don't fade or you'll have to get a new pair." Shar then gave me a wicked "You missed it" look.

"Fine," Toti snipped. "Is that it?"

Toti and the others left for their scheduled positions in the Club. Shortly after, Shar escorted me on my inspection tour. Shar had little problem pointing out a Bunny's mistakes I had overlooked, foot not lifted enough in the Dip or the tray order slightly off. Yet Shar gladly ignored several Room Directors' errors that I noted. And Shar seemed to distance herself from a Room Director's angry, uncalled-for insults blasted at a Bunny. I was appalled when I heard comments like "Do something about your hair. You look like a witch." Or "Your brain is no bigger than a pea. You can be replaced."

At one point I pulled Chris Malloy aside and dressed him out. His response, "They make more money than I do so I expect perfection. You should expect perfection, too."

I wanted to drag him off the floor. Instead I decided to include the episode in my report that went to Barry Fleishman. "We'll discuss this further later, Mr. Malloy." I'd soon see who had the upper hand after I informed Barry. But at the sound of Malloy's bitter, deriding laugh, I placed my hand on the back of my neck to stop the prickling sensation and I stalked from the area.

Away from Malloy, Shar made it clear that I needed to watch myself around the Room Directors. "If they have it out for you or a Bunny, they will make it rough on both of you. Those macho guys don't like women making more money than they do. And they don't like a woman telling them what to do—especially when the Room Directors have college degrees and the girl doesn't."

I smiled, "I guess Chris and his band of merry men will have to get used to it. Besides, several girls are working their way through college, and there are a few who have degrees like Carlie."

"Ummm, the nun," Shar smirked.

I studied Shar's face which had lost the self-assured glow that I admired when I first arrived. Something was festering in Shar. But what? I finally answered, "If I'm going to do my job right, I can't let people like Malloy control me, or demean the Bunnies. I won't allow him to take out his own personal insecurities on innocent, but effective women. I will expect any director's report to be a useful evaluation, not a girl's death sentence." I hesitated, then added, "I hope as my boss you'd support me."

"You have a lot to learn, kiddo." Shar walked to the door. She turned and said in a more mellow tone, "Let's have dinner in the bar and call it a day. Tomorrow we'll check out the new show to critique. So don't make any plans for the evening."

As usual, Shar's sudden change of mind perplexed me. The

ground never felt steady with her around.

Back at my hotel, the clerk told me I'd have to vacate my room by Monday because all the rooms had been booked for a convention. I somehow nodded as pleasantly as though this news were the most normal thing in the world and walked to the elevator like a zombie. Then tears stung my eyes. How much more could I take? I had no apartment yet, which meant I had to find another temporary hotel over the weekend. The notion of searching for another room was exhausting. Then I brightened. I'd get my first paycheck on Friday and just in time because I only had $1.30 left.

I fell asleep while watching TV with my hand in the box of chocolates the Bunnies gave me as a welcome gift. At 5 am the phone rang. Clark was calling from his bed at Caesars Motel where he often crashed after a late night rather than go home. My heart pounded wildly as I listened to him say, "I'm blue. I miss you. I love you."

At first I wanted to quit Playboy right that second and race back to L.A., but later, after a shower and breakfast I admitted that it was nice to know someone loved me, but I had to stick it out for the money if nothing else. I also knew nothing had changed between Clark and me. He would eventually leave Caesar's and go home to his wife. He always did.

Chapter Five

The Real Thing

To all my new brood—thanks ever so much for your warm wel-
come and for all the help you've given me. I'm sure I'm going to love
it here! Please feel free to come and talk to me any time. I'd like to
get to know you all better-and there'll never be a time when I'll be
too busy to talk to you (after all, I'm a female, aren't I?), Alyce. First
Page, Bunny Schedule

I placed the last of the schedule I had typed on top of the pile.
"Thanks, Carlie. I doubt I'd have gotten this out on time if you hadn't
helped. Can you believe how many different excuses the girls can
come up with to get on another shift or position? And what about the
girls who just don't show up at all? And since when is a fight with a
boyfriend a reason not to come to work?" I could feel the burn from
my neck to my forehead. I blew air up at my bangs and then inhaled
to cool off. "Isn't there a work ethic?"

Carlie shrugged and shook her head in disgust. "As for the girls, I
don't understand them either. But I'm glad to help anytime, especially for you."

"You're a doll. I could sure use more like you." I studied Carlie for
a few moments. Since my own training earlier Carlie had become the
friend I so desperately needed, a woman I could confide in without
the fear that what I told her would become the next day's rumor. Perhaps that loyalty had been learned in Carlie's religious training, her
chosen career before Playboy. Carlie had told me she had needed to
breathe and to experience a real life. So she left the convent, but
never expected she'd be taking in as much new air as she was by

working for Playboy. Carlie admitted she enjoyed the thrilling, risky and challenging job. And it showed because she was a dependable Bunny, a good trainer and a friend.

"What do you mean, Carlie, especially for me?" I dared to delve deeper.

Carlie leaned back into her chair. "At first I suspected you'd be like Coco." She stopped.

I leaned close. "You can be straight with me. We're friends, aren't we?" I placed the schedules in the out box for distribution. "And," I said as an afterthought, "we've already acknowledged that there aren't many in the Hutch we can be honest with. So let's have it."

Carlie smiled. "Coco always played favorites and spent most of her time telling her own tales of woe. She rarely had time to listen to our problems like you do. And she never had a single solution to offer." Carlie shook her head. Then her face brightened, "You always seem to have a good answer or at least a shoulder to cry on. Your door is always open."

It would always be open for Carlie. What would I have done without at least one good friend? Playboy was tolerable because of her.

I watched Carlie rise, so graceful. "See you later for my inspection," she curtsied and left. Even as a Bunny, Carlie maintained the quiet dignity of a cloistered nun and the allure of childlike innocence. She'd been promoted to the black costume shortly after training because she never missed a day, because of her beauty and because she maintained her cool under all circumstances.

I saw this firsthand one time, when a wealthy regular, but drunk, keyholder kept grabbing Carlie as she delivered his order. Though Carlie reported his behavior to Chris Malloy, he did nothing to stop it. Apparently he feared losing the business of a prominent Chicago businessman. So the drunk didn't give up. Carlie decided to take the situation into her own hands.

As I had arrived on the scene to inspect, Carlie was delivering his scotch on the rocks. Just as she removed the glass from her tray she tripped ever so slightly and dumped the drink in his crotch. From where I stood Carlie appeared to do it deliberately, but I doubted others would guess. Carlie was good.

The drunk jumped up. His bright red face radiated both anger and disbelief. Carlie handed him a napkin. "I'm so sorry. I've never been that clumsy before," she said softly with a demure smile.

The drunk threw the napkin onto the table and left. Once I found out the whole story, I could only praise Carlie for handling the man the best way she could given the circumstances. Then I marched over to Malloy and confronted him for not dealing with the problem.

"Look, Alyce, the man is a wealthy patron and Mr. Hefner's friend," Chris defended himself.

"I don't care if he is God himself. You know the rules. Hands off the Bunnies." I lowered my voice. "If I see this happening again, I'll report your inability to do your job."

Malloy's lips tightened across his clenched teeth and he spit back, "If you hired a better quality girl, we wouldn't have this problem."

"How much better than a former nun?"

Malloy leaned closer to me. "Even a nun can be a hooker." His thin lips seemed pasted into a permanent grin that mocked everything I said or did. Yet I knew that same mouth could spit angry, nasty words without warning.

I counted to ten. "Are you accusing me of hiring prostitutes or just that I condone the part time job?" I didn't wait for an answer. "Perhaps you're telling me you're jealous because you didn't think of being a pimp yourself." I adjusted his bow tie and checked the room to see if anyone else had been listening. No one seemed to notice our heated conversation. "You need to get a grip on the rules, Mr. Malloy. No more playing favorites and no more tricks to get rid of a girl you couldn't get into your own bed."

"You obviously haven't heard the latest from International." Malloy's grin was more of a sneer. "Management is looking for a Bunny who is prostituting. They must have some evidence to pursue it. I'm surprised you didn't know."

Though I was stunned, I didn't let on. "Keep that to yourself for now and do your real job. You're no cop." I started for the stairs back to my office when Malloy asked, "Are you going to give Carlie any demerits?"

I turned and faced him smiling, "Not for doing your job."

In my eagerness to be an accessible manager, I had suggested I would be available any time for the Bunnies, but I sometimes questioned whether my door was opened too wide. I often found myself engulfed by chatty Bunnies. In a short time they'd made me keep my promise to get to know each one of them intimately and sometimes told me more than I really wanted to know. For instance, on those too frequent occasions when one of the girls needed an abortion, I surely was the Mother Rabbit.

Natalie proved to be only the first. When she came to my office before going on the floor, she asked me, "Do you have time to talk?"

"Sure, I always have time for a Bunny," I assured her even if it wasn't true on every occasion. I noted Natalie appeared pale and a little heavy. Since I didn't know her well I decided not to dwell on those two negative points until they became overly evident to the Room Directors. After all, Natalie could just be on her period.

Natalie stood in front of me. "I need to get an abortion," she barely whispered. "And the other girls said you had the doctor's name and phone number."

"That's illegal." After my own trip to a back-alley doctor in Mexico for an abortion years before, I nearly bled to death. "Besides, why don't you use a contraceptive?"

"I have a diaphragm," she shrugged. "Sometimes I forget." Natalie's eyes became rimmed in red. I felt the sting in my own.

"I also thought he wanted the baby. He didn't." A tear slipped from one eye. "He threatened to leave if I have it."

I realized Natalie would have to pull herself together before the lunch crowd showed. Would that even be possible?

"How would I know where to get this doctor's name?" I wanted to be cautious though I knew I'd give Natalie the information if I had it. I had no desire to see any other woman go through what I did.

Natalie pointed to the Rolodex on my desk. "It's there. Under A for abortion."

I thumbed through the cards. Sure enough I found the number. I wrote it down and handed it to Natalie. "Try to remember your diaphragm the next time."

"Thank you."

"Now go freshen up and get to your station," I directed with a hint of tenderness. "I'll call the Room Director and let him know I held you up."

The next day Natalie brought me a box of Whitman Samplers and a Thank You note. I would come to discover the Bunnies would always show their appreciation in a like manner.

I was on my own for the first time in the two months I'd been at the Club. Both Shar and Babs, my so-called assistant, had the day off. I really felt at home at Playboy working alone, and found the day going much more smoothly, particularly when not fielding Shar's insults and constant references to my nemesis, Coco. As for Babs, for as little work as my alleged assistant did, she might as well take the rest of her life off. Shortly after Babs had been hired, she announced she was pregnant. Babs occupied her time with planning showers, buying baby clothes, and holding conversations about rearing children. She had no time to type and distribute anything. If I had my way we wouldn't rehire Babs after her maternity leave. Instead I'd find an assistant of my own choosing looking for a career outside the home. But Babs could have the upper hand because she had been hand-picked by Keith.

Three girls popped in the door. "Hi," one called out. "Can we have lunch here with you?"

Pleased they wanted to spend their free time with me, I agreed. Though I'd planned to get going on my rounds and finish up some other paper work, I couldn't refuse the three Bunnies when they had also brought a sandwich for me to eat. So I cleaned an area at the small oblong conference table and motioned to them to gather around. "Pardon the dust," I said. "No money in the budget I guess for the cleaners to take care of my office."

I resigned myself to the notion that my plan to work less than an eleven-hour day would go unfulfilled again. I would have to get into a shorter routine when the boys arrived. Carl and Greg's move to Chicago had been delayed because I hadn't found a place to live.

The Bunnies, Toti, Renee, and Ellie, seemed so chummy. In reality, they were as different from each other as if they had been raised on separate continents. "How did you three get to be such good friends?" I asked, not able to sidetrack my curiosity.

Renee spoke first. "Toti and I are from the same neighborhood back in Indiana."

"Renee got me hired here," Toti added. As Keith's current fling, Renee would have pull. That probably explained why Toti worked as a Bunny when Shar and Keith didn't think she was pretty enough.

"And you, Ellie?"

"I met Renee when we lived in the Mansion. I still do, at least for another week."

As they munched their sandwiches, I assessed the girls. Renee certainly outshone the other two girls, even without all the help from artificial aids. Though Ellie had a fresh, girl-next-door-look so appealing to many men, Renee possessed classic glamour and sophistication. Her startling waist-length black hair highlighted with natural auburn streaks was an enticing contrast to her porcelain skin. Each of these two had qualities to please every keyholder's taste, no doubt. Unfortunately, I sided with Shar about Toti.

Though attractive, Toti had none of the exceptional beauty or charm of the other two. She did the least amount required in the job and rarely volunteered for extra hours. But who could blame her. She came to Playboy as a welfare mother of two children she'd had by the time she reached nineteen. Sadly her history was not unlike that of several other Bunnies abandoned by their lovers at the birth of the first child. Toti's boyfriend at least stayed until the second one arrived. She didn't make the $600-$800 a month that classy Renee brought in, but she did make a far better salary than she would have done waiting tables elsewhere or working at the Kresge dime store. Plus she had health benefits.

I finished my meal and freshened my lipstick. "Ellie, why are you leaving the Mansion?"

Ellie was silent for a few moments. She seemed to be preparing her answer carefully. "I have enough money to live on my own, now," she answered. "And far away from that prying house mother."

"Mrs. Bundy isn't all that bad. She's just following Mr. Hefner's rules," Toti defended.

Ellie spun around to face Toti. "I need more space. Leave it at that. I also can now pay more than $50.00 a month for rent, thanks to Playboy and . . ." She threw her half-eaten sandwich into the trash. "I gotta get ready for my shift." Ellie left the office.

Toti shrugged at Renee and me. "She must have the red curse."

"You think her period affects her attitude 30 days a month?" Renee responded, sounding snide.

Was there a rift between Renee and Ellie? I started to pose the question when Toti said, "You're only upset with Ellie because she doesn't think I'm Bunny material."

Renee reached across the table and patted Toti's hand. "Of course you are. Besides you need this job more than she does. She'd never think beyond herself as you have."

I didn't interrupt, sure Renee referred to Toti becoming the guardian of her seven-year-old sister when her mother died suddenly a few months ago. I empathized because I, too, had found myself in the same position with my sister Tekkie. That alone could be why I protected Toti from Shar's often vicious attacks about her Bunny Image.

I rose. "It's time for you two to get a move on. I'll walk with you. I like to watch you get ready because it gives me tips on how to help my own looks."

"You don't need help," Renee offered.

I chuckled. "Thank you, but not everyone thinks that way I'm afraid."

"Right. Shar doesn't think so," Toti spurted out, then covered her mouth.

Surely my reddening tell-tale freckles set off an alarm in the two Bunnies.

"What I mean," Toti continued. "Shar says you're super intelligent and that's true and we all respect that. But she says sometimes your brains get in the way of your looks."

I noted for the first time that Toti's voice sounded like a Munchkin from *The Wizard of Oz*.

Toti sighed. "I'm sorry. I shouldn't be talking behind her back, but sometimes she, well, she can be difficult."

"We're all difficult one time or another," I consoled. Once again, Shar had shown her insensitivity.

"Now that you've started, we might as well tell Alyce the rest." Renee turned from Toti and faced me. "Shar keeps reminding us that you won't be here long because Coco is coming back. Most of us don't want her back because things have run so much more smoothly since you came."

"Shar tells us not to get too close to you because you'll be transferred." Toti's face seemed to register the reality of the warning once those words flowed from her. "Where will you go, Alyce?" She asked almost in tears.

I didn't answer right away. Then I said, "I'm not going anywhere. I'm sure Coco's return is just a rumor." I walked to the door. "Come on, you two pouty-faced girls. We have jobs to do." I must confront Shar about all this garbage. Idle and nasty gossip only made the day-to-day operation unstable.

I followed the two girls to the dressing room. The small chamber vibrated with the Bunny's youthful energy. Several girls, including Ellie, sat before the long mirror and transformed themselves from everydayness to gorgeous showgirls. The sight always amazed me. But today I learned a new trick. I laughed when I saw the other use for the Bunny tails. The less-endowed girls stuffed one in each bra to boost their breast size.

I couldn't help comparing myself to the girls preparing for their shift. Granted they all looked more seductive with help from a perfect makeup application, hairpieces to enhance fine hair and conceal any problems and a costume that squeezed a twenty-seven inch waist down to twenty inches. But one other day in the dressing room, Bunny Jane came in at the end of her shift and as she undressed, she exposed raw and bloody slashes where the uniform stays had pierced her body. I pointed to them and Jane acknowledged, "It's the price we pay to fulfill men's fantasies." She leaned over and took off her spikes. As she rubbed her blistered feet she said, "I don't think God meant for these little piggies to be crammed into such towering points." She tossed her heels into a locker.

Since that day I looked the other way when Bunnies ripped stays out of their costumes although I should have given them demerits for alterations not acceptable in the manual. Blistered feet and scarred torsos were a normal part of the daily routine for a Bunny. Yet when I looked at myself, I only saw that nose. At this moment I vowed to take care of it as soon as I could work it out financially.

As each girl finished her ritual, I inspected her. I fluffed Ellie's tail, ordered Toti to clean her shoes and suggested that Sally get her hair piece dyed again because the color didn't quite match her own hair. But mostly they all passed. As always, I marveled at each girl's remarkable metamorphosis. I equated the transformation to the difference between a dandelion and a rose.

Though I dreaded doing so I pulled Toti aside. "Are you gaining weight? Not that you are too heavy, but you might want to watch it. You know how Shar and Barry are about weight." Toti's eyes reddened. I hated this part of the job. Yet my position required such brutal scrutiny and truth. If I didn't nip problems in the bud, a Room Director would scream about the girl's inadequate looks. Sometimes he'd tell Barry before he put it in his report to me, especially if the Room Director wanted to get rid of a girl.

Toti pulled herself together and said, "I'll watch it." She fled to her station.

Once the dressing room had emptied, I went back to my office to check messages and to give the girls time to get to their stations before I made a round through the Club. No sooner had I sat down—as always careful to avoid the unreliable back—than Barry raced through the doorway faster than his short legs appeared able to carry him. "I need Adrian Ingstrom's telephone number."

"Why?" I asked. Barry rarely acted without some sinister motive. "You can talk to her when she comes to work."

"I need it now," he shouted and then said more quietly, "I really need it now. But you can't tell anyone I asked for it, understood?"

I nodded.

"And hurry." Barry paced. "I've got to get back to the Playmate Bar. A friend is waiting."

I flipped through the Rolodex. Could it be true? That Barry needed to reach Adrian to set her up with one of his friends? I had heard the gossip, but assumed it couldn't be genuine because management made it clear that there could be no fraternizing between Bunnies and guests. Or could the number be for Barry himself? I had also heard he dated Bunnies and I had noticed he made sure Adrian got preferred posts. I handed him the number. What else could I do?

He snatched the paper from my hand and started for the door. "Oh, by the way," Barry turned back to me. "What do you know about the effect on my four-month old son if he's been exposed to whooping cough?"

As I explained, I felt honored Barry thought of me as a real mother, not just a woman who played that role at the Club. Yet I did wonder why he hadn't asked his own wife. Unless of course Barry's son was with him at a location neither should have been. Perhaps Adrian's apartment before her recent move. I'll bet that was it, I thought, and now I wanted to spit at Barry for cheating on his wife and for taking advantage of his position. I myself knew what it was like to have a husband who cheated on me. Yet I needed to be careful about condemning Barry on hearsay.

When I finished explaining, Barry held up the paper with Adrian's number on it, "Thanks." He reached for the doorknob and stopped again. "One more thing, you're doing a good job here. You're bright, organized and the girls like you. You're also looking good, more hip. But you should have your nose fixed." With that he was out the door in a flash.

I considered throwing the ashtray at him. Instead I flipped through my desk calendar counting the weeks until my health insurance went into full effect. Perhaps my once diagnosed deviated septum could get corrected at the same time so I could get an entire nose job for nearly free. "I'll show you, little bald man, who has brains *and* beauty."

As soon as I said that I felt sorry for him. Originally he had worked as a bartender. Most stayed in that position, but Barry, even without a college degree, apparently did a good enough job to catch International's attention and management decided to groom him for his current position. So I didn't understand why he wasn't more careful about his extracurricular activities. Never mind, I told myself as I got back to work. Just remember he's an insecure bully.

Once on the floor my confidence soared. Men made no bones about staring at and asking Room Directors about me. I over-heard one say to another, "Check it out." I gathered I stood out because I was tall, attractive—and clothed. The difference when compared to the Bunnies gave me an air of importance and mystique. I allowed myself to revel in it for exactly thirty seconds then I chastised myself for caring how any man felt about me. I shouldn't and wouldn't count on anyone to support my two sons and me. Angelo hadn't and Clark made no effort. I had long since ruled out depending on any man. And I wouldn't let myself be like the Bunnies who believed they were better than others because they had a man. Now I wanted more than that from my life.

Happy to arrive at the end of my room inspections without any hassle, I made a final check in the Playroom. If all went well, I could get out of the Club before 8 pm for the first time in weeks. I needed to get back to the hotel—the second since my arrival—to pack. Against my better judgment I had decided to move into the same townhouse complex where Barry and his wife lived. I didn't like having my daily life played out in his view but I didn't have a choice. Other places either were too expensive or too far away from public transportation. It was bad enough that I would have to take an advance on my wages to pay for the unexpected $220.00 security deposit plus the connection fees for the telephone and utilities. But I needed the boys with me. Plus they would enjoy living only two blocks from Lake Michigan and a block from Lincoln Park which borders the lake.

Toti, her face red and tear-streaked, ran past me. I reached out to stop her, but the Bunny wrenched free. Chris Malloy was the culprit once again. There he stood, leaning against the bar as though nothing had happened, observing every movement in the room. As much as the man irritated me, though, I never failed to be slightly distracted by his remarkable eyelashes. No man had the right to such luxuriant lashes. Their abundance became even more noticeable in the bar lights that focused on them like a stage spot. Though I wanted to maintain an air of authority, I caught myself recalling past discussions. After Gloria Steinem's undercover expose of the Playboy Club, men including Malloy charged feminists with penis envy. Little did Malloy realize it wasn't his penis women wanted, it was his eyelashes. And only his eyelashes.

I readied myself to do battle.

When I reached Malloy, he stood up straight and raised both hands as if to stop me. "She's screwing up every order, Alyce." Of course he anticipated my question. His face still showed a hint of anger from his run-in with Toti. "I'm justified in being upset. Toti asks for the wrong drinks which means we waste money because she's not listening to the keyholder. Then she asks for the drinks in the wrong order, and so on. Toti can't keep this up or we'll lose customers."

"Did it ever occur to you something might be wrong with her? She's a far better employee than you're portraying." I turned my back to the bar so I could observe the other Bunnies on the floor.

"Did it ever occur to you, Mrs. Bonura, that's your job, not mine? If she can't serve 10 people in 10 minutes and get it right, Toti shouldn't be working here."

I whipped around to bring my face within inches of his own. "Did it ever occur to you it's both our jobs? Did it ever occur to you she might need more training and not a reaming out in front of these customers?" I waved my arm at the full room. "As in all businesses," I added, "an employee's well-being will make or break an organization. And didn't your mother ever tell you that you catch more bees with honey than vinegar? Now you'll have to work the floor short. Too late to get a reserve."

Without waiting for an answer I left to have a talk with Toti. I didn't get far before I nearly toppled Shar to the floor as we met rounding a corner. I caught a glimpse of Shar's boyfriend, Brian. His abrupt departure and Shar's teary eyes spoke of a recent argument.

"Oh," Shar yelped. "You startled me."

"I thought you were off today." I knew I sounded edgy from my confrontation with Malloy, and now this—had Shar come to the Club to check up on me?

Shar flipped her thumb at her lover's disappearing back and said, "You just missed Brian. We had dinner here before he had to get back to Detroit." Shar gazed after him, her mood going from sad to star struck in seconds. "Isn't he the greatest?"

"Yeah, the greatest," I almost snarled. If it wasn't Brian she bragged about, it was one of her new dresses, like the last one for which she spent $55.00—a fortune and a third of my weekly take home pay. Had my envy shown? "You seemed upset a minute ago. Is everything ok?" I secretly hoped it wasn't, then caught myself. When did I ever get so catty?

"Yes," Shar answered and then seemed to disappear into another space before she added, "I miss Brian so much when he's gone, that's all."

"I've gotta go, Shar. I need to tend to a Bunny incident and get home. See you later."

"Anything I can help with?" Shar sounded genuine for the first time since I met her.

"No, I can handle it." I didn't need any more interference in my tasks. And Shar would only mess things up more than Malloy had.

I was too late. Toti couldn't be found. Too bad because now I would have to give her demerits for leaving without permission, let alone for the mess she left her post in. It would be exactly the right fuel Malloy needed to mount a case to terminate her for violations of Bunny Image. Hard to argue against such a nebulous trait, but attitude and her weight gain fit the picture. Yet I would have to wait until tomorrow to deal with this issue, after I signed the lease and arranged for movers to tote all my goods now in storage to my new home. Thank goodness my Playboy day didn't start until 11 am.

Chapter Six

Trust

For us it is the Good Life. It doesn't matter that all American young men don't live like Playboy heroes; what matters is that we think they do. For us Playboy is the symbol of your good life. The Playboy Paper September 1967

The phone rang as the last box was hauled away by the movers. Toti's voice surprised me. "What's up?" I tried to sound cheerful, knowing what laid ahead for Toti.

"I need to see you today. In private." Toti sounded as though she'd been up all night crying.

"Sure thing. I'll be at the Club about an hour later than usual. When would you like to meet?"

"Then. I'll be waiting for you." Toti hung up without a good-by, which wasn't characteristic of her normal self. Her voice held more distress than a usual row with her boyfriend would bring on.

I hurried over to my new townhouse. I had to a take a taxi, a luxury for which I didn't have the funds. Plus I'd had to pay $23.00 a month to store my furniture and $89.00 to have it moved to the townhouse. Playboy only agreed to pay for the move. Would my finances ever get to the place I didn't have to count each penny and calculate practically to the hour when a payment was due? A few more weeks of steady income should get me over the hump. But could I make it?

As I grabbed the handle of the taxi door, an impeccably dressed woman stopped me. "Have you ever modeled?" she asked.

I was so stunned I could only answer, "No." What a morning! I really couldn't dally. I certainly didn't have the time to discuss a career change.

The woman gave me a card and said, "If you think you'd like to, I'd love to have you come to my agency."

Flustered, but also flattered, I thanked the woman and said I couldn't talk right then because I was late for work. Nevertheless, the woman did wave good-by as my cab sped off. I stuffed the card in my purse to think about another day. The hours I already worked would never allow me to take even a part-time modeling position. Yet the offer had all the magical promise of scene from a movie like *My Fair Lady*.

I rushed the movers and as soon as I paid them, I hopped a bus to Playboy. The trip that day seemed to take forever. What could be causing Toti's anguish?

As promised, Toti waited for me in my office. Curled in the corner of the couch, the Bunny resembled a sleeping child. She sat up when I approached her. I saw the misery I had heard earlier in Toti's voice. The Bunny's red and swollen face made her barely recognizable. I had enough personal experience to realize much of the discoloration and swelling came not so much from crying but from a beating. I'd looked that way myself.

I sat next to Toti and took hold of her small, tense hand. "Tell me what's going on."

Toti kept her head bent toward the floor as though examining the carpet pattern. Like figures in a still life, neither of us moved. The quiet was disturbed only by the sound of a car's horn from the street below.

I dared not disturb her for fear Toti would recoil and become forever silent. I anticipated a terrible revelation. I could be patient to give Toti the time she needed.

After nearly fifteen minutes, Toti took her hand from mine. She stood and faced me. She lifted the man's shirt she wore over slacks. Suddenly I felt as though my breath had been punched out of my own body. The skin on Toti's slightly swollen stomach and chest was a labyrinth of yellow, greenish-purple and black-blue patterns.

"What happened?" I gasped, willing myself not to turn from the sight.

Tears hung from Toti's chin. "George, my boyfriend."

"He did this? But why?" I flashed back to my own embarrassment all those years ago when I showed up with tell-tale bruises and found myself making up one excuse after another for how it happened.

"He doesn't want our baby." Toti lowered her shirt and wiped the tears away with the back of her hand. Though normally not a beauty, at that moment her face appeared so disfigured from the pain she harbored, Toti seemed like a grotesque rendering for a horror show.

My own heart remembered such a time. I shared Toti's uncontrollable grief. "What does he want?"

Toti collapsed onto the couch. She folded her legs to her chest and clasped her arms around them. She laid her head on her knees. "He wants me to get rid of the baby. He says I have too many responsibilities already."

"Including him. Toti, when was the last time he worked?" I had been aware that once Toti let George, her third lover, move in with her, he hadn't worked since, which made it about six months.

"It won't matter if he works or not. If I can't get an abortion, he'll leave me." Toti sobbed openly.

I leaned back and looked across the disheveled office to the opposite wall so in need of paint that layers of past colors poked through worn and peeling areas. "What can I do to help?" I sighed, resigning myself to the answer.

Toti glanced at the Rolodex on my desk. "Give me the name and number of the doctor."

I didn't have to ask her what doctor.

"I can't," I answered.

Toti's whole body tensed as she glared at me with such venom I doubted I would ever shake it from my memory. "You mean you won't. I'm not one of the favorites and this will be a good way to get rid of me. Fire me because I'm pregnant. Renee would get the information."

I circled my arm around Toti's shoulders and pulled her close. I secretly agreed with Toti that no girlfriend of management would have to endure a pregnancy. But in that case it would be to avoid a scandal and perhaps an unwanted divorce, rather than to preserve the relationship and the girl's job. "Toti, I can't give out that information any longer because a former Bunny is facing felony charges as an accomplice to abortion. International is walking on eggshells now and probably still will long after the case is settled. We're all being watched. No more abortions."

A recent confidential memo had been sent out about the subject. Even at that moment the uncaring harshness of it hurt. The Bunny being charged was on record as terminated from Playboy and could not be rehired. She had also been described as "the little silver-blonde with the over-size chest measurement."

Toti threw off my arm and jumped up. "Then that means George will leave and I'll be out of a job. What will I do then? How will I support me and my kids—ask my dead sister?"

I reached for her, but Toti fled. I fought down the vomit rising into my throat. For the first time in years I felt completely helpless.

After almost an hour, I finally left the couch and started my real day. With all that had happened with Toti I hadn't noticed the mixed bouquet in a vase on my desk. I picked up the attached card, sure the flowers had come from Clark. To my amazement, Barry had sent them as an apology for his irrational conduct the day before. Once again he commented about the good job I had been doing. His actions typified those of an abuser like my own former husband. Each time the offender hurt his prey, whether emotionally or physically, he'd beg forgiveness to keep the victim in his control.

I decided to use the fleeting gesture to get Barry to tell me the truth about Coco. So I walked the block to his office at headquarters to thank Barry in person.

International hadn't cried budget crunch when they'd decorated Barry's office. The oversized furniture in dark mahogany dwarfed him. Still I was envious of the paisley print sofa and matching chair and the window with the uninterrupted city view. What did it take to get a space like that?

Balls! The real ones.

I rapped on the door jam. Barry looked up from the latest edition of the *Playboy Magazine*. "Good afternoon," he said without taking the cigar from his mouth. "What brings you all the way here, sweetheart? Nothin' serious, I hope." Barry pushed his glasses to his forehead. Then he slid the magazine on top of a file and motioned me in.

He propped his feet on his desk, leaned back in his chair and scratched his crotch.

His degrading gesture stopped me in my tracks. Barry smiled and said, "Sit. Sit."

I moved slowly forward. "I'll only be a minute." I sat in a leather chair.

"Well, what is it?" Did I detect irritation so soon?

"First. . ." I leaned gracefully back in the chair and crossed my legs, showing enough to get Barry's attention. "I want to thank you for the beautiful flowers you sent. You really didn't have to."

Barry batted the air as he answered, "No problem. You deserve them, sweetheart. I like to make sure my employees know their value." He still had a New York accent though he'd been in Chicago for years.

I jumped on that opening. "That reminds me of another situation. One less appealing than a bouquet, I'm afraid."

Barry's forehead turned a deep pink. Did he think I had some dirt on him "What's the gossip now?" he asked and scratched his crotch again.

"Shar says Coco is coming back. I need to know the truth." I paused to avoid sounding testy. "As you know, if she comes back, I'm out of a job."

"Shar's always opening her big mouth about one thing or another." Barry cocked his head to the side. "She's still angry with me for breaking up with her and marrying someone else."

I hadn't known that little tidbit, but it didn't surprise me. In the first week at Playboy I had been alerted to most of the affairs. Corporate headquarters was a Peyton Place. "Okay, perhaps, but is she telling me the truth?"

"No!" Barry's angry voice had become one of his most notable and unpleasant traits. "I told you before, Coco is not taking back her job, your job, and," he lowered his voice, "I also told you that Shar is on her way out. Didn't I tell you that you had a great chance at getting Shar's job?" He sucked his cigar and made a smacking noise before puffing a billow of smoke upward. "Besides do you think we'd waste all that money to train you for nothin'?"

"By the looks of my office, no one spends any money."

Barry took a hard drag from his cigar before squashing it out in the ashtray. I expected I'd pushed too far. "Have you ever lived in New York City?" he asked.

"No," I answered, caught off guard as he abruptly dove into another subject. "But I've been there many times. Why do you ask?"

"I'm thinking of going back there to take over the Club. If you'd go along too, you'd make that transfer easy."

"But that's not the point of today's conversation, is it?" I really didn't want Coco in the same club with me in any capacity. "I mean," I pressed further, "Coco could come back if I'm promoted to Bunny Director, right?"

"Well, uh, technically, I suppose so. But I haven't heard that." Barry moved a stapler from one corner to another. His phone rang. When he answered I took the opportunity to leave before he became even less forthcoming or I set him off on another tirade. He'd have to give me a box of Godiva Chocolates for that. Yet I wondered about the New York question.

Back at the Club, I couldn't help but resent its contrast to headquarters' offices. The narrow, dim hallway didn't match the sleek, modern decor of International. Before entering my own personal dungeon I smelled the ever-present mix of cigarette smoke and White Shoulders Perfume and glanced down the hall to Shar's office. I could hear her talking with someone. This was as good a time as any for confrontation. What difference would it make? I either had a permanent job at the Chicago Playboy Club or I didn't. Once I faced my boss, I would then have to take care of another unpleasant task— Toti. I needed to call in a reserve girl to fill in for her. At least for the moment Toti still had a job.

As I walked toward Shar's office I pondered Toti's predicament. How long could I hold out before I'd have to let her go? She had already gained enough weight to have a problem fitting into her costume. Soon everyone would notice the obvious signs of pregnancy. Little got by the scrutiny of the other Bunnies, let alone the male employees who noted every flaw and scored each women according to her beauty. Enough of Toti for the moment. I had to get down to Shar's motives for telling me Coco would be back as Bunny Mother.

I walked through the open door just as Shar hung up the telephone. The Do-Not-Disturb sign dangled from the doorknob. Shar used that when she watched her afternoon soap operas. The usual smoke-fog floated through the room. I sneezed six times before I could acknowledge Shar's greeting. Shar offered a tissue. I nodded and blew my nose. I dabbed my eyes, careful not to disturb the false eyelashes.

"What's up kiddo?" Shar sounded too cheerful. "Sit." Then she sounded like Barry.

I sat across the desk from Shar. "This is going to be difficult, but. . ."

"Life is difficult most of the time." Shar lit another cigarette. She was smoking more than usual the past few weeks.

I bit my lower lip, which never held lipstick because of that habit. I shifted my legs and finally said. "Ok, here it goes."

Shar's forehead furrowed. Her smile melted away as she inhaled from her cigarette. The area around her mouth showed hard, permanent creases from the habit.

"You know how the gossip is around here."

Shar nodded as she blew the smoke out her nose and then her mouth.

"First of all, I'm concerned about my position here. You have told me Coco is coming back as the Bunny Mother, but Barry says otherwise." I waited for a response which didn't happen. So I continued. "Barry did admit Coco could come back but in another capacity and then he mentioned New York City to me."

Shar took several more drags before she said a word. "Barry plays both sides. He knows as well as I do Coco's coming back because pregnant or not, she's one of Hef's favorites. Ya know the type—cute, bubbly, a yes-girl, but not too bright." Shar chuckled. "That's why she keeps getting pregnant."

Exasperated again by how Shar circumvented my questions, I became even more blunt. What had I to lose? "Tell me the truth for once, Shar. I'm tired of being kept in the dark."

"Coco's coming back." Shar crushed her cigarette into the ashtray and lit another one. "At the moment, no decision has been made in what position, but I wouldn't get too settled if I were you, kiddo."

Shar looked tired, her skin drawn and ashen, not the normal glow. Even her makeup appeared less perfect.

"You don't look well." I made every effort to sound soothing, concerned.

"I'm fine. Some days more than others the job gets to me, though."

I thought I could see uncharacteristic tears forming. And did I note Shar's chin quiver?

"Is that all?" Shar almost whispered.

I couldn't tell if Shar was sincere or if she was acting this way to stop my interrogation. I decided to take a chance on the acting. "No. What's going to happen to me?"

"You're too bright and they've put a lotta money into you. So don't worry. You'll still be a Bunny Mother, but maybe not here." Shar's voice had hardened to matter-a-fact rather all sympathy gone.

"Didn't anyone think to ask me what I wanted? Didn't anyone think about how another move would affect my sons?" I stood so fast my chair teetered backward and wobbled before it righted itself. "Doesn't anyone here see women as more than an object?"

"Sshh, keep your voice down." Shar raised her finger to her lips and motioned for me to sit again. I remained standing. "Hef doesn't think he gives that impression. He thinks Playboy is the best opportunity for the girls—all of us. Where else would we get these salaries and benefits?"

Shar's defense rang true, but still I didn't see myself or any other woman as a commodity. I thought Playboy did. "So I just do my job like a good little girl and wait to see where the shoe falls."

"Basically," Shar stood, "that's it. Now I've gotta get to a meeting."

I walked to the door with Shar. "I do have one other thing."

Shar's impatient sigh sounded like air being let out of a tire. "Well, let me have it, kiddo."

"My name's Alyce, Shar. Try to use it."

Shar stepped back from me and widened her eyes to tease me.

"I've also heard other rumors." I couldn't stop now. "You're forever referring to me as the brain and noting I'm not pretty enough to be with Playboy. Is that why I'm being railroaded?"

"Slow down, girl," Shar almost shouted as she pulled me back in and closed her office door so no one else could hear. "I'm impressed with your intelligence. And to tell the truth, you could improve your looks. Who can't? But I'm not the one pushing that issue. Your buddy Barry is. He wants your nose fixed, pure and simple. Brains are for the men around here, doll, I mean Alyce."

Neither Shar nor Barry spoke like the modeling agent. Who was right? Didn't matter, the nose as they all knew it would be gone soon.

Shar opened the door, "Now I must go. We have more pressing problems at the moment. We need to find the Bunny who is a hooker on the side." Just like that my problems were irrelevant. "Any ideas? I think it's Nadine. You know the vamp who calls in sick all the time?"

"You mean the Gift Shop Bunny, don't you?" I didn't hide my sarcasm.

"Yeah, her." Shar said as she rolled her head from side to side. "She's alone a lot. So she'd have the opportunity to slip the information to a john."

Shar turned away, leaving me to bite my lower lip to stop myself from crying.

Chris Malloy had mentioned management's hunt for a prostitute among the Bunnies, but he thought it was Carlie. At the rate he and Shar were headed the investigation would net all 70 plus Bunnies who worked for Chicago Playboy Club. When would someone let the Bunny Mother in on the investigation? Did they think I got a percentage, that I could be a madam?

"You let me know if you find that mysterious lady of the night," I said. "Lord knows why you didn't tell me about management's concern. I only supervise the Bunnies, right?"

Shar stopped. She faced me. "Watch your tone. I thought Barry told you."

"Perhaps you and Barry need to put your hatchets aside so each of you know what the other is really doing." With that I went to my office.

I slammed the door so hard the only picture in the room fell off the wall. I slumped into my desk chair and pulled the modeling agency card from my purse. I left it there on my desk as a happy reminder of a possible new career until another administrative position came along. That is if I would be forced from Playboy.

The week's schedule stared at me from the middle of the blotter. I thumbed through the 15 pages until I landed on the correct day. I called the listed reserve girl to fill in for Toti explaining Toti had a cold and would be out for a while.

I finished the payroll, happy that the week neared its end. Ten more days and the boys would be with me. They'd have to start school a couple of weeks late, but I couldn't move them until I put the townhouse in order. The new environment for Carl and Greg would be tough enough without the delayed start, but they were resilient and would manage. I slid the payroll in the outbox and headed out to the Club.

Barry stopped me and asked me to join him for a drink when I finished my room inspections. Though I said I needed to start organizing my townhouse and had hoped to get home early, he insisted.

"You're the boss." Giving in, I smiled and told him I'd be back in a half hour.

When I reached the main level, the last of my inspections, I heard an uproar coming from the Cartoon Corner. I arrived on the scene just in time to hear one of three men seated at a table call Sadie a Nigger. She passed me crying as Joel, the Room Director, told the member to pay his bill and leave. As I watched, open-mouthed, one of the member's guests stood and punched Joel in the mouth, sending him through the service door—just as the night bartender came the other way. Then Joel caught his balance and swung back, and the second guest joined in the brawl. When the bartender saw that, he and the busboy jumped in the fracas. Finally, the unruly guests were subdued and escorted out of the Club to the cheers of other patrons and employees.

I turned to Joel and asked, "What started this?"

"I cautioned the member and his guests not to use their fingers to pick food off the buffet. They objected because even though they had already been told. They ignored me and continued to do the same."

"Nasty cut on your mouth." I interrupted. "You need to take care of that."

Joel dabbed at his bloody lip with a hanky and continued, "I told them that they had to leave the Club. The member pulled me aside and begged me to reconsider because he was closing on a big deal."

"From what I just saw they obviously still didn't behave themselves." I chuckled.

"No, but I did let them stay, and asked Sadie to wait on them. I even told Sadie to get them plates of food from the buffet. The rest you saw."

"I'm always amazed," I said. "I'll talk with Sadie and get her back on the floor."

Within minutes of their conversation, Sadie was back at her station, showing no sign of hurt feelings. What a trouper!

As promised, I met Barry. "What kept you so long?" Barry sounded annoyed.

"Oh nothing. Just a little misunderstanding that had to be worked out." I ordered a much needed Rob Roy and opted to have a plate of food so I wouldn't get tipsy.

Barry sipped his martini and said, "After our discussion earlier, I need to get something off my chest."

What little of it there is, I wanted to say. But of course I held my tongue and waited for the worst.

"Oh, and what is that?"

Barry looked around to make sure no one was listening. "You probably got wind of the spiteful rumors about me."

I had no idea how to respond so I took a bite of food to fill my mouth. I'd heard so many.

"Pretty dress, by the way, sweetheart," Barry commented out of the blue.

I gulped my drink. "You can call me Alyce." What was Barry up to?

Barry paused for a moment. "People talk a lot around here, but you know that already. So you probably also heard that I have been dating a Bunny."

Just one? I dabbed my napkin over my mouth to hide my smirk.

"Well, it's not so. I'm a happily married man with a baby son, a lovely wife and a job I can't afford to lose." He finished his martini in one huge gulp and signaled for another. "I just wanted to set things straight."

"Thank you," I said. "I'm glad you confided in me, and now I really must get home." I stood and said, "Good night."

The Bunny with Barry's drink distracted him. If he noticed my departure, I couldn't tell. What else would I expect from him? At least I didn't have to prolong my farewell.

I reluctantly pushed open the door to the townhouse. My welcome would be nearly 100 boxes to unpack, again. That seemed a never-ending part of my life. With my own job in jeopardy, it might not be over soon.

I made myself a cup of tea and browsed through the mail, setting the bills aside and unsealing a letter from Clark, the first in over a week. As in his past letters he went on for three pages about his daily activities and closed with his usual self-pitying words, "I'm so lonely. I miss you. I love you. No more post cards. Please write a letter. I'm so proud of you. We all want to hear the latest. "

I folded the letter and returned it to the envelope. I didn't have time to write a letter but if I did, it wouldn't be kind. My patience was wearing thin.

In every room, daunting stacks of boxes lined the walls almost to the ceiling. I decided to begin in the kitchen. I needed that room more than any other to function, but instead of opening a box, I sat at the Formica topped table and cried. Clark had no idea what loneliness was.

By 1:00 am, I had only unpacked four boxes. The process had been slowed by the dirt. Landlords Mr. and Mrs. Bill Anderson, both in their mid-fifties, had promised the townhouse would get a thorough cleaning before I moved in. But it appeared they'd either forgotten or their definition of thorough differed from mine.

At that meeting with the landlords, the topic quickly went from maintenance responsibilities to Mr. Anderson's perverse curiosity. "I have ways to find out everything my tenants are doing." His mouth formed a half smile as he raised his right eyebrow.

His expression made my skin crawl. I signed the longest lease I had ever seen and got up to leave, but Mr. Anderson hadn't finished his say. "I'm familiar with those Bunnies." Was there drool at the corner of his mouth? Several Playboy employees other than Barry lived at the complex. Had Mr. Anderson spied on them? I pictured him on a box outside one of my windows, peering in.

"Yes, well, I must get back to work."

I made it to the door before he spoke again.

"They're nothing but sex-crazed screwballs."

I turned to look at him.

His eyes were wide and shining at the thought. Mr. Anderson clearly wanted to believe that. He wanted the Bunnies and all associated with the Playboy Club to be titillating, rather than hard working.

In other words more juicy than boring. I decided not to burst his fantasy bubble. Besides, I had real, less provocative work to do—the schedule.

Though I had nothing to hide, certainly no late night orgies, my drapes would be closed once dusk appeared. I had no desire to have that dirty old man peeking in my windows.

I again woke up around 4:00 am to TV static. I had fallen asleep curled in the corner of the couch, the only uncluttered spot I could find. I stretched my aching limbs and climbed the stairs to my bedroom. I grabbed a pillow and blanket from a box on the unmade bed. Once in my nightgown I fell onto the bed and slept.

The telephone awakened me around 9:00 am. Too drowsy to even focus on the receiver, I nearly knocked the whole unit to the floor.

Renee was on the other end, sobbing. She told me to get to the Club immediately. "There's trouble," Renee said and blew her nose. "It's Toti. And it's bad, but I don't want to tell you over the telephone."

"I'll be right in." I splashed water on my face and dressed. I'd fix my hair and makeup at the Club.

All sorts of scenarios rushed through my mind as I rode the bus to work. George beat Toti bad enough to put her in the hospital. One of her children was ill or perhaps even missing. Or had Toti tried unsuccessfully to abort the baby on her own? My thoughts again flashed back to another time. I rested my hand on my stomach and recalled my own nightmare as vividly as though it happened yesterday.

In 1962, I had an abortion in Mexico, the only place I could get the procedure done unless I used a coat hanger. My neighbor, Mrs. Garcia, had done that and nearly bled to death. My abortion was botched. I hemorrhaged. I would have done as well with a hanger. I had to chance being turned over to the police or bleed to death. I drove myself to the emergency hospital. Jail time would be better than dying. Whether they believed my story, that I miscarried, I never knew. Fortunately no one pried further. Clark never had known he fathered the child.

So into my own world, I almost missed my stop. I ran to the Club and once inside the lobby I opted to take the stairs, two at a time, rather than wait for the elevator and its lumbering ascent. With each step up, I prepared myself for Toti's own botched abortion.

Renee stood at the window in my office gazing at the brick wall across the alley. For the first time, I truly observed Renee's extraordinary beauty, even without makeup and with hair pulled into a youthful ponytail. Standing in the brutal sunlight, somehow the natural Renee looked more ravishing than usual.

When Renee heard me, she ran to me, hugging me so hard against her chest, I gasped. "She didn't come to me," Renee sobbed. Her body shuddered against me. "In the end Toti didn't trust me."

"In the end?" I backed away. "What do you mean, in the end?"

Renee lowered her head. She stayed like that until her shoulders stopped shaking and she had gained composure. "Toti hung herself yesterday afternoon. She put her kids on a bus to Indiana to her mother's and then she went back to her townhouse and hung herself in the basement."

I fell onto the couch. I couldn't stop my tears this time or the intensely personal memories Toti's death recalled. "Who found her?"

"I did. I have a key to her place. When she didn't answer her phone or return my messages, I knew something was terribly wrong." Renee sat next to me and lit a cigarette.

At that moment I wished I smoked, too, especially when the vision of my own mother's body being cut down from a basement rafter came to me.

"Toti came to me yesterday for help." Saying her name stung my tongue. I put my face into the palms of my hands and sobbed as hard as Renee had earlier. "I couldn't help her." I rocked back and forth and repeated, "I couldn't help her." The second time I spoke the words I thought of my own mother. I couldn't help her either. I failed both women.

Renee leaned back and murmured, "I don't think anyone could." She rubbed my back in small, caring circles. "Toti had made too many mistakes and she couldn't see any other way out."

I again thought of my mother. She hadn't made mistakes that I knew of, except getting married too young to a man not suited to her. I now knew my mother also suffered from depression, which in the 1950's no one dared to discuss. But, Toti? She must have had other alternatives.

Chapter Seven

Insane Routine

Effective immediately unescorted women will be allowed in all Playboy Clubs at all operating hours in all rooms. Slight exception: in the Playmate Bar, unescorted women will be permitted at the table and at the bar itself after 3:00 P.M. (The Playmate Bar will be a male-only sanctuary from 11:00 A.M. until 3:00 P.M.). It goes without saying the ladies must be in possession of either the Playboy Key or their Playmate Card. International will soon be doing a promotion regarding this new policy. Interoffice Memo

The Bunnies collected money for a flower arrangement and sent it to Toti's funeral in Indiana. With Renee's influence, International set up a special fund to help Toti's mother pay for the funeral expenses and support Toti's children. The girls, even Shar, wanted to do anything they could so that the entire burden wouldn't be placed on Toti's mother who had little money and would now be the children's guardian.

I couldn't help think poor Toti could have used that kind of support while she lived, not when she lay six feet under. I had become so much more cynical each day over the past three months I hardly accepted the girls' and management's generosity as genuine. In fact within day's reality set back in. Their magnanimity soon became a fleeting memory.

A week after Toti's suicide Bunny Jenny graduated from college and accepted a social worker position in Boston. On her last day at the Club the Bunnies and staff celebrated Jenny's success and good fortune with a cake and punch in the conference room. During the festivities, someone stole her wallet containing the money from her last paycheck. Jenny was also a single mother with a ten-year-old son to feed. No one except me stepped forward to assist her and I had only little I could offer. A disappointed and teary-eyed Jenny thanked me for my thoughtfulness but said she had enough money saved and child support to get her through until she settled in Boston. Jenny had made it known she had been one of the lucky divorcees who actually collected child support without a hassle. Yet she also said, "I loved those girls and would have done anything for them. I can't believe one of them took the cash." Then she sounded more hopeful when she added, "It could have been someone else. Maybe a bus boy."

I could only nod. Given the attitudes of Shar, Barry and Chris Malloy, my own view of the staff had altered. I wouldn't put it past anyone at the Club to steal or cheat.

Though Jenny's story had a happy ending, my own sadness about how devious people could be no matter where they lived or worked seemed to drag me so far down I could hardly move from behind my desk that whole day. I finally forced myself to leave my secure surroundings and drop off paperwork at the payroll department. Stella, the head clerk, greeted me in her usual manner, "Where the hell ya been? I've been waitin' too damn long for this shit."

I studied the aging, foul-mouthed woman who always reminded me of a rough and tumble gun moll from the '20's. Stella's too-bright dyed red hair often matched the anger brewing in her face, emphasizing the cigarette-induced wrinkles. Holding back an urge to laugh, I answered, "The way things are going this week, you're lucky to even get this."

While in the accounting office, I picked up the pay scale of all Playboy employees for no other reason than to make myself aware. Paula, Stella's assistant, fetched the chart for me. Paula, who audited the bar checks, appeared as out of place in Playboy as Stella but in an entirely different way. Paula more closely fit the librarian stereotype—quiet, congenial, middle aged and plump, wearing black winged glasses, jersey print dresses and her hair in a bun at the nape of her neck. But, however opposite in temperament and appearance Paula and Stella could be found from 1:30 to 3:00 pm every day in the Bunny lounge watching soap operas. I should have brought the paperwork to Stella there to see if she'd chastise me for tardiness. Not likely. I wondered if either woman compared herself to the beauties they saw each day the way I so often did.

Back in my office I thumbed through each employee category and discovered to my delight the $175.00 salary I received was at the top of the Bunny Mother scale. My spirits soared for a moment, then dropped like a roller coaster as I thought about Shar. She had never shared this information with me. Wouldn't that alone prove I wouldn't be transferred elsewhere? International obviously thought I had the skills worth that kind of money. Perhaps Shar hadn't liked the competition, my big nose and all.

I checked off one more day on the calendar. Only eight more days and the boys would be with me. Would I be able to get the apartment ready in time for their arrival? The boys' homecoming should be special, but they should decorate their own room themselves. It was their place after all. I sacrificed and gave them the larger of the two bedrooms. While on their aunt's farm in upstate New York all summer, the boys had become used to sharing accommodations. But they still needed adequate space.

"Eight more days," I reminded myself. I wished I could head to the airport right that minute. I had many sightseeing adventures planned for the three of us, and of course the boys had to enroll in school. I had heard many negative tales about the school Carl would attend, but I had no choice. Where else could I move? Carl was intelligent and sensible. I doubted he'd get involved with drugs or gangs.

The phone rang. Chris Malloy interrupted my review of my sons' new lives. "What the hell is going on?" he yelled without explaining what he meant.

"Got me," I almost snickered at his absurd behavior.

"We're four girls short and no replacements in sight. Plus we have a private party in the Playroom in an hour." Malloy paused. "Well?"

"Bummer." I covered my unsympathetic sarcasm quickly. "Babs was supposed to check the schedule. Has she left?"

"I haven't seen her all day. She's probably at another baby shower." I could hear Malloy's deep, almost panicked breathing.

"It looks like I won't get out of here on time again." I sighed. "I'll get on it. But you won't have replacements for at least an hour. You might have to use some of the girls here now for the party."

"Don't take too long," Malloy ordered and hung up.

I grabbed the schedule and reached for the telephone at the same time. I called Bab's extension. No answer. I called Bab's home and got the answering machine. "Damn," I slammed the receiver down. Babs had left me holding the bag once again. I planned to write a disciplinary letter to her and place a copy in her personnel folder after counseling her in person. I expected that I could count on Bab's many excuses as always. My assistant's usual rationale for errors ran something like, "I don't make up the schedule" or "I'm not the Bunny Mother." It never occurred to Babs that as the assistant she acted on behalf of me in my absence. Fortunately, in less than a week that ding-bat would be off on maternity leave and Brooke Sterling, the new girl I had hired, would be in Bab's place. It was almost harder to wait for that day than the boys' arrival.

After an hour I had covered the absent Bunnies with the reserve girls and left for the night. On my way home I picked up a deep-dish pizza for which Chicago was famous. While eating I watched *Laugh-In* on a TV Renee had loaned to me until my own was fixed. Luckily it was the only item damaged in the move. Glad to take my mind off the day's events, I laughed so hard a few times I spit food from my mouth, especially at Goldie Hawn's kooky antics. The wacky humor got my mind off the not so funny routine at the Playboy Club.

Normally I listened to my beloved Dodgers, but their games weren't broadcast in Cub and White Sox Country. Either I had to give up my favorite sport or become a Cub or Sox fan. For now I would watch and listen to the TV as I worked around the rental.

When I finished the pizza I tackled the unpacking, a task I couldn't put off any longer. After storing all the linens, making the boys' beds and stocking the bathroom, I went to bed. As I reached for the light on the bed table, I saw the stack of mail which I had forgotten. Perhaps on purpose. Clark's letter lay on top. I hadn't heard from him in over a week. I'd discovered I didn't mind. This letter contained the usual news and love-sick messages. I reacted little. Maybe he now loved me more than I loved him. Maybe as I had become unattainable, I'd become more desirable. Did it matter anymore? I let the letter drop to the floor and turned out the light.

At my office the next morning I found several Bunnies had already gathered for inspection. Babs had not shown up as scheduled which was no surprise. I caught the tail end of a juicy conversation. One Bunny, Charlene, handed each of the others a piece of paper with a name and telephone number written down. "This is the guy I told you about who's bitchen in bed."

As each took the information, Jane asked, "Is he as good as that farmer who showed up for brown-shoes-white-socks night?"

"Umm, umm. Now that was some dude," Charlene said. "Almost makes me wanna move to a farm. But trust me, this here guy tops even the farm boy."

Charlene, a blond beauty and hard worker, came from a strong Polish background. Her sense of humor often got me through an otherwise grueling day.

All the Bunnies laughed. "Want the name, Alyce?" Charlene shouted out.

I walked to my desk and laid my purse in the drawer. "What on earth are you up to?"

The girls giggled as they looked at each other. Charlene finally explained, "When one of us finds a gas in bed, you know, the best, we share him. The dude never minds and if he's not attached, what's the harm?"

For a moment I had no answer. "I'm no swinger, I'm afraid. Especially since the men in my life are due here in a few days. But you girls have fun while you can."

Near the end of inspection I asked, "By the way, what does 'brown-shoes-white-socks night' mean?"

"That's Saturday night when all the farmers come to the Club. The businessmen have all gone home for the weekend. So many show up we have to add more tables in each room."

I giggled. "That's good to know."

"We make a lotta money on Saturdays. It's like those boys are set free into a world they never saw before." Charlene lowered her hands down her body and struck a model's pose. "I should know. I come from a farm. Besides, we can deal with their dress code."

"Is making all that money on Saturdays a reason why some of you don't show up for work the rest of your schedule?" I turned serious and sat.

"Some Bunnies," Jane answered. "But not all of us."

"I know and I'm sorry if I sounded too accusing." I shrugged.

"Sometimes though, I think the girls don't care how hard it is to run this place, especially when they give lame excuses for not coming to work."

"Yeah, well, we hope we're not them," Charlene said with almost teary eyes.

"No, certainly not you."

Just as I sent the last Bunny to her station, Barry burst through the door in his usual Road Runner manner. No hello, no how are you. "Get Sadie off the elevator," he ordered. "She's not pretty enough for that post."

"You mean the Black girl Mr. Hefner wanted me to hire?" If Barry had heard my snide question, he ignored it. Perhaps Sadie, a dignified and true beauty, rebuffed his advances. Barry could be a persistent clod even though he made it clear he was a happily married man in his third marriage with a new son, and even though he had Adrian secretly on the side.

I could feel the man's hot breath as he leaned over my desk. "She'll still work here and accommodate Hef's need to integrate the Clubs. She just can't run the elevator."

"Yes, sir." I saluted.

"Put Nancie Yee on the elevator. That should make Hef happy." Barry spun on his heels and sped to the door. He stopped turned back and ordered, "You need to hire more Bunnies. Make sure some of them are minorities." Then like a flash of lightning he was gone.

"Whew! Do you ever slow down?" I asked as Barry's jacket disappeared in a blur.

Though I had yet to meet the reclusive Hugh Hefner, I knew he had already helped break the color barrier, especially in the American South, by recruiting and integrating black entertainers. He took chances. He even lost money when keyholders boycotted some Clubs after he hired minority Bunnies. I had to respect the man for having the courage of his convictions even if he was rarely seen by anyone. He ran his "empire" as he called it from the quarters in the Playboy Mansion several blocks from the Club and corporate offices. Hefner appeared in public on few occasions, to appear on TV or to open a new Club. Another Howard Hughes. Both were tycoon-playboy-recluses.

Before I could check the schedule to make the changes Barry ordered, my phone rang again. This time it was Monique stuck in New York City because her flight had been cancelled. She had been on loan to the New York Club for the past two weeks. When I asked why she hadn't made plans to come back a day earlier after she was off the New York schedule, Monique said, "Oh, I wanted to hang out for a while."

I couldn't give her demerits since I had sent her to New York and the girl had no control over the airlines. So I was stuck again. I had to call in a reserve. Lucky for me, Nancie Yee was on the reserve list so she could accommodate Barry—Nancie on the elevator and Sadie in the Penthouse.

No sooner had that been solved, my phone rang again. Time ticked by and I hadn't yet made my room inspections. This call came from a keyholder who was also a dentist. At first I thought he was calling about a dental appointment, but realized how silly that was since his office help would do that. Instead he asked, "Is Jane at work? I tried to call her at home, but didn't get an answer. We're supposed to meet after her shift and I need to find out what time."

After I asked several questions, I discovered he was not Jane's own dentist. He had met the Bunny the other night at the Club and she gave him her telephone number which of course was against the rules. "I'll let Jane know you called," I told the dentist without revealing Jane's misconduct. "She can't take personal calls unless they are emergencies." I paused. "Does she have your telephone number?"

"Yes, she does. Thank you. I'll wait for her call then." He hung up.

Though hard to prove wrongdoing on his part, the dentist should have been aware of Playboy's rules. Bunnies cannot date keyholders or any other patron. Had he and Jane thought I didn't know the regulations? Or, perhaps they'd hoped I'd ignore the Playboy edict that one time? They were wrong. Jane had to be suspended after her shift. Jane's misconduct could possibly seal her fate at Playboy since Barry wanted to get rid of her anyway. Her latest antic gave him the fuel he needed. Maybe she had also spurned Barry's advances.

"Damn." I picked up the schedule. "Another change and we're already 10 girls short," I mumbled to myself as though I talked to my assistant, the elusive Babs. "And if we find the prostitute we'll be 11 girls down. I must get some new girls hired pronto."

Off on my rounds of the Club, hopeful everything would be quiet, I didn't get any farther than the Living Room at shift change. With every table filled, guests clamoring for attention and an impatient line of patrons waiting to get in, there was no room for error. As soon as I stepped into the room Bunny Carol complained, "Patti doesn't want to buy my checks. She got all upset when I tried to tell her what stations I worked."

Patti saw the two of us talking and came over. "I don't know what Carol told you but I never said I wouldn't buy her checks. She knows we have to pick up all the open tabs from the girls going off duty. She asked me if I'd rather buy them or work them out. I told her," Patti sneered at Carol, "I didn't care."

"It's your attitude that stinks," Carol said. "You should just tell me what you want."

"Hold on." I stepped between the two Bunnies, who never did get along, and spoke with quiet authority. "Neither of you is portraying a Bunny Image to this room filled with eager members and their guests. So I suggest we straighten this out and get back to serving drinks." I paused. "Or perhaps you'd rather get demerits for your attitudes?"

Both shook their heads. Patti opened her mouth but shut it quickly. I settled the issue by telling Patti to buy the checks and let Carol tell her about the stations. The check problem solved, Patti again got upset because she couldn't understand the fast-talking Carol. By that time all her stations were fouled up and the members started yelling for their drinks.

They would have to wait because Carmen let loose her tray near the bar and fled from the room. I stopped her at the door. Carmen told me that Bunny Lil wouldn't break a twenty-dollar-bill to buy Carmen's checks. "I'm just fed up with these bitches."

I let her go for the day but told her, "You'll get demerits for both your actions and your mouth. This is not like you. We'll talk more tomorrow."

Everything on Carmen's tray including the checks had been hurtled about the room. Lil's attitude and the mess with Carol and Patti set off the other Bunnies who kept dropping items and mixing up drink orders.

Finally, I made Lil buy the checks she could find strewn across the floor. I helped pick up the mess from Carmen's tray, and then I called the Bunny dressing room to get Bunnies on the floor earlier.

Those Bunnies marched on the scene like a riot patrol and went from table to table trying to straighten out the drinks and tabs. It took almost an hour for the room to come back to order. In the end, Mona still went around the room with a key found on the floor from Carmen's tray, trying to find the holder.

It was the wildest thing I had ever witnessed. Yet more amazing, no guests left.

Back in the sanctity of my office, I thought my problems for the day had ended with the Living Room melee until Carlie pushed through the door. She was not quite ready for inspection although she was due on the floor in fifteen minutes. I focused on a blueish-green shading on Carlie's upper right arm. Carlie placed a hand over it and said, "I need to talk to you."

"Sure. Sit down." I walked over to the couch and motioned for Carlie to follow. "You have time before you go to your station."

Carlie sat next to me. "It's about my schedule." Her youthful face, now lined with worry, seemed to age before me. Its bloom was gone. Her tired eyes were shrouded in darkness.

"Do you need some time off?" I asked. "Because you never take any and you do deserve it."

"No, no." Carlie almost whispered. "It's just that. . ." She gulped.

"Take your time. We're not busy today," I said attempting to soothe her yet recalling the melee I'd just left. "So you can get to the floor a little late."

Carlie raised her head. I could feel the sadness in her almost empty gaze. Where had Carlie's sparkle gone? And when?

"I can't work in the same room as Chris Malloy," Carlie finally said. "I really have to switch stations with another girl." She twisted her hairpiece in shaking hands. "He's always hassling me. He makes me nervous."

I thought for a few minutes. I'd heard rumors that Malloy had been hard on Carlie, picking on her for no apparent reason. Then he accused her of being the prostitute. From what I saw before me, there had to be much more going on than Malloy's obvious dislike. If that weren't enough, I would soon have to confront Carlie about her weight loss. She had gotten too thin and that didn't meet Bunny Image.

I walked to my desk and picked up the schedule as I sat. "I'll put you in the Gift Shop tonight and let Jane work the floor." I called the Bunny dressing room.

Jane pitched a fit. "I don't work the floor."

"I know. It's hard work and you'd rather not put yourself out in that way." I hadn't planned to sound so annoyed, but then Jane deserved it.

Jane obviously sensed not to push me too far and acquiesced. "Ok, no problem."

Could Jane be the hooker? After all, she did give out her telephone number.

I turned my attention back to Carlie. "You know you're not just an employee, but a friend. I sense there is much more going on than you're letting me know. You must tell me what's really happening."

Carlie's weak smile transformed her from a glamorous Bunny to a troubled child. As she opened her mouth to speak, Daisy raced into the room shouting, "Look!" She lifted up her blouse to show me her new breasts. Daisy had just returned from Los Angeles where she received silicone shots. "Aren't they great?"

While I looked on in shock, Carlie slipped out of the office. I peered around Daisy's long legs that stretched from her pink short shorts down into white go-go boots to say something, but Carlie had already disappeared.

"Well?" Daisy's persistence annoyed me.

"They're perfect. You should be quite happy. But," I said, "Daisy, please check to see who's in here before you barge in." I didn't want to give away any details about Carlie and tried to make my instruction sound like general information. "I might have been in a personal conversation."

"Sorry, but I'm so excited about the new me." Daisy's smile filled her face, which made me more aware of the cloud around Carlie.

"I'm glad they turned out the way you had hoped." I tried to sound upbeat. I knew how important larger breasts were to Daisy, a tall girl whose breasts never grew much bigger than the ones she had been born with. "You'll have to see Catalina to get fitted for a new costume."

"I'm on my way there now." Daisy waved and skipped out of the office.

"If only new boobs could change everyone's lives." I then made a mental note to delve further into the Carlie and Malloy situation.

I started for the door to make room inspections and was nearly bowled over by Mona. "My brother has been in a bad car accident. He's critical and may not make it." Mascara blackened tears made tiny lines down each cheek. She held her false eyelashes in her hand. "I've gotta go to Ohio, now. And my husband Mike is at a meeting. I can't reach him."

I circled an arm around Mona's shoulder. "I'll ask Hef for the limo to take you. Will Mike know where you are?" I led Mona to a chair. Mona slowly lowered herself using the arms as a brace as though she might have been injured herself.

"I left a message at the school," Mona said as I dialed Hef's office.

Hefner's executive assistant and latest girlfriend, Bobbie, answered. She screened all Hefner's calls and protected him from any unwanted intrusions. Hef's choice surprised me because Bobbie resembled Audrey Hepburn rather than Brigitte Bardot, Hef's usual type. Bobbie also had brains and didn't compare to the other office help like Stella and Paula.

I explained Mona's situation. "Please ask Mr. Hefner if he would send the limousine and driver around to take her to the airport."

"I'm sorry, but Mr. Hefner can't be disturbed. He's getting his hair cut." Bobbie's answer was polite and direct.

"What?" I yelled louder than planned. "Did you hear what I said? We have an emergency."

"Yes, I heard you, but obviously you did not understand me. Mr. Hefner left orders not to be disturbed because he is having his hair cut."

I slammed down the receiver. "The hedonist. I hope I never meet him." Then I remembered Mona and regretted my words. "I'll call a cab."

Mona nodded as she dried the dark streaks from her cheeks.

I hadn't really been that surprised by Bobbie's steadfast refusal to put the call through. I remembered one time searching for Barry during a Club emergency only to be told, "I'm sorry but Mr. Fleishman is playing Risk with Mr. Hefner and can't be disturbed." Barry and the other players' command performances lasted three days.

"Call me as soon as you have any news about your brother's condition," I said.

Mona smiled. "Thank you for caring." She hugged me and left.

I wanted to march over to the mansion and slug Hef. Instead I went into the Club to make rounds. I'd deal with a replacement for Mona later.

Chris Malloy busied himself when I came through. He hastily nodded at me and went about speaking to the bartender. Though I knew I should speak to him, I decided not to press it at that moment. I attributed my edginess and outspoken anger over Carlie, Hef and Mona to the fact my period was due any time. Everything seemed worse and out of control at that time of month and I didn't want to appear that way to Malloy. No matter, at least I still got my period unlike some of the girls who worked for me who at that very moment had to decide whether to seek an illegal abortion or have a baby alone and lose their jobs. Some choice.

When I got to the Penthouse, Rick Califf, a recent transfer from Los Angeles, was on duty. He had been promoted from bartender to a Room Director and made a pleasant addition to the Chicago staff. "Here is our brilliant and beautiful Bunny Mother." Rick's greeting was a far cry from the usual I got, especially from Malloy. "How's it going?"

His boyish charm lifted my spirits. "Not too bad. How about you?"

"No negatives to report." Rick only disclosed the Bunnies' most egregious errors. He'd rather handle the small stuff with the girls personally to give them a chance to correct the problem. In most cases, the Room Directors complained about a Bunny's appearance— messy hair, makeup needed freshening, weight problems—more than her attitude anyway.

Rick almost smelled like he just came off the beach after a day of sun and surfing. His laid back yet perky persona, familiar California characteristics to me, lifted the spirits of anyone in Rick's presence. I immediately felt better after our conversation and pushed Malloy to the back of my mind for the moment. If Rick hadn't been so much younger, I would break both social and Playboy rules and ask him out. Instead I left for the evening filled with more optimism than normal. I also now looked forward to going to my own place instead of a hotel room, even when it meant I had to clean it. I'd forgotten how good it felt to have a home and sleep in my own bed.

The day had come. I rode to the airport in a downpour praying the weather wouldn't delay my sons' plane. At another time I would have asked for the limo, but after the Mona incident, I decided not to try though it would have been fun to pick the boys up in style.

I paced the waiting area for the tardy plane. After an hour, it finally taxied to the door. My heart pounded so hard, my chest moved to its rhythm. The door to the gangway opened. Passengers pressed forward and into the waiting arms of their loved ones. I eyed each person and then the door and then looked back to the crowd. Had I missed my sons? Flashes of another such time surfaced. Angelo wouldn't do this again, would he? He only kept them the last time to punish me anyway. If he did it again, this time he'd protect the boys from my kidnapping them as I had so many years ago.

As I approached the stewardess in the doorway to question her, the two boys, farm tans fading, raced up to me. "Thank God you're here." I smothered them in kisses on their noses, cheeks and eyes. "I've missed you so."

Greg's smile filled his face. "Did you think we weren't coming?"

"No, but the plane was late." My mind fastened on a moonlit night several years past when the boys and I fled across the dirt road to my parked car and into the night. I had sped as fast and as far away from Angelo as possible.

I held both boys at arm's length. "You've each grown a foot. And look at those muscles." I squeezed each boy's biceps. "Uncle Paul must've worked you hard."

Carl flexed his biceps. "It wasn't bad. The food was good and a lot."

I envied Marie's wholesome farm cooking, with everything including the bread made from scratch. Though I did pride myself on my cooking, I wouldn't be able to promise such dining. I simply didn't have the time. We'd all have to get used to nights of fast food and eating at a few fun Chicago spots. But first, I'd have to get paid. My funds were stretched as thin as onion skin. I couldn't count on Angelo's child support payment, because he sent it when and if he felt like and often not the whole sum. Then there was the $100 gas deposit I had to pay. I planned to call the company to ask why so much when the townhouse was heated with electric.

"When do we get Fraulein?" Greg asked. He broke my nonstop worrisome thoughts.

"Aunt Tekkie is shipping her tomorrow. We'll pick her up around six tomorrow evening." I ruffled his brush cut. At eleven, he nearly reached my shoulder.

"Dad buzzed our heads," Greg said. "He told us he didn't want no hippie sissies for sons." Greg lowered his head so that his chin nearly touched his chest.

"It didn't matter," Carl interjected. "He never was around anyway. But Aunt Marie wanted to know if you'd let us stay with her, seeing how we're starting school late. Besides Dad's living in an apartment because his new wife kicked him out."

"Well, that has nothing to do with you two." Yet I was still concerned that Greg had let it slip out earlier that he had told Angelo I lived in Chicago now. Fear still scraped along my spine like a sharp razor. Would Angelo once again chase them down especially since he lived so close? I prayed that too many years had passed for Angelo to care about either punishing me or getting me back. He had found other ways to penalize me. How hard could it be to dig up $25.00 a week for his sons? Angelo probably thought he also got back at me when he never sent gifts or cards for the boys birthdays or Christmas. I couldn't bear Carl and Greg to suffer from Angelo's neglect. They already felt abandoned by their father. So often, to protect Carl and Greg, I'd get the boys something and tell them the gifts or cards were from their father.

Pushing those thoughts to the back of my mind I dared ask, "Do you want to stay with Aunt Marie and Uncle Paul?" The frequent question came again: had I made the right decision to move the boys to Chicago? I wanted them with me and nowhere near their father's influence. To my relief and pleasure both boys shook their heads no.

"Good." I rubbed Greg's head again. "Well, there's one thing for certain, your hair will grow back," I proclaimed. The last time I saw the boys they sported the same haircut as the popular British group, The Beatles. "Now let's get your luggage and go home."

Chapter Eight

Beating the Bushes for Bunnies

$50 REWARD
If you spot a girl who fits the following description we'll pay you $50 when she has been employed as a Playboy Bunny for 3 months! HEIGHT: Between 5 and 6 feet tall. WEIGHT: Just right! AGE: 18 or over. NOTICEABLE CHARACTERISTICS: Pretty face, the prettier the better. Men and women turn to look at her as she goes by. Figure must be nicely proportioned. Personality: charming. Anyone reporting the name, address or phone number of this wanted person should contact the Bunny Mother at the Chicago Playboy Club. Recruiting Flyer, 1966.

I gave Carl and Greg a tour of the Club the day after their arrival. They wore the new matching crew neck sweaters I bought earlier that week. Flamboyant Greg fit right in. He loved the Club's glitz. Quiet, serious Carl didn't want a return trip. Carl was especially turned off by Ellie's attention while Greg wallowed in it.

Ellie's provocative behavior bothered me too, particularly after I had found Ellie's business cards earlier. I settled the boys in my office with trays of food from the buffet. While they gobbled all they could, I went to the dressing room to talk with the Bunny. "Can you explain these?" I handed the cards to Ellie and sat beside her before a mirror.

Ellie shrugged. "They're my cards. I wondered where I left them."

"I found them on the gift shop counter in a holder. It appeared they were deliberately placed for the keyholders to retrieve." I had hoped for some kind of confession.

Ellie appeared unruffled. "Thank you," she smiled and tucked the cards into her purse.

We looked at each other in the mirror rather than face-to-face. "I hope you aren't getting supplemental employment by handing out those cards. I'm sure you're not using them to get dates." Did Ellie's shoulders tense?

Ellie continued to apply her makeup. "I'm not breaking any rules, if that's what you're asking."

"Yes, and I'm glad to hear you say you're not." I didn't quite believe the fresh-faced young girl. "I have one other thing."

Ellie put down her blush brush and turned to me. "What else could there be?"

"I don't want you flirting with my sons, just as I don't want you to flirt with any keyholder or employee."

"Ha! Your sons seemed interested." She turned back to the mirror. "I didn't force anything on them." Ellie sounded defiant.

"Just be careful. My sons are only 11 and 14 years old. Greg is outgoing and excited by everything. Carl is shy and too serious for. . ."

"The likes of me?" Ellie finished my sentence.

"For anyone your age and in this job. Don't read too much into their youthful exuberance and curiosity." I stood. "Keep those cards out of the Club."

"Yes'm," Ellie mocked.

I had found the hooker. Now how would I prove it?

Returning to my office I found Carl had slumped into the couch while Greg was spinning in my desk chair. Surely Greg had gone through all the desk drawers and papers on top. He couldn't help himself from prying. Thank goodness he hadn't taken anything apart to see how it worked the way he had done many times in the past. I smiled. It still amazed me to have them here.

"How about seeing some of Chicago?" I asked.

Greg stopped spinning and Carl jumped up. Both screamed, "Yeah!"

Carl made it to the door before I retrieved my purse. He obviously wanted to get out of the Club.

We rode the bus to the Loop to do some window shopping. Then we took in an early movie, *How to Steal a Million,* during which I made mental notes about clothes, make-up and hair styles. After the boys and I had a quick dinner at Todd's Steak House we rode a shuttle to the airport and picked up Fraulein.

When Fraulein spotted the boys and me she wagged her tail so hard it became a blur. We walked the midget German Shepherd for a few minutes before piling into a cab and riding back to the townhouse. Once Fraulein had eaten, we walked her for over an hour through the nearby park, which didn't have a name but was one blessing in our new neighborhood. The evening chill predicted an early winter. It had already dropped down to 48 degrees with winds whipping like the infamous Santa Anas in Southern California. The difference was the Santa Anas were warm. Even Fraulein shivered. In fact, she was so cold she finally refused to walk farther so the group had to turn back. I found the warmth of the red and gold autumn leaves such a contradiction to the temperature I could hardly enjoy their beauty.

I also could hardly believe Greg's birthday, October 15, was just days away, which meant even cooler weather soon would follow. The whole family needed to think about proper winter clothing. The townhouse wasn't much warmer than the outside temperature. I had to find out why the furnace produced so little heat. Even though I turned it up we had to stay bundled in sweaters and heavy socks. So, along with contacting the kids' schools, I had to call the gas company about that $100 deposit and get the janitor to look at the furnace. My "to-do" list for Monday grew.

Sunday morning started with a welcome quiet. When I heard the boys' muffled voices, I could hardly contain my happiness. My sons and of course Fraulein were back with me.

We had one more day of pure pleasure before a routine would start. The boys must be enrolled in school Monday. So that Sunday would be special. After showers, dressing and a quick breakfast of cereal, we went on a four-hour bus tour of Chicago, which started at the Conrad Hilton Hotel. Carl in his Playboy sweater drew stares from everyone, including the female tour guide when we boarded the bus, making me aware of how much he'd matured over the summer. After eating in a downtown cafeteria, we rode a bus home. Though tired from our day's adventure, we walked Fraulein and prepared for the first day at school.

Still no check from Angelo. I counted my money. Not much left after our whirlwind two days in Chicago. Greg's birthday would be a scanty celebration. And with Carl's less than a month after, thank goodness I had already bought a few special, reasonably priced gifts, mostly Playboy memorabilia. I'd make arrangements for a special dinner at the Club too. If Angelo's past performance meant anything he would not call the boys, send them a card or a gift. He'd most likely be too busy purchasing another motorcycle or playing pool to remember his sons.

I promised the boys I'd make up for the lack of birthday gifts at Christmas. I would deal with the other money problems tomorrow. So I tucked in the boys and Fraulein for the night and collapsed into bed, sad my weekend had ended.

Both schools were within walking distance of the townhouse. Greg's appeared normal, but he had to be held back a half year because their curriculum was different from California. Also the school didn't serve lunch so he had to come home each day or find some place nearby to eat, which concerned me. The clerk told me he could bring a lunch and milk would be served to him when the weather was too bad for him to leave the campus. Still Greg could be easily distracted and once home might not get back to school for the afternoon classes.

On the other hand, a uniformed police officer patrolled Carl's school. Nervous about what that meant, I questioned the officer. "Keeps the riff-raff out," he explained. "The school's decent though."

Although the officer's answer didn't comfort me, the school itself didn't look bad. Besides I had no choice. Carl had to stay. While I waited to fill out papers in the main office, two boys were suspended for reasons unknown to me. Two others were brought in for smoking in the bathroom. The assistant principal was anything but soft on them.

I completed the necessary forms. The clerk asked from where Carl had transferred. When I said Los Angeles, I overheard two girls who were helping in the office whisper. One asked stunned, "He's from California?" The other asked, "Is that his mother?" The first one responded, "It can't be his mother." Flattered, I smiled.

After another hour wait, Carl and I were introduced to the Assistant Principal, who after grunting a brief greeting with no handshake, led us to the counselor's office. I left Carl with the counselor to set up his schedule and headed to the Club. As I walked the empty school hall, I fought back tears knowing how hard it was for Carl to adjust to something new, unlike Greg who simply rolled with the punches or made the modifications necessary to get along. Today, I felt like I had when I'd left Carl on his first day of kindergarten in L.A.

I reached the Club a few minutes past my normal 11:00 am start time. Getting the boys registered had taken the entire morning. Before I could get to my office Barry stopped me. "Make sure Adrian is not on the schedule tonight. Do anything to get a reserve in to take her place."

"We're so short now, Barry. How do you expect me to fill in? Besides, why does she need the shift off?" I knew the answer but enjoyed watching Barry's forehead turn pink and bead in sweat.

"Just do as I say. That's all you need to know." He skittered away on his little feet.

"Yes, sir."

I called the house—the dorm in Hugh Hefner's mansion—and found Lydia, a reserve, to fill in for Adrian. I then checked my own calendar for the times I had scheduled the girls interviewing for Bunny positions. Only ten had called after Playboy's unprecedented efforts to solicit applicants. Not only had I run ads in several newspapers, but flyers had been posted at colleges throughout Illinois, Wisconsin, Michigan and Indiana. I had even handed my business card to potential candidates in restaurants, on the bus, at the hairdresser and in various department stores. Most recipients had more interest in my role than in being a Bunny. "I can't believe that's what you do," was the general response, followed by a tiresome litany of questions.

I had been under the impression, at least as Shar and Barry postulated, that girls throughout the country couldn't wait for the chance to be a glamorous Bunny. So where were the eager applicants—on vacation? Few beauties beat the path to my Chicago office for interviews.

"Well, let me see what this batch of applicants has." I had already interviewed five others. Only two had any potential. I had to fill at least 18 spots. Plus, for the V.I.P. Room, I needed two foreign-born who spoke their native language and English with an accent. On top of that, Barry and Keith had to approve every girl I selected. I often wondered why they didn't just interview all applicants since they had final say. I simply screened them for my bosses who apparently didn't trust my judgment.

Before I tackled the Bunny problem I had to wade in to my own personal issues. I called the gas company and happily discovered they had made a mistake and I needed only a $25 deposit by October 25. I could handle that. Next I called Mr. Anderson about the furnace. The landlord begged off responsibility as I had expected. "It worked ok with the other renters," he said.

After several minutes of negotiating, Mr. Anderson agreed to send the janitor over to see what could be wrong. "But you may have to pay for the repair."

Too tired to argue any further with the miser, I simply said, "I've got another call. We'll talk about this another time."

As soon as I ended that conversation, the telephone rang. Claire's father was on the line. Claire was a new Bunny hired by Keith Hefner who found her in the Boston Bunny Hunt. She was scheduled for training next Monday. I could hardly believe what Claire's father told me. Sixteen-year-old Claire had run away from her Ohio home. He wanted her back. He threatened to call the police if Playboy didn't make arrangements for her safe and immediate return.

After I assured the caller I would handle the problem immediately, I hung up and called Keith. I had a hard time stifling a laugh as I listened to Keith ramble on. "She looks older," he said. That meant Claire had large breasts. He finally concluded with, "From now on we should get each girl's birth certificate before she's hired. Better yet have them mail a copy directly from the county office where they were born. That way they can't forge the damn thing." He slammed the phone down as though it had been I who caused the problem, not he.

No sooner had I finished that call, Barry phoned. "Do you want me to change the schedule again?" I asked.

"No, no," he yelled. "Mr. Hefner just called me highly upset because he had to ride the helicopter to the Lake Geneva promo with Bobbie Kay."

"And?" I already knew that management had two goals: to use the most beautiful Bunnies for promotions and to sell liquor at the Club. I heard an exasperated sigh and I imagined him biting down on the ever-present cigar.

"Mr. Hefner doesn't think she's very pretty. You know he only wants pretty girls at his side."

"Yes. If there is one thing I have learned, it's that." I stuck my tongue out at the receiver. "But I must remind you, Shar hired Bobbie Kay and felt she was pretty enough to be a Door Bunny. And you approved."

"Just don't have her with Mr. Hefner again." He too slammed the phone down so hard the sound rang in my ear. Nevertheless, I took great pleasure in his frustration. Imagine how upset he would have been if I had told him about Claire.

Beautiful Kelly, who got away with anything because she fit the Bunny Image, had been scheduled to ride the helicopter with Hugh. He would have been very happy with that choice, but Kelly decided she didn't want to ride in the helicopter if she had to go to the opening and serve. That also meant swapping all the costume colors.

It got worse after that. Renee had to back out of the promotion because Keith wanted her to go with him to New Orleans for the weekend. Of course no one said "no" to Keith. So the six girls needed for the Geneva Promotion had dwindled to four. With some scrambling and another costume change I found two more, only to have Sally not show up at all. She, too, usually got away with anything because she was going to be a Playmate. She told me, "I can't go because I drank too much and fell in the bathtub. I knocked myself out."

At the moment if I could have spanked her, I would have. So many girls were spoiled and only wanted to work when it suited them. They didn't seem to think being a Bunny meant they had to actually show up for the job. And Barry, a narcissist to the core, thought about nothing but his own gratification.

So now it was back to hiring new Bunnies. If I only had 10 applicants to see and Bobbie Kay hadn't been pretty enough, how on earth would I fill the vacancies? Good news, though, my new assistant started work that morning. Yet that added to my already over-booked schedule. The sooner Carlie and I had Brooke Sterling trained the better for everyone.

Shar popped into the office. "Are you interviewing today? Because Lord knows we need some Bunnies."

I gave her a frown-smile. "Yes, I am. I had thought getting new Bunnies would be a lot easier than it is."

"Not when you've got the likes of Ellie and Jane tellin' the applicants that all they need are big tits and the ability to carry a ten-pound tray." Shar sounded as though she could scratch their eyes out. For one, she and I were in synch.

"I did hire one new girl a while back who fits the first part of those qualifications. She's a 44 E, if there is such a thing." I laughed out loud at the vision. "In fact, when she went to a costume fitting, her breasts were so soft they kept flopping out. She'd dip, one would ease over the top. She'd walk, another slipped out. Worse yet I remember the night she did the twist on the piano bar. Her costume split and fell to her knees. What a sight!" Now my laughter became uncontrollable, until I noted Shar hadn't paid attention.

Shar lit a cigarette and sat opposite me. "Where's the glamour in any of that—big breasts, lugging heavy trays? It's a tough job, especially when ya have those Room Directors either making passes at ya or callin ya a lazy slut because the girl won't go out with them." Shar took three or four quick drags. She flicked the ashes and took more puffs.

"Are you ok?" I dared to ask. I thought I caught an alcohol odor and Shar's words were slurred. Plus she certainly had a different outlook from my first session with her when I was new to the Club.

"No, no I'm not." Shar stubbed her cigarette out and lit another one. "I've been asked to leave Playboy."

My next words had to be chosen carefully. I didn't want to reveal either my pleasure or relief. I wanted to sound concerned, sad. "Why? I mean I had no idea."

"Politics, kiddo. You'll see." Shar stood. She looked at the tip of her cigarette, took one final drag and put it out. "I need a change of scenery anyway. You will too, I'm afraid." Her bitterness showed in her face, which seemed to age right then in front of me. "It's jusht Barry's way of getting back for me dumpin' him a year ago."

My mouth dropped open. "You and Barry? I had no idea." Of course Barry had already told me about the affair but he claimed he ended it.

"Schurprise, schurprise." Shar almost toppled to the floor.

I caught an arm and steadied her. "When's your last day?" I asked with the intention of planning a party.

"Today."

"What?" I couldn't believe International would be that uncaring.

"Yeah, well, International, mostly Barry, doesn't want to keep any disgruntled people around who might start trouble." Shar started for the door and turned back to me. "You always reminded me of Laren Bacall, ya know. Same style, sophistication."

"Thank you," I mumbled, embarrassed now by my own ill feelings toward Shar. Pity for her began to creep in.

"See ya, then, doll," Shar waved and left.

I sorted through my mixed emotions. I felt sorry for Shar, but also couldn't help think that her termination could be the event I had waited for. I would now become the Bunny Director as Barry had intimated. I could hardly stand the suspense.

Someone rapped at the door. My first applicant had arrived.

By 3:00 pm I had interviewed all 10 applicants. They had also donned costumes to ensure each had the figure Barry and Keith sought. In the end, I referred seven to my male bosses, knowing full well they wouldn't accept all of them. A gorgeous eighth girl came close until a handgun spilled from her dropped purse. I decided not to take a chance the girl would use the weapon at the wrong place and time.

I did take a chance on Brenda, a housewife and mother. Though plain, I saw something in her I couldn't put my finger on. "I need the job to put my husband through college," she said with calm and dignity. "I know I'm not the image Playboy wants, but I'm a hard worker and will do what is needed to improve my looks."

I included her in the final seven applicants and crossed my fingers.

Barry rushed into my office shouting, "Before you do another thing, call Adrian and tell her she's back on the schedule."

"What? You seem to think that's all I have to do today."

"Sorry, but she gotta work tonight. By the way we need to remodel this office."

"I know. You've said that before." I didn't hide my agitation.

"I've also said you're doing a good job. We like to reward our good employees." Barry paced back and forth in front of my desk.

I detected he had more to say. "Is there anything else, Barry? You seem upset." I had hoped he would let me know about Shar.

"I'm not upset," he spit at me. "Only five girls you interviewed are good enough. That one from Cleveland is too hard and the one from Peoria looks like a hippie."

"They're the best of what applied." I stated firmly. I had no intention of offering an excuse. "Perhaps we need to do better PR about the job."

"NO!" he shouted louder. Something surely bothered him more than usual. "Just hire what Hef wants: a girl with a full face, not thin, not skinny, not as tall as, and therefore in competition with, the male, an accent on a full figure, narrow waist, full hips, a very robust and healthy-looking girl. How hard's that?" He paused and went on, "She's a guy's idealization of women—a pin-up concept."

"Good luck!" I couldn't resist. "Most of us fall into the more normal female category. Rarely up to that kind of man's fantasy."

Barry's face had turned a deep red. I might have crossed the line. And with a cheap shot. If I were truthful I'd admit even I wanted to fulfill that fantasy.

"Keep lookin,' doll. That's your job. And don't forget about Adrian." As always he was out the door in a whirl of dust. He never mentioned Shar.

My temples pounded. I had heard Barry's wife Shelly wanted Shar's job because they needed money. I couldn't imagine what they knew about being broke. Yet I understood all too well that politically Shelly had a better chance to get the position.

The good news? Brenda made it. How? Who cared?

I turned my attention to Adrian and called her. In our conversation Adrian told me she had no intention of coming to work that day. "I have other plans—a very important date. I intend to keep it even if you give me a no show."

Perhaps she too had been manipulating Barry for the Bunny Director's job. I certainly seemed to be getting more paranoid by the day. Did I think everyone wanted that job—my job?

I realized I couldn't discipline Adrian for what I had caused due to Barry's crazy indecision. "So be it," I said to the phone as I hung up the receiver. "But you don't know that your date has other plans."

When I discovered it was already 6:00 pm and I hadn't even spoken to my new assistant, I raced from my office to the Penthouse where training took place. Brooke and Carlie had just finished the session. I apologized for my delay and explained I had been tied up with interviews. I promised my full attention to Brooke the next day. "You have no idea how much I need you."

Before I did anything else, I called the boys to make sure they were home from school and had found their dinner. I reminded them to walk Fraulein in the park before it got dark. "Remember to pick up her poop," I told Carl. Getting home no earlier than 8:00 pm each night would be the hardest part of my job. At least I had weekends off and could get my sons ready for school every morning.

Once satisfied with the home front, I took Brooke with me to make room inspections. Everything went well until Chris Malloy came to our table while we ate dinner. I introduced them. He nodded, but because he was preoccupied he said nothing to her. Instead Malloy directed his attention to me. "You know that new Bunny, Karen, you hired?"

"Yes." I could hear the rage in his voice. I decided I wouldn't let it get to me.

"Well, she looks like a dishwasher."

"Now, Mr. Malloy, I don't know quite how to respond to that since we do have some pretty good looking dishwashers employed at the Club."

Brooke put her fork down and looked from me to him as we each spoke. She cleared her throat a couple of times but neither Malloy nor I paid attention.

Malloy teetered back onto his heels. Then he leaned closer to me. "You know exactly what I mean." I felt a hint of warm air with every word he spoke.

"No, Mr. Malloy, I don't. So please write your concerns in your report and make your observation very clear. Because as far I as can see, there is nothing wrong with her."

He opened his mouth to rebut my directive when all three jumped at a loud clatter from the table of four men seated nearby. "Shi-i-i-i-t!"

I turned to the sound. It took every bit of energy not to laugh at what I saw. One man at the table had a cherry draped over an ear, and an orange slice balanced on his head while ice cubes lined one shoulder. The man who had apparently yelled had a crotch filled with beer that dripped from a turned over bottle. He jumped away from the table to avoid the remaining spray and tilted the table again only to topple the other Singapore Sling, forming a lake filled with citrus.

I whispered to Brooke, "Bunny Karen, the dishwasher, missed her dip."

Karen rounded the table several times dabbing up the spillage without getting too personal, and repeated, "I'm sorry." Dab, dab. "I'm sorry."

Malloy glared at me and then ordered Karen to leave the floor. "No," he yelled. "Stay and help clean up."

When the four men decided to remain despite the mishap, Karen retrieved a Room Director's jacket two sizes too small for the one keyholder to wear and offered to pay for the cleaning of his own. The other man with the wet pants returned to his seat. When he sat, the chair squished and foamed. Amazing as it seemed none of the four men were angry and Karen continued to serve them drinks on the house.

As Brooke and I were leaving the area, Barry and his young wife came in. He made a quick introduction and hastened to a table. So this was why Barry wanted Adrian at work. He wouldn't make his date with her that night. He had other plans. Meanwhile Adrian probably waited in her apartment dressed and perfumed to perfection. When would these girls learn that married men aren't reliable? I answered my own question with a question. How many years had I waited for Clark?

"Time to get home to my sons, Brooke," I mentioned when we gathered our things in my office. "Tomorrow we'll go over the schedule. I'll work out a draft tonight."

"Are all your days like this one?" she asked.

"No, worse. But you'll get used to it." I couldn't help it. Now I sounded like Shar.

The single mother of a five-year-old girl, Brooke received a divorce settlement that was considered small, given that her husband invented the lie detector. While the elevator carried us down to the lobby earlier, Brooke described the millionaire inventor as a miser with kinky sex habits. I had a brief lapse into a silly thought. Had

Brooke's millionaire also given kickbacks to Playboy to use the test? International seemed to order one for every employee infraction known to man.

Yet despite the miser, Brooke clearly had money, perhaps inherited. I wondered why Brooke wanted to work. Every inch of her projected wealth. She wore only the latest styles in designer silk, linen and leather. I envied Brooke's very "now" look; one I myself couldn't afford. Everything Brooke chose flattered her full, firm figure and her auburn, shoulder-length flip. Even her face held the subtle seductiveness of a Geisha. Yet Brooke, a college graduate, appeared to be a genuine person—none of the airs or phoniness that Shar had displayed. Brooke was comfortable in her own skin and appeared not to be threatened by another good-looking, skilled woman or man.

When we started our descent to the lobby a keyholder stopped me. "I'm told you're the Bunny Mother."

"Yes, and this is my assistant." I motioned to Brooke.

"It must be fun to be the Bunny Mother." The keyholder stepped close to us.

"It's more fun to say you are than to be one," I blurted before I thought about Brooke standing at my side. There I went again. What kind of impression would that make?

"Well, you're pretty enough to be a Bunny," he said, his glance moving from my chest to my face. "Although you might be a little old."

I had to press my arms at my sides to stop from hitting the idiot. I decided to focus on his original compliment when he asked, "Do you have any children?"

Odd question. He might have had too much to drink.

"Yes. Seventy daughters," I answered. A Hutch filled with female Bunnies.

The man stepped backwards. "Whew. That's a lot of mouths to feed." He wobbled away.

Every man Brooke and I passed as we headed to the lobby stared at us. I hoped some of their gazes fell on me.

The boys surprised me by not only eating the dinner I had left, but cleaning the entire kitchen. Fraulein appeared content in the warm apartment. The janitor had fixed a broken part on the furnace. His note said he would let the landlord know I hadn't been at fault and the part was deteriorated from age. Things seemed to be looking up until I discovered the oil supplier forgot to deliver fuel and Chicago would only have a high of 43 degrees. I had to plead with him to deliver it before the boys and I froze.

Before I tackled the schedule, a task I already realized would never get done at my office, I sat with the boys for a game of Crazy Eights.

"So how did it go at school today?" I shuffled and dealt while I waited for the boys' responses.

"Fine," Carl answered, picking up his five cards.

"Ok," Greg added. He, too, buried his nose in the hand I'd dealt.

I placed the undealt cards in a stack face down, turned over the top one—a King of Hearts—and placed it next to the stack.

Carl drew from the stack. He triumphantly slapped a Ten of Hearts on the king.

Neither elaborated on their school day, but I sensed they hadn't found their place yet. We all faced that adjustment in our new environments and we must be patient.

Greg perked up. "I got a job at the drugstore on the corner." He slapped a ten of hearts on the stack without drawing a new card. Would he end up with no cards first?

"What?" I was stunned. "You're too young to work." I knew that hadn't made a difference in the past. Greg always made some arrangement with a local business to do odd jobs in exchange for goods or payment under the table.

We each picked up and discarded at a frenzied pace, trying to be the first to have no cards left. As we played the game we also talked.

"I clean up and deliver for the owner. It's ok." Greg beamed. He loved to work because school bored him. A job gave him an outlet for all his otherwise untamable energy. "He gives me a buck an hour and food if I want," Greg added.

"What's the owner's name?" I questioned. "And when can I meet him?" I drew a card, but couldn't discard any. The number of cards in my hand was increasing.

"It's the same as the drugstore —Newton's. You can come by any time." Greg lifted his empty hands. He managed to rid himself of every card while Carl and I held at least two more than we started with.

Carl had been silent throughout the whole card game. It didn't matter. Greg won as he seemed to always do.

"What about you, Carl?" I rubbed his head. "How was your day?"

"I want to go back to California. I miss the ocean and this weather is nowhere." His eyes reddened and filled. "I don't belong here."

I placed my arm around his shoulder. Carl shrugged it off and cleared the table. "I'm going to bed."

"Carl, let's give it a little while." I grabbed his hand. "You'll meet some boys and things will be better."

"Yeah," he answered but stared at his feet. Then he lumbered off.

Brooke and I reviewed the schedule I had tried to put together. "One of the things that will become very clear," I picked up the paper and waved it at Brooke, "this is impossible."

"How do you mean?" Brooke turned a page of scribbled, almost illegible row of names, assignments and times.

"As you know, we're 18 girls short and that's not counting the re-serves—part time—girls we need. Then Gail only wants to work two days so she can keep up her modeling jobs and promotions. Teresa was so upset over her boyfriend problems she flew to California yesterday without completing her shift or telling me she wouldn't be here for the rest of the week. I had to find out from a Room Director that she'd left the floor. Then I learned from her roommate that Teresa was in California."

"Man, what a bummer."

"I'm not finished. Sarah's mother called to tell us Sarah can't work nights because she's too young to be in the city after dark." I paused for a moment to check my notes on the schedule's margin. "Let's see," I dragged my finger down the line. "Oh yeah, Monique won't be in because her boyfriend Mike beat her up." I looked up from the paper. "It's not the first time either. Apparently this time he caught Monique in his apartment elevator going to a party without him."

Brooke shrugged. "And?"

"Mike pulled her into his apartment and slapped her around. Monique, bleeding and with a blackened and swollen eye, fled to her sister's. Then Monique and her sister Sheila went back to Mike's place and started in on him. The three brawled. When neighbors banged on Mike's door to complain, Mike fled from the scene holding his bloodied nose. The two sisters were right behind him." To Brooke this must have sounded like a script for *The Young and the Restless*.

Brooke's mouth hung open. Then she asked, "That will be the end of Mike, right?"

"Doubt it. Monique has gone back to him in the past when he tossed her around."

Brooke shook her head. "I hope Mike's banged up as well."

"Me, too," I agreed. "But his plumber's job doesn't require good looks so he can still go to work, unlike Monique. But I'm still not finished with today's excuses for no shows. Before you came into the office, Marylou called to tell me she had an abortion and an ingrown toe nail removed so wouldn't be back for a few days." I shook my head. "Just last week she told me she had had enough of abortions and was keeping this baby. On top of that, Sadie called and she also had an abortion. I hope it wasn't the same father." I snickered.

Brooke's eyebrows raised into her hairline. "Same father?"

"I'll tell you some other time about passing around the name of a man good in bed," I responded but wanted to laugh at the absurdity of it all.

"I can hardly wait to hear that story but don't these girls know anything about birth control?" Brooke laid the schedule on the desk and sat.

"I asked the very same question. The best I can tell, they either forget or they really do want a baby. The silly girls think they'll get their current men to make commitments to them when confronted with their paternity. It rarely happens. I can't tell you how many abortions take place in the month. Maybe one a week." I shrugged and shook my head again. "I probably don't even know the number anyway."

"But abortions are illegal. How do they . . .?" Brooke waved her hand. "Never mind. I don't want to know."

I returned to real work issues. "We have a special event to deal with this week." I reached under the desk and produced a straw hat, the kind with about three-inches of straw strands hanging around the rim.

"Is this part of my initiation into the Club?" Brooke grabbed the hat and plopped it on her head. She quickly removed it and put her finger through one of the two holes in the crown. "Playboy couldn't afford a new one?"

I smiled. "The hats are for the Bunnies to wear. International is celebrating the Jamaica Club. The holes are for the Bunnies' ears."

Brooke and I stared at each other. Overwhelmed by the insanity of it all, we laughed. Then we laughed some more. We couldn't stop until the phone rang.

My face must have gone gray as I listened to the voice on the other end. I hung up and said to Brooke, "I've got to go to the Mansion. Hold down the fort as best you can for the next hour. Start calling the reserve girls, even Adrian, to replace Lydia. You better make that two reserve girls. Georgia also called to get off tonight's schedule because her boyfriend's not working as he thought and she wants to be with him." I took a deep breath. "I told her I couldn't do that, but I bet she's a no show."

"I can handle it, but what's up with Lydia?"

"She overdosed again." I could feel my face tighten into a deep frown. "I'd like to find out who supplied the drugs this time."

"Oh, God." Brooke lifted her manicured hand to her mouth.

The uncanny silence in the Mansion contrasted with the first time I had been invited there to a party. Though I had hardly been able to manage the traditional 1:00 am starting time, my curiosity had gotten the better of me. Plus my presence had been part of the Bunny Mother's role—a command performance. I left well before the party heated up at 4:00 am when the invited entertainers and Bunnies got off work. I'd guessed Hefner had forgotten about the other working stiffs; the ones who had regular hours and couldn't sleep, eat and work anytime they wanted the way he could. From what the girls told me afterwards, the event sounded sordid. I knew I'd get another chance to observe the goings on myself during the upcoming holiday soirees already in the planning stages.

This day, however, I walked up the flight of stairs to the foyer without anyone checking a guest list. The empty first floor great hall with its two-story ceiling seemed cold, although the paneled walls were hung with expensive and often colorful abstract art. The huge room surely was intended for the royalty Hefner viewed himself to be. The last time I entered here the space had been occupied by so many party-goers I barely saw the infamous proprietor. Never in one place for more than a minute or two, Hef had glided through the adoring crowd holding the ubiquitous Pepsi in one hand, a pipe in the other and wearing his signature silk pajamas. His brief appearances at these galas had become notorious. He usually retreated to his own private quarters for intimate conversations with those lucky enough to be courted. Hef's aim had always been to put on parties that would make headlines and history. He succeeded because everyone wanted to get invited to the ultimate bachelor pad.

I climbed the stairs to the fourth-floor dorm at the top of the Mansion. Though not a requirement of the job, several Bunnies lived in these quarters until they found other arrangements when their finances allowed. As I hurried upwards, I realized there was no ambulance outside, no sign of any emergency medical personnel inside and I heard not a sound. Once I reached the top floor, whispers floated from the dorm area. As soon as I placed my hand on the door knob, Mrs. Bundy, the House Mother appeared.

"It took you long enough." Mrs. Bundy filled the doorway. Ever persistent and with hands on her broad hips, she asked, "Did you know that Lydia used drugs?"

I had heard the rumors and had in fact sent Lydia home just the week before for being high. I never learned her source though I had some suspects—Lucas, a night busboy for one. I would never tell Mrs. Bundy. Someone in management would offer a lie detector test to Lydia and any other person on their list of recalcitrant employees to find the supplier. It would be a roundup of those who had fallen out of favor and whom International looked for any excuse to fire. Lie detector tests had become the instrument of choice in the hunt for thieves, prostitutes, drug and alcohol abusers, whatever.

"Well, Alyce, did you know about Lydia or not?" Mrs. Bundy was actually tapping her foot.

"No, not really. Only rumors." I pressed by the House Mother and found Lydia sprawled naked across her bed attended by a woman in a nurse's outfit and a man in street clothes.

Mrs. Bundy followed so close to me I could feel her breath shift my hair. "You know I run a clean place here," Mrs. Bundy whined. "I don't abide drinking, men in the rooms, drugs, no nonsense at all."

"Yes, I know." I also remembered Mrs. Bundy rode havoc over any girl she didn't like for one reason or another, but particularly if the girl didn't fear her.

When I introduced myself I discovered the man was a doctor called in such cases. He would keep the information to himself so it wouldn't become headlines or part of a police investigation. What other secrets had he not revealed? "Will she be alright?" I leaned over Lydia's bare body.

"Yes," the doctor answered.

"What did she take?" I caught myself from saying "this time." No point confessing to the House Mother-snoop.

"As best we can tell, several sleeping pills," he nodded to an empty bottle on the bed table, "and a lot of alcohol." The doctor dropped Lydia's wrist, which slapped against the sheet. He faced me. "Is she having any unusual problems?"

"Define unusual, Doctor." I didn't wait for answer. "Many of these girls suffer from broken hearts, unwanted pregnancies, divorces, money problems, depression. They have no idea what the real world is about. Would you, if you lived in a place like this mansion—built to feed a male's fantasy?" As I talked I became angrier. "Sorry. Is there anything else I can do right now?"

Mrs. Bundy, not the doctor, answered. "Get her out of this house. She has one week to find another place to live."

"How charitable of you, Mrs. Bundy."

"Well, if she hadn't squandered her money on that stuff," Mrs. Bundy smirked and pointed to the empty bottle on the floor, "she could afford to live anywhere. She makes enough money."

What a House Mother. Mrs. Bundy had no clue about what made people tick or how to help them. "If that's all, I've got work to do. And please cover the girl, for God's sake," I said as I stalked out of the room.

Mrs. Bundy called after me, "One week. Remember. Or I'll be forced to have her fired."

"Witch," I mumbled.

Greg came to the Club to have lunch because schools were closed for Election Tuesday. Also because of elections no alcohol could be served but that didn't stop members from patronizing the Club. Rather they substituted orange and tomato juices. By the time I left in the evening, though the country would still be led by a Democratic President, Lyndon B. Johnson, the Republicans were sure to win every local election. I felt guilty that I really didn't care about who won what. I was overwhelmed enough in my struggle to survive each day. For the rest of the country, the Viet Nam War seemed the most salient issue. On a personal level, I had come to think more about women's rights and the feminist movement. Playboy certainly had taught me that in the eyes of this organization at least, many women were nothing more than expendable tits and asses.

After my unusually slow day, I took Greg bowling, which he always loved. He had become so proficient that now I could never beat him. But no matter how exhausted I was, which seemed more often than not, I always enjoyed my outings with Greg and he needed the private attention. Without our special time he most likely would find some less productive way to occupy himself. I feared he would reach out to his less savory peers or perhaps even fall into drugs or alcohol.

Carl had an appointment with his tutor so he couldn't make the bowling trip. Carl had reading problems. Over the past two years Carl had suffered because he couldn't learn like his classmates. One day in L.A. he had come home sobbing. He threw his books against the wall and screamed, "Why did God make me so stupid?"

It took only one Chicago tutor to determine Carl not only was bright, but he needed reading glasses. In just a few short weeks, Carl's attitude toward school changed from never wanting to attend to thinking perhaps it wasn't so bad. I now had hopes he would change his dreams from being a farmer, a solitary job, and instead go to college. Having glasses had altered his whole life.

Though happy about the finding, I was furious with the nasty counselors and teachers in L.A. who had ridiculed him rather than searching for the root of the problem. Plus I chastised myself for being so self-absorbed I hadn't found the solution myself. What kind of mother was I?

Chapter Nine

Single Mothers

The Big Bunny is at the heart of what motivates most men. What we have tapped is a combination of status and sex. It is romance, it is the maximum image that a man has of himself in terms of what he wants to accomplish, in terms of prestige. The romantic image where women are concerned, the business image where men are concerned. It's his pot at the end of the rainbow, it's what the guy works for." Hugh Hefner from the book BIG BUNNY written by Joe Goldberg and published by Ballantine Books

Barry circled his arm around my shoulder, a gesture he had never made before. It didn't take long for me to ascertain his meaning. Coco stepped into the office behind him.

"Hi," she said and waved. "I'm back."

I pulled away from Barry and glared. I could feel my lips form a thin, tight line. The blood pulsed in my temples. I said nothing and waited to hear Barry's next lie.

"Coco will be training the new Bunny Director, Judy Wax, when she comes on board next Monday." Barry circled his arm around my shoulder and squeezed, I assumed as an attempt to console me. "Coco has more experience."

This time I couldn't move. The room spun. What was going on? Dare I ask what would become of me and Coco once this Wax person showed up? "Who is Judy Wax?" I finally asked and eased out of Barry's clutch again.

"She's a poet. She wrote the poetry for Playboy Calendars for the past 14 years. She's the wife of the magazine's editor." Barry's shrug said the rest. Just as Shar claimed—politics. She had been right all along.

"And Coco?" I ventured another question to Barry. "Where will she go when Miss Wax gets here?"

"Didn't you know I was coming back?" Coco meandered toward me, making no attempt to hide her disdain for the meager office remodeling I had been allowed to make.

Barry pushed his shades to the top of his head. I preferred them in their proper place. At least then they hid his betraying eyes.

"No, I didn't. It's obvious I'm not in the loop." How could I have trusted this slime bag? The answers cascaded through my mind: because I wanted to believe that I had a chance at a profitable career with Playboy, Inc. That I'd been hired because of my skills. That the Playboy Clubs had grown too fast and International needed experienced, well-trained administrators not promoted from the ranks of unprepared Bunnies and bartenders. That my sons and I could have a decent home. That I wouldn't be haunted by the possibility the utilities would be turned off because I couldn't pay the bills.

I clenched my fists so tightly my nails pressed into the skin of my palms. I needed time to think. Then I remembered my journal and chuckled to myself. Maybe one day I would expose all the lunatics in the Playboy Asylum Inc. My daily diary had been my solace since before I got to Chicago. I spent hours writing in it every night. My entries helped me work through many crises. It looked like that process would get me through the Coco and Judy Wax disaster as well.

Once I mulled all this over, I decided to be as gracious as possible. To Barry's evident surprise, I smiled. I didn't want to make waves or show hard feelings until my health benefits went into effect in a couple of months. I had to work six months before I would be covered. Once the insurance became available I'd have my nose done. After that I'd decide my next move. I did have concerns about Coco's interactions with the Bunnies. Who would come out the victor when it came to managing them? I didn't look forward to that battle.

After a few moments Barry asked Coco to leave so he could talk to me. His sudden show of boldness was unusual. On other occasions when he had dropped such a bombshell Barry had run away with his tail between his legs.

I appraised Coco as she left. No sign of giving birth. Coco managed to recapture her youthful figure, though her outfit seemed too mod for her age. Perhaps she chose to wear the mini skirt and boots to reassure management that Playboy hadn't made a mistake by taking her back. Certainly the tight turtleneck tucked in and cinched at the waist with a large leather belt would guarantee Barry's support.

"What is it now, Barry?" I walked to my desk chair and sat. Barry followed but stood to one side, his back to the door.

"You know how I feel about you."

I simply nodded. If I started in on how I really felt, we'd be there for a few hours. Time I couldn't waste. Barry had already taken up enough of my time for this day.

He lit a cigar. "Usually you do a good job. But damn, you think you're running your own Club over here."

"Usually?" I ventured. Was that supposed to be a compliment "Are you going to give me the 'Get Your Hair and Clothes fixed' lecture again?"

"No, no." He waved his cigar back and forth. Ashes dropped to the floor. "You look fine. But you let the Bunnies run all over you."

"What?" I shouted. "I hope you have an example."

"In fact I do, though I was planning to make today's session one where we talk about your future with Playboy."

"Save it for another time." I fumed. I stood and walked toward Barry. He showed his cowardliness and backed up.

"Ok. I'll give you a recent situation. You let three Bunnies back out of the Jamaica promotion which left us short for a special event."

"Wrong!" I leaned toward him. He, in response, bent further backward. I enjoyed how I towered over him. "One girl never agreed to take part, another had her dates mixed up and had an auto show to do." My voice rose so it even hurt my own ears. "And a third girl did the spot as planned."

Barry's blush traveled further up his neck to his forehead with each explanation. He didn't apologize for misunderstanding. Instead he plunged into another management grievance. "What about all the girls who show up late at their stations?"

"I'm not sure who you're talking about, but I keep a list of who is tardy twice or more in a week." I threw the list at Barry. He wasn't quick enough to catch it so several pages scattered to the floor. As he picked them up I came within inches of him so that when he stood up to face me our noses nearly touched.

"By the way, the tardy girls had never promoted Jamaica before.

Neither have I. None of us knew about the hats. Another loop I was left out of." I leaned even closer to Barry. "It was another last minute whim dreamed up by International."

Berry resumed his slow shuffle backward. I kept a steady voice and inched forward with each of his retreating steps. "When the girls discovered the addition to their costume, they had to remove their hair pieces, cut holes for their ears and reassemble themselves. Next time it might help if you or someone at International would clue us in."

"Well, well." Barry put out his cigar near the door, clearly happy to be at the exit.

But I wasn't about to let him go yet. "Before you get on my case about those stupid beads International ordered, I've told the Bunnies not to give them out because they bleed. And the banana chips are soggy. You don't want to disappoint the keyholders, do you?"

Barry shook his head and opened his mouth. I broke in first. "One more thing. I don't give up on the Bunnies so easily. I continue to work with the ones I think are salvageable until it's proved they can't or don't want to do the job. I gain their trust. If they don't meet our standards, I let them go. Got the picture?"

By this time Barry had one foot in the hall. "I guess I came up here for nothing." He smiled sheepishly. Perhaps he was attempting to soften the situation.

"No, Barry, you came here to tell me someone has taken my job. It doesn't matter which one—Bunny Mother or Bunny Director."

Barry made it into the hall. "It wasn't my decision. I knew Coco was coming back because she had been given a short leave to have her baby, but I didn't think she'd come back here."

I didn't answer. I glared at him with such intensity my eyes stung. Right now I didn't trust him or many others at Playboy.

Barry pulled his shades over his eyes. "I know there will be a good spot for you."

"Good-by, Barry. As long as I'm still the Bunny Mother I've got work to do."

He made quick steps to the stairs. I slammed the door and went back to my desk. "Damn them!" I sifted through the papers and talked to myself. "Only a short time more. About six months should do it so I don't have to take the boys out of school. Plus my nose will be done courtesy of Playboy. I can do six months. I hope."

Shortly after Barry left my office, Brooke appeared. "You look like you lost your best friend," she said.

"No." I bit my lower lip to stop the quivering. "But I may have lost my job."

"What?" Brooke's voice echoed down the hall. She slapped her hand over her mouth and closed the door. "Tell me everything."

I wanted to have faith in Brooke. I really liked her. I sensed from our first meeting we could be friends. So I let my guard down and bared my soul. I not only recounted my whole Playboy experience, including what had just happened, but once I started I divulged personal history. I described my mother's suicide ten years earlier and how I often had similar urges to take my own life when things got tough, which right now, seemed like always. "I miss my mother desperately," I whispered.

I faced the window and stared at the wall. I didn't want Brooke to see my tears. I didn't want her to see how weak I could be. Here I was, defeated and alone again. Any hope for a bright future had just evaporated. Even though I should stop my outburst, that I should position myself to be more of a mentor to Brooke, I just took a deep breath and went on, now in depth about my former husband's abuse and how I went into hiding to free myself and my sons. "Then there's my kid sister, Tekkie. Since our father died four years before our mother, she had no one to care for her. Tekkie was only thirteen then. So I became her guardian. I had to be her mother. Tekkie's in college now." Momentarily I brightened. At least my sister had made it to college. At least she had a chance at a happy future.

I revealed my affair with Clark. I finished my story by telling Brooke about rarely getting child support payments and how I was always broke. "Now this," I turned away from the window. "I guess I sound like the rest of the girls at Playboy."

An hour fled by before my sad eyes met Brooke's. Only then did I realize she hadn't said a word. Instead Brooke wiped tears from her own cheeks. She walked to me and gave me a hug. Neither of us said another word. I had found a true friend. I didn't think I would ever regret being honest with her.

We heard a knock at the door. It opened before we could separate.

Two men came into the room. One announced, "I'm Kurt Forbes with the F.B.I." He pointed to the other. "He's agent Dick Clemens." Both produced identifications. "May we?" Forbes motioned into the office.

What next? I quickly wiped away any evidence of a tear away. "Yes. Please sit." I introduced Brooke and myself. I chuckled to myself when I noted both agents dressed in what appeared to be the F.B.I. uniform: navy suits, white shirts, blue-striped ties and wing tip shoes. Both sported nondescript brown hair cuts like Herbert Hoover's, receding hairline and all. They fit the image of every agent I'd seen in the news or the movies.

I was sure they had come about Lydia's attempted suicide. Perhaps the agents were hunting for the person who kept supplying her with pills. Or maybe it was about the doctor who performed the abortions. "A visit from the F.B.I. is quite unexpected," I commented as I took a seat at my desk still cautious not to lean too far back. The chair had never been repaired. The agents smiled as automatically as if someone had whispered in their ears to cue them. Brooke eased into a chair next to the agents and opposite me.

Forbes, obviously the senior agent, spoke, "We need to talk with one of the Bunnies. Her name is Ellie Conrad."

Ellie! "We have an Ellie working here but that's not her last name," I said.

Forbes handed me a picture. A smiling Bunny Ellie, ears and all, peered back. "Yes. She works here. What has she done?" I immediately thought of the alleged prostitution ring.

"Nothing to our knowledge." Forbes slid the picture back into his attaché.

"I'm confused, then."

"We need to question Ellie about a man who passed bad checks in Las Vegas. He had her name."

I let them know that Ellie wouldn't be in until the next shift. I'd arrange for them to meet in my office. Meanwhile, I too was curious about how the man got Ellie's name. Yet I feared confiding my suspicions about Ellie's possible prostitution to the agents. I didn't want to accuse her of something about which I hadn't enough evidence. Not yet anyway.

No sooner had the F.B.I. agents left, Barry came down the hall.

"We'll never get the schedule done at this rate," Brooke complained. "Is your office always like this?"

"Yes. That's why I usually end up doing the schedule at home."

"Sorry to interrupt. I needed to deal with one other issue," Barry said as he eyed Brooke.

"She'll stay." My firmness left no room for argument.

"Fine," Barry conceded. Though he closed the door, he stayed near it.

"You know that little problem with Adrian?"

I acknowledged with raised eyebrows.

"Well, I want her terminated for Bunny Image." Barry reached for the doorknob.

I stepped near him and stopped his hand.

"Barry, she's a perfect Bunny."

I held my hand on his and eased myself between Barry and the door so he couldn't escape, a position I seemed to find myself in often. He wiped moisture from his forehead. Then froze in place.

"If you and Adrian have a personal problem, you need to deal with it. It is unreasonable to tell me to get rid of a good and much needed Bunny because you got caught with your pants down." There. The gauntlet was thrown. After Barry's earlier blow, I had nothing to lose.

Barry pushed my hand aside and squeezed back into the room. When he faced me, his face was stony. His lips barely moved when he opened it to speak. Though I had frequently been the recipient of Barry's many outbursts, I hadn't seen him this angry. "I'm the boss," he said. "You and every other girl in this place will do as I say. I want Adrian gone by the end of the week. Clear?"

"Everything is quite clear," I answered in a tone that could chill the dead.

Barry left.

Brooke again sat with her mouth flopped opened but once she gathered her composure she complimented me. "I can't believe what you have to go through each day. You are such a special person."

Her generosity nearly reduced me to tears for the second time that day. "At least you're on my side." I willed my voice to stay calm. "Now let's get to the schedule. Later this afternoon you get another treat."

Brooke raised her eyebrows.

"Bunny Council. You get to hear the girls' gripes." I pulled out the schedule that was showing so many names crossed out already.

"You mean there's more than what we hear every day?" Brooke sounded amazed.

"Yep. Hard to believe, isn't it?" I looked up from the mess staring at me from the schedule. "Most will be about the Room Directors who seem to be on a mission to destroy any Bunny who won't ball them." I shrugged. "Or maybe they envy the attention."

"I can hardly wait." Brooke's sarcasm made me smile. "We had our problems in the Peace Corps, but nothing like this," Brooke added.

"Different breed, I guess." I slipped into thought for a few seconds. "When Coco and Shar were here together, they had to either order or specifically select girls to attend the meetings. Shar lectured me about my volunteer system. She said no one would show up." I handed Brooke a copy of the schedule and smiled, if a little grimly. "So far there has been standing room only for the meetings and many times we end up with great ideas for promotionals or about work issues."

As we worked on the schedule, I again noticed how great Brooke looked. Though I really liked her, I felt intimidated by her beauty and fashion sense. I'd never look that good and couldn't afford the help needed to achieve that kind of style.

Oh, quit it. I told myself. When would I stop comparing myself to other women?

Before the Bunny Council met, I spoke with Adrian. To my surprise, she had suspected Barry planned to get rid of her. She explained that the night he stood her up, she decided to return to a lover, Rod, who recently had come back into her life. He lived in California and wanted to marry her. Better yet, he had always been the love of her life. He had a great job and she wouldn't have to work if she didn't want to. They both wanted children. "I'm going to be Mrs. Cleaver," Adrian chuckled. "I took this job for the money and to get away from Rod who had been so indecisive about our relationship. Then Barry put so much pressure on me that I either had to be his mistress or give up being a Bunny. I'm one of the lucky girls. Barry certainly helped me make my decision to go with Rod when he came back into my life."

I envied Adrian. Riding off into the California sunset with her knight. She deserved it. Still, why couldn't I have a happy-ever-after life with Clark? How did these girls, good, bad, pretty or not, get the guy? Suddenly, I was terribly homesick for Los Angeles.

The Bunny Council took my mind off the day's bad news that had piled up like a snow drift. This time a majority of the girls appeared, filling the cramped space with long legs and Go-go boots and compounding the closeness with a collection of Channel #5, Bellodgia, and Jean Naté.

Jane opened the discussion with a blockbuster. "All they see are whores," she said.

After that the floodgates opened and I, playing counselor, found myself in the midst of a group therapy session. It was more intense than a regular meeting, except for including the usual job complaints about Room Directors. I hoped it wouldn't scare Brooke away.

"Yeah," Nadine said. "Why can't they treat us like ladies? Being a Bunny is like any other job." They were the Room Directors. This was a common complaint.

"Bill thinks we want it that way," Mona said as she tucked one long slender leg under her. "He actually joked about balling me after I did the twist on the piano. He knows that dancing's part of the job."

I wrote a note to speak with Bill about his crude behavior. Others had also complained.

Tom, one of the Room Directors, attended the meeting, a requirement just like periodic attendance at Bunny Training. But sadly, the Room Directors often only wanted to hear the dirt. He did make a good observation, though, in response to the Bunnies. "Each Room Director is different," he began, "just like each Bunny. There are a lot more Bunnies to adjust to. Some shifts are worse than others and I agree we shouldn't take our problems out on the girls, but we are only human, like you." He eyed each girl in the room. "You also know it's an uphill battle for many of the Room Directors, with them trying to forget you make more money than they do. They are young and less experienced than the senior Bunnies, yet most have college degrees."

A few girls shifted in their chairs, one blew her nose while others stared at him. I thought Tom had been diplomatic, but I sensed some disagreement. Soon Sadie spoke. "The Room Directors should try being a single mother getting no child support payments from men just like them. If they want to earn more money tell them to wait on the tables in three-inch heels and a corset."

"Or perhaps you'd like to be treated like a commodity rather than a human being," Carlie piped up. "Besides, I have a degree, as do many others."

"Human being? Let me tell you what that means to a colored woman like me," Sadie lamented. "You know when I went to New Orleans to work for a couple of weeks?"

"Uh huh," the girls chimed and nodded.

"Well, not only could I not take the same cab as Jane over there, the freakin' keyholders boycotted the Club." Sadie paused long enough for the whole scene to sink in. "The Bunny Mother told me to play down my lips, as though that would help." She glared at Tom with her magnificent, dark eyes, anger causing her cheeks to go deep brown. "You want that part of my life?"

"Same thing happened in Cincinnati," Nadine offered. "We all thought from the publicity, the town looked forward to seeing the Chicago Club Bunnies. Instead, the keyholders and others picketed outside the lobby door with signs that said *Nigger, Go Back to Chicago*. And instead of a tip, one guy wrote *boo* in the space." She took a long slow breath and stared at Tom. "If you think that's bad, at the hotel where we stayed the receptionist gave out our room numbers and men pounded at our doors all night." She stood and placed her hands on her hips. "We went there to help out. The Club got caught short when the girls walked off the job in a protest over firing a Bunny for dating a manager. Two Room Directors and a Night Manager also dated Bunnies so they walked too. It was a fiasco for which I paid dearly."

Nadine collapsed onto a chair. No one else moved until German Heidi piped up, "Even I was told to go home by a keyholder in the V.I.P. Room at that Club. It's no different here." Heidi's accent became more pronounced as she talked. "My accent." She shrugged. "I'm called *Nazi*."

Tom held his hands up in an apology. "I didn't mean you girls aren't worth every penny you get. I'm tryin' to tell you that Room Directors have problems they need to deal with too."

Always the diplomat I thought. "Anything else on this subject?" I asked. One girl snapped her gum.

"Well, then," Tom said, "I need to get on the floor. Thank you for your time."

"He had his nose done," Mona announced as Tom escaped through the door.

The girls laughed again as one called out, "No reason the boys can't get as pretty as the girls. Besides, he's not the only one."

Within minutes of Tom's departure the girls resumed their rapid fire. One issue followed another. They were all personal.

Heidi spoke first. "I guess I'd feel the same as those guys. We also make more money than you, Alyce. I couldn't be a Bunny Mother because of that."

I wanted to tell Heidi she might not be a Bunny either much longer if the Room Directors caught her hiking up a check to get a bigger tip again. Instead I said, "I think of this job as training for a future career move. I've learned how to deal with just about every situation imaginable and with all sorts of people. You should look at your jobs in the same way."

"I don't know how you take it sometimes," Candy sympathized.

"That's why you're Tom's favorite—you're soooo sweet," Nadine said to her, and the others laughed.

"Ah ha! We've managed to get back to the male topic," Ellie shouted as she jumped up. "Let me tell you a thing or two. All men play favorites and all men cheat. They're just no damn good."

"Only the ones we Bunnies get." Sadie sounded so sad. "Take me for instance. I'm tired of getting rid of pregnancies."

Almost every girl echoed their agreement.

"You got that right," Nadine added. "What's your take, Alyce?"

"I don't believe only Bunnies get stuck with the worst. You're more honest about the situations with each other than most women. It depends if a person really loves the other." I stopped for a moment because I knew I referred to Clark and me. "Or whether the cheating was a common thing or something that happened in a weak moment. I mean sometimes we find someone and fall in love without looking for it."

Quiet Joan put in her two cents. "It's not only men who cheat. What about Bunny LeeAnn who pretended to be out of town, but was still in Chicago with her lover?"

The room filled with uproarious laughter as several added more to the story. "Yeah, she almost got caught because her husband needed the car and he thought it was parked at the airport."

"She called me to move it from downtown to the airport."

"We all asked her why she doesn't quit her marriage and run off with her lover. She told us that she loved her husband and her boyfriend loved his wife. They were just having a thing."

"A THING! What the hell is that supposed to mean?"

"Joan, you shouldn't bad mouth LeeAnn. You dumped your man 'cause he got orders for Viet Nam," Sadie chided. "Then you started up with a guy too old to get drafted. Oh, yeah, and I forgot the old guy has money."

Joan lowered her head and fiddled with the buttons on her sweater. "I know it looks bad." The tip of her nose turned red as one tear slipped from the corner of her eye. "But I couldn't bear it if he got killed over there. I just couldn't handle it."

"Did ya ever think about what he wanted?" Ellie asked. "Being in that jungle, the boy needed something to comfort him. You coulda even gone over with the other Bunnies to entertain the troops. Weren't you gonna be adopted by his unit as their official pinup?"

"Yeah, well." Joan swiped at a tear. "It's over."

The room fell silent until the Bunny snapped her gum again.

"I came pretty close to getting married and keeping my baby with Herbie," Sadie piped up. "But he had other ideas. He went back to his wife." Sadie grimaced. "And I went back to the doctor." Sadie did have a two-year-old daughter from another affair. "Though I'd like to have a whole houseful of kids," she told the group, her eyes became distant. "I'm grateful for Cecilia. But she's as much work as a dozen."

"Ha!" The girls jumped at the loud challenge from Mona. "My man dumped me for the seventeen-year-old he got pregnant. Her daddy probably came after him with a big ol' shot gun. He sure never wanted the babies I carried."

"Maybe it's good some of these no-good macho clods dumped us. If they didn't, we'd be supporting them for the rest of our lives," Ellie added.

"I shouldda let my father choke the cheap SOB when he had a chance," Sadie said. "We all lived together along with Herbie's brother. One day my father and the brother got into it—they did every day." Sadie lit a cigarette. "That time it got outta hand. They were slapping each other around. Herbie tried to separate the two. My father got so furious, he wrapped his big ol' steel worker's hand around that boy's throat." She took a long, hard pull on her cigarette, then blew smoke from her mouth for what seemed like minutes. All eyes focused on her. "I shouldda never stopped dear ol' Dad."

Though I had been well aware that many Bunnies supported their boyfriends, fearing they'd run off otherwise, I wondered if Ellie referred to her pimp. Of course I still hadn't collected enough proof to support the prostitution allegation. Suddenly my memory filled with the day I cocked a shotgun and aimed it at Angelo after a particularly bitter fight. Thank God the gun didn't work.

"When will we learn? As it is, we can't even get our own bills paid." Sadie turned to the quiet girls and asked why they hadn't said anything.

One answered, "I guess we can't compete with your goings-on."

"The new girls sure are square." Sadie thumbed in their direction but faced me.

"Give them six months," I tittered.

The other girls agreed.

"I'm not as square as my brother," one new Bunny said. She had said nothing until then. "He's married to a divorced woman and sleeps on the sofa Saturday nights so he can take communion on Sunday."

"Now that is square," Sadie admitted. The others couldn't stop laughing.

I looked at the room filled with girls none of them yet twenty-five-years old. How did they all get themselves in those positions? A few, the college girls, kept their mouths closed. Maybe they thought they were better than the rest. I finally said, "Perhaps we're all running away from bad relationships and looking for ones we hope will be better. If we put more weight into our own self worth, we'd be better off. We deserve it."

All eyes were focused on me. Silence again. "Well, it's getting late and some of you must get ready for work." I broke the momentary lull in the conversation.

"Not all men are that bad." Everyone turned to look in the direction of the gentle voice. Brenda, the newly hired Bunny, stood near the door. Brenda no longer looked like the housewife I hired. With hair and makeup miracles and the incomparable costume, Brenda now resembled a voluptuous movie star. She had amazed me when she showed up for her first inspection, not only because of her total makeover, but especially because of her hair. The natural blond hair was dyed brunette, which made her piercing blue eyes stand out. That unusual move would also give Brenda an advantage on the floor. Members would surely take notice.

"My husband has never cheated. He thinks my transformation," she turned around, "is wonderful. He can't brag enough about me and show me off." Brenda's bright smile only added to her new-found beauty. "I'm thrilled myself with the results."

The girls held their tongues. I nodded my approval. "May I add that I think you look marvelous?"

A few girls nodded in agreement. The others no doubt were jealous.

"Thanks for a great session," I said. "Now let's get back to work."

As the girls ambled from the room, many stopped to thank me for understanding. "You really are our mother," Mona said. I wondered if they felt that way about Coco.

Brooke stood slowly and stretched. "What a day for you. I do hope my time with Playboy goes better."

"Don't take the Chicago Club Bunny Mother job, then," I almost snarled. "Let's get back to the office, finish up what loose ends we can and go home to our children."

"Good idea. But do you ever hear any good news?"

"One time," I started as I stuffed the council notes into a file folder. "Now I say happiness is when a busboy tells me I am the best Bunny Mother ever because I don't complain when there's no silverware for my lunch."

"What?" Brooke laughed heartily.

"Yeah. Apparently, the dishwasher showed up for work late and didn't get the silverware done on time. What little the kitchen had was kept for the paying lunch crowd." As I looked up from the conference table, I couldn't help but smile. "Thank goodness, I ordered a sandwich."

Brooke shook her head. We walked to the door arm and arm.

Once back in my office, I received a call from Tom, who wanted to know what the Bunnies said about him after he left. He sounded disappointed when I told him the truth. "Your name never came up again except for a complaint that you play favorites on occasion. We've discussed that problem before, haven't we?"

"Yes, yes, we have," Tom's voice drifted. "Gotta go." He hung up.

Saturday morning. Finally some sun streaked into my bedroom through the parted drapes. It had been days since I last saw its brightness. I hardly remembered going to bed. I'd fallen asleep again fully clothed on the couch watching TV long after Carl and Greg had gone to sleep. I wasn't surprised to find myself still dressed in my work clothes. I must have fumbled my way up the stairs and into bed half asleep and unaware. I'd done that before, too.

Now, I couldn't get out of bed. My whole being felt too heavy for one person to move. I was exhausted from working ten or more-hour days and depressed because I had no money and maybe no job. I also had not received a child support payment. Sure, the paperwork could hold up payments when I moved, but four months?

I forced myself to sit up and snatched my purse from the bed table. I pulled out my wallet. I fingered the $17.50. Had anyone seen me take it from petty cash? I'd never done anything like that before. Yet faced with not a dime to my name, little food in the house and two boys needing adventure, I had to lift the money—as a loan, of course. I'd pay it back either with the child support payment or my paycheck.

I replaced the money and my purse. I heaved my legs over the side of the bed. My feet thumped against the floor like two cement blocks. Using both arms, I propelled myself upwards. I couldn't let my sons see how depressed I had become or how broke. Carl and Greg needed to think everything would be fine.

I could barely wash my face. I labored with makeup. Putting on my face had become a daily task I had trained myself to perform knowing I could meet someone from work at any time. I always had to look close to my best even if I was only doing laundry. Thinking of laundry, once the boys and I ate breakfast, I had to tackle that, which lay in giant piles in both bedrooms. Until that moment I hadn't thought how I'd transport the dirty clothing the two blocks to the laundromat.

I pulled on a turtleneck sweater and slacks that had become a size too big. I had lost weight I didn't need to since my tenure began at Playboy. Stress, no doubt. If I had any money to spare I'd buy some decent clothes. Several Bunnies had hinted they'd take me shopping. Even they thought I needed some help.

An hour later Carl, Greg and I each carried two pillowcases stuffed with dirty items. Though the air was cold and the wind whipped from the shore, the sun's warmth cheered the walk. That cheerfulness passed all too soon. When I put money into a machine for bleach, I neither received the bleach nor my money back. When Carl put $2.00 into the money changer, he only got $1.75 back. I complained to the clerk about the errors but to no avail. "I'm not telling the boss," the clerk snarled, "because he always complains the money's short anyway." How could I argue with that kind of logic? The clerk couldn't see any problem with me paying for someone else's errors.

Two hours after that and nine loads finished, we trekked back to the townhouse. I wrote a letter to the laundromat's owner about how I had been cheated. That task completed I offered up an adventure, a bus ride downtown and a visit to the Museum of Science and Industry. Maybe this was frivolous, but I felt compelled to give my sons a fun day so they would be less homesick. So I used almost the whole remainder of the stolen funds to take the boys to a steak house for dinner. Fortunately the boys passed on a movie because none suited their tastes. More important, I didn't have enough money.

While window shopping, Greg spotted a model car set which cost $50.00. He practically got down on his knees and begged for it. He was so disappointed I couldn't afford such an exorbitant toy I promised I'd buy it for Christmas praying inwardly I could keep my pledge. I desperately wanted to have enough financial stability so I didn't have to resort to borrowing cash from the Playboy fund.

Back at the house, we walked Fraulein, played cards and ate popcorn, sharing a handful at a time with the dog. Satisfied with the day's events and lack of work interruptions we went to sleep. Before I gave into my fatigue, I wrote about the last couple of days in my journal. I underlined the last sentence: *I must find a way out.*

After two hours of writing I put the journal into a drawer and slid into bed, relishing being in my nightgown for the first time in a week.

Drowsy, I could hardly believe it when the phone rang. I checked the time. "1:30 in the morning," I mumbled and reached for the receiver.

The Room Director Tom was shouting so loudly, I held the phone away from my ear. "Calm down," I said. "You realize what time it is and that you've awakened me from a sound sleep?"

"Yes, well, maybe you or Brooke should work more weekends."

"Forget changing policy for the moment and tell me what has you so upset."

His several minutes of gibberish practically put me to sleep again. He finally gave the reason for his intrusion. "I don't want Kerie on the door."

"You called me for this?" I was awake suddenly, and very angry.

"Well, yes. I want Sonja to come in."

"Are you afraid to ask her yourself at a decent hour which is exactly what you should've thought about when you called me? Some people sleep at this hour."

"Will you handle it, then?" Tom's mission obviously wouldn't be side-tracked. He hung up without an apology for the late call.

The boys and I spent a peaceful Sunday devoted to putting away the laundry, cleaning the townhouse and challenging Greg to another game of Crazy Eights. Then later, while the boys played with some new acquaintances, I finished the schedule and wrote in my journal. When I got to the part about the petty cash, my hands became clammy.

We had enough food for three days. I splurged the last time I had grocery shopped, buying a pot roast on sale so I could prepare a delicious Sunday dinner. I had once cooked on a regular basis when my hours had been more normal. In California when I couldn't get the cooking done, my sister filled in as chef so there had always been a balanced and shared dinner every night. It had been one small piece of sanity in my life. Now, tonight, and for the first time in a while we sat at dinner like a real family and enjoyed the roast.

Chapter Ten

Lunch With Mrs. Bundy

To protect Playboy Clubs from possible libel or slander suits, great care must be exercised when terminating an employee suspected of prostitution, dishonesty, or use of narcotics. When there is reasonable suspicion of these offenses, the employee should be summarily dismissed and told only that he is not a satisfactory employee in his work habits, or in the case of a Bunny, told she no longer represents the Bunny Image. The employee should not be advised of the specified allegation nor asked to take a polygraph. Interoffice memo 1966

Greg unexpectedly appeared in my office. I thought by the looks of his puffed eyes, he had been crying. To avoid embarrassing him, I didn't ask him about why he dropped in. Instead I said, "What fun to have you visit!"

He gave me a quick half smile. "Carl and his buddy won't let me hang with them," he said, forcing back a sniffle. "They think they're too old for me and that I'm a pain."

To help ease his dejection I ordered dinner for us, which we would eat at my desk. While we waited for the food, I thought about my sons' less than perfect lives in Chicago. First, Huey, a neighbor and Carl's only friend, concerned me. He seemed to have parents who didn't keep tabs on him which brought out undesirable behavior. For instance he had no idea about curfews and couldn't be persuaded to stay out of the junkyard. "It's only junk," he'd say, offering up a trophy he'd pilfered on one of his nightly scavenger hunts. "They'll never miss it," he added.

On weekends, I kept an eye on the two boys so Huey wouldn't persuade Carl to do something foolish. Carl rejected most of my suggestions for after-school activities separate from Huey. "He's my only friend," Carl whined.

"You'll meet others if you go," I prodded, but to no avail. Carl wanted nothing else but to return to the California beaches and his surfboard. I was usually surprised when he went to the tutor without a fuss.

Greg brought me back to the present when he mentioned he wasn't needed at Newton's Drug Store that day, and he had no neighborhood friends so he didn't have anything to do.

"Most kids at school live too far to walk," he said.

Fortunately Greg's mood improved with each mouthful of cheeseburger and gulp of Pepsi, though he preferred RC Cola. Greg's hair had grown over his ears. I needed to get it trimmed.

My thoughts wandered from a haircut to a larger reality. Greg might start skipping school as he had in Los Angeles. Memories of dropping him off at the front door to his L.A. elementary school and him sneaking out the side door came to mind. No one let me know until several weeks of his absences had been calculated. Greg needed more challenging assignments to keep his attention. When such tasks hadn't materialized, his boredom translated into fidgety behavior, which his teacher described as unruliness. My attempts to explain that Greg had above-normal intelligence and energy that could be satisfied with a little more attention and extra constructive activity, his teacher balked. "That means more work for me. Perhaps you should send him to private school."

I wished I had the funds to do exactly that so Greg's creativity would flourish rather than be misunderstood and stifled. One of my missions had to be finding Greg a friend close by our house.

Most days he'd been occupied at Newton's, which kept him, and of course me worry free. I hadn't thought there might not be work for him.

"Let's go bowling this weekend," I offered.

Greg beamed. "But Carl doesn't like to do that." His smile faded.

"Then he'll have to stay home with Fraulein." I could afford bowling after I got my check from Playboy and there was always the possibility of a support payment. Perhaps one day I wouldn't have to do mental math just to take my son bowling. But when?

Once our meals had been consumed, Greg took the bus home. I promised to follow shortly after. Barring any unforeseen no-shows, disagreements between the Room Directors and the girls on the floor, and spur of the moment demands from Hugh Hefner, I'd keep my vow to Greg.

Speaking of unreasonable demands, Hef had six Bunnies on call this week to model new costume colors. The girls chosen to model sat around doing nothing. They couldn't go on the floor or work a normal shift until Hef called for them. The waiting was now in its third day. When I raised my concern to Barry about the inconvenience and waste of Bunny labor and wages, he told me, "Mr. Hefner will get to it when he has the time."

"Didn't he ever hear of appointments?" I ranted. "Doesn't he realize we can't be at his beck and call like indentured servants? Did it ever occur to him that he is the only one who can sleep as long as he wants and the rest of us work in the morning? Doesn't he know we have a business to run?"

"That's how Hef runs his business," Barry answered.

"From a fantasy tower in his pajamas," I retorted.

Barry shrugged. "He's the boss."

End of discussion. The girls bided their time until the master beckoned.

It didn't take long for the first problem to materialize. Priscilla came in for inspection. She told me she had reconciled with her husband—her second marriage—of three months.

"That's great." I genuinely meant that.

"Yeah, but I have this doctor's note, too."

I read it. Priscilla had to work days and not in a strenuous position because of her female problems. That meant she had to work the gift shop. "The modification will have to wait until tomorrow."

"I know." Priscilla didn't leave.

"Do you have something else to say?" I asked.

"Yeah." She bit her lower lip. "If I want to keep my husband, I have to stay on days. He's jealous of my night hours. In fact, he really wants me to quit altogether."

"Why?" I wondered if Priscilla had given him any reason for the jealousy. I surely had become suspicious of the Bunnies.

"The other night I worked the Piano Bar so I could be near my uncle and my mother who is in a wheelchair. You know my Mom keeps my seven-year-old daughter. They brought my kid brother, only eighteen, in for his last night before he ships out to Viet Nam with his Marine unit."

Priscilla stopped. Her lower lip quivered. If she started crying she'd have to do her makeup again.

I nodded. "I know it's been tough for you."

She took a deep breath and continued, "My husband dropped by just as one member flirted with me. It was harmless and meaningless but that did it."

"As I said, I'll make the change tomorrow, but I can't guarantee it will be permanent. It depends on how our new girls work out."

"Thanks." She left.

Priscilla's husband had pushed her into being a Playmate to get the $5000 payment. Once she did that, he took the money and spent every cent. After that she had no choice but to become a Bunny to support herself and her husband just as he expected. He had no intention of working. She had it tough all right. Yet she turned out to be a fantastic Bunny and earned a great deal in tips using a trick no other Bunny ever mastered.

On those Saturday nights when the showrooms were packed with extra tables filled with farm boys, Priscilla carried two laden trays, one in each hand. When she'd reach a table, she'd kneel on one knee and balance one tray on the other knee while she served from the second tray. What a feat! Well, I thought, when her husband discovers she won't earn that kind of money on days, he'll probably make her go back to nights which would be great for the Club.

For some reason that brought Brenda to mind. As a new girl, Brenda was superb. She would fill in. She not only would be willing to switch stations, but she'd work twice as hard. Brenda had turned out to be a gem and a life saver at times like this, thanks also to her happy supportive husband, a rare situation.

Brenda almost hadn't made it through training, however. Her first night on the floor, as she had been instructed in class, Brenda asked a member, "May I see your key, sir?"

"I'm Hugh Hefner," the man answered.

She smiled demurely. "I still need to see your key."

The Bunny working with her, pulled her aside and explained, "Mr. Hefner doesn't have a key. He owns the Club."

After that Brenda had been so nervous when she delivered the tray to his table, she dumped its contents onto the training Bunny who was walking in front of her. Things got better as the evening went on and with each shift she improved. Brenda became one of the best Bunnies.

Anyone would be better than me doing the job. On too many occasions I had to work the gift shop or coat room to free up those Bunnies for the floor. I didn't plan on volunteering that night.

After Lydia's overdose, I arranged to have lunch with Mrs. Bundy at the mansion. The housemother's accusations about most girls living in the dorm had to be nipped in the bud. Mrs. Bundy's negative attitude needn't be added to my growing list of miseries.

Before I could leave my office for the appointment, though, my telephone rang. It always seemed to be the case when I needed to leave. I doubted there would become a time in this job when my day moved forward as planned and without interruptions. My annoyed tone when I answered didn't set the appropriate stage for the conversation that followed.

Bunny LeeAnn's husband was calling to rant on about how he wanted his wife to quit that day and be taken off the schedule. "I make enough money to support us."

LeeAnn had told me her husband drank up both their wages.

"And I'm tired of hearing about her aching muscles." His voice screeched now. "I've had enough!"

I mustered as much control as possible to reason with him. "It would be difficult to fill in for her until I make up the new schedule," I explained. "Do you think she could finish out the week?"

"I told you I've had enough! I get plenty of aggravation dealing with people just like you all day." He sounded irrational.

I had no plan to defend myself to such an agitated person, especially when I hadn't the faintest idea what he was talking about. "Then you understand my position," I ventured an appeal to his own perceived business sense. "You wouldn't quit your own job without notice."

My ploy failed.

"I'm self employed," he said.

I gave up on the notion of saving LeeAnn's job, but I convinced the husband to let her stay for the week, promising not to use her if there was a reserve girl available. I doubted LeeAnn had any say in her own life. Lunch with Mrs. Bundy would be a relief when compared to the likes of LeeAnn's husband.

Mrs. Bundy greeted me on the stairs before I reached the dorms. My determination to have a pleasant encounter melted away as soon as I spotted the plump and pompous middle-aged woman. Hands on her hips, mouth pursed in her usual disapproval, Mrs. Bundy looked every bit the person who the girls reported had a mind looking for dirt.

"You're late again." Mrs. Bundy tapped her Oxford-clad foot. Her face formed a mass of craggy lines, the residue of everything that ever angered her over her nearly fifty years of life.

So much for courtesies. "I'm sorry. However, my agenda isn't always at my discretion as your timetable apparently is."

She grunted and turned. "Lunch is ready," she called out over her shoulder.

I assumed I was supposed to follow. The woman would be a casting director's dream in the role of any college dorm housemother. As I loped behind, I glimpsed Hef scooting through the hall. As expected, he was unshaven, wore his usual pajamas, clenched a pipe between his teeth and held a Pepsi in one hand and papers in the other. Though he glanced at us, he made no attempt to acknowledge us.

I sat in the chair Mrs. Bundy pointed to that was opposite her own. I knew the Mansion's kitchen operated twenty-four-hours a day to accommodate both Hef's odd habits and his guests' needs. It also proved to be a perk for Mrs. Bundy and any girl living in the dorms. They had complete access to the amenities for a small price.

"The girls who live here are very lucky," Mrs. Bundy actually smiled as she said this. Her crooked teeth showed no sign of her ever having smoked. In fact she frowned on "the filthy habit" as she termed it. "They not only have a safe place to sleep, but good food at their disposal. And of course on Sunday evenings Mr. Hefner invites them to view movies with him when he shows one."

I knew all this and more. Mrs. Bundy didn't mention that if Hef, in his pajamas unless other guests had been invited, decided not to watch the movie he had planned, no one could view it until he left the room. Although he ate popcorn during the showing, the girls couldn't share any until he had finished what he wanted. The whole scene seemed uncomfortably similar to a pack of wolves with Hef as the alpha male.

Mrs. Bundy spoke in a whisper to share her next information. "I checked Lydia's area and closet as I now do every day—for drugs and alcohol." She rearranged a bobby pin that held her bun.

I nodded and then took a forkful of Cobb salad.

"Everything is gone. Her closet is empty." Mrs. Bundy sounded astounded by this fact.

"You did tell her leave in a week," I reminded her.

"Yes, but I also gave her an extension. I didn't want her on the streets. Has she shown up for work?"

"I gave her a couple weeks off to get herself together. She's due in tomorrow." I sipped my ice tea, but wished for a Rob Roy to help me through this encounter.

Mrs. Bundy took her first bite of salad. By her large size, I doubted she ate salads often. "Please keep me informed. She probably moved to the Algonquin with Mandy. It's reasonable."

Though I caught a hint of surprising compassion in Mrs. Bundy's voice, I still wouldn't share my last conversation with Lydia. When I visited the Bunny in the hospital the day after her attempted suicide I learned that Lydia had placed her only child up for adoption two years earlier. Her boyfriend (and the father) didn't want the bother of a child and Lydia couldn't face raising the baby without a man.

"Now," she explained, "I'm pregnant again. He took off even though I told him I would get an abortion. He's living with a nineteen-year-old." Tears streamed down her pale cheeks. "He never lived with me."

The young woman sobbed, "I'm such a loser. What kind of mother would I make anyhow?" She pounded her fist into the sheet. "If I don't have this baby, I'll be too old soon. And I'm getting too old for Playboy too." She choked back a cough. "No one wants me, do they?" Lydia's eyes begged me for an answer. "I'll have to work at the Gaslight like the other ex-Bunnies. You know the saying—old Bunnies don't die, they work at the Gaslight." She managed a weak smile.

I held back a chuckle when Lydia mentioned the Gaslight, a rather raunchy club where the waitresses wore skimpy outfits styled after those from the old west bar rooms. The usual rowdy crowd left equally skimpy tips so the girls never made the money they had at Playboy. But age never stopped them from keeping a job at the Gaslight.

I focused back on Lydia's pained face as I wiped her forehead with a cool damp cloth. Lydia waved it away and moaned so loudly it echoed down the hall. A nurse scrambled to the bedside. She told me to leave. I never had the chance to give Lydia an answer.

"Not only does Lydia drink too much, so does Sally." I snapped out of my reverie. Mrs. Bundy apparently had finished her tirade about Lydia and dove right into other smut she had on the girls. Her list of complaints seemed unending. "I found liquor stashed in Sally's closet, too."

I tried to look interested. I buttered a roll.

"Sally's not clean either."

"What do you mean?" I asked, knowing full well others had complained about her, including Catalina. She refused to clean or repair Sally's costumes as required after each shift because Sally never wore her bikini underpants so the crotch was soiled.

"She never bathes. You must know she wears a wig or a hair piece so she doesn't have to wash her hair." Mrs. Bundy clicked her tongue in disgust. "She smells too, and tries to cover it up with a cheap cologne."

I felt sorry for Sally because she never had money and cleaned apartments to make ends meet. Her wealthy husband skipped out on her and didn't pay child support, but Sally wouldn't discuss him. Meanwhile her mother was taking care of Sally's son and Sally had to pay her $150 a month to do it. Yet I had a more selfish motive not to confront Sally. I needed every one of the Bunnies. Now with even Mrs. Bundy bringing it up, the confrontation seemed unavoidable.

"Kathy slipped and let me know that many of the girls use marijuana." Mrs. Bundy didn't wait for me to respond to the Sally issue and kept right on with her list of concerns. "I tried to find evidence but I haven't yet." The House Mother hesitated with a sly look that indicated she thought I would give her some clues. "Well, Kathy lies about everything. She said she went to college but she barely graduated from high school."

The image of Mrs. Bundy donning riot gear to search the rooms of presumable offenders flashed into my head. I no doubt would use marijuana too if I had to face that House Mother every day. And probably stash away liquor, too.

"Do you know some of the girls sneak men in here?" Mrs. Bundy leaned across the table and whispered, "I've even found contraceptives."

"No!" My sarcasm went unnoticed. How could Mrs. Bundy identify any birth control methods? Though she used the married title, I had never heard a word about a real Mr. Bundy.

"You may think my concerns are trivial but these girls are far from home and are easily enticed into no good." She sounded like a prurient Sunday school teacher. "I'm sure you know how much I respect Mr. Hefner, but Cassie told me she thinks he keeps her around just for his friends. What do you think she meant by that?"

I shrugged, "Don't know." Yet, I was certain Mrs. Bundy understood the situation as clearly as I did. Hefner often accommodated his good friends and colleagues by setting up dates with Bunnies. Beyond that, who knows what happened. It would only be speculation.

"I'm not sure I can control what the girls do in their free time. As far as the Mansion rules, you're in charge. You already decide who can live here or not with Mr. Hefner's approval. You can also choose who stays." I stood. "Thank you for lunch. I must get back to work. I enjoyed sharing this time far more than that which we spent over Lydia."

Mrs. Bundy's face registered disappointment. She must have thought I would confirm her findings or in the very least add to them.

I found Jane hunched over her knees sitting on the couch in my office. Chris Malloy hovered above her. The veins at his temples pulsed in angry rhythm and his fists were clenched so tightly at his sides his knuckles turned white. Both looked up when they heard me come through the door. Jane's swollen and red-rimmed eyes spoke volumes about her distress.

"What's going on?" I took hesitant steps toward the odd couple.

Malloy wasted no time in answering. "She," he pointed an accusing finger at Jane, "stole money from the gift shop."

The $17.50 flashed into my head and sparked a reminder. I must put the money back.

Jane, dressed in costume, sobbed an unintelligible response. She tore her Bunny ears from her head and threw them on the floor. Her hairpiece flopped to one side. She began to resemble a drunk rather than a showgirl.

"Leave this to me," I told Malloy.

"Are you sure you can handle it? She's admitted the whole thing, but without taking a lie detector test." Malloy paused long enough to glare at Jane. "Since she didn't do that and refused to give a statement in writing, she may not be truthful when it comes time to fire her."

I chose to ignore Malloy's acerbity. "I'll give you a full report after Jane and I talk." I held the door open for him. "Meanwhile, write up your charge. Besides, we only discharge for Bunny Image, remember?" I wanted Malloy to understand the absurdity of Playboy's personnel regulations.

"I want it on record that I'd rather have been present when you two talked." Malloy tossed an envelope at me. I checked the contents.

"It's the $50.00 she took," he said over his shoulder as he left in a huff.

I sat next to Jane. I picked up the ears and gave them back. "Can you tell me what this is all about?"

She wiped her nose with the back of her hand like a little girl. I grabbed the tissues and offered them to her. Jane took a couple and blew. Then she sniffled a few deep breaths and began, "I needed money for food. My husband took off with another girl about two months ago."

"I had no idea," I interjected, my heart beating harder. I was no stranger to needing money for food.

"He left me with his bills, the house note and the kids. I don't know where he is and don't care. But I didn't know what else to do." Jane started crying again.

"Do you have any family who can help you out for a while?"

"I sent my kids to my mother a week ago. She wasn't happy about it. Hell, she never wanted her own kids." Jane gazed off. "She never wanted me to marry my husband either."

I remembered a similar situation with my own mother when I told her I was pregnant by Angelo. My mother and I became estranged

when I eloped, ignoring my mother's pleas. Jane and I both would
have been better off if we'd listened to our mothers. Yet I wouldn't
want a life without Carl and Greg.

"So what's in store for me? Are you going to call the police?" Jane
asked.

"Is it the only time you've taken money from the gift shop?"

"Yes, but everybody does. Maybe not as much as I did." She had
cried so much Jane sounded like she had a bad cold. "I bet Mr.
Malloy isn't all that pure."

"I'm not sure any of us are." I hesitated, not wanting to get into
what everyone else did. I mulled over my options for Jane which
weren't many. "I'll have to suspend you and give a report to International. If I don't, Malloy will. His interpretation will be far more in-
criminating."

Jane sobbed harder than before. "What will I do for money until
the house sells? If it sells. I'll probably lose it."

I thought for a moment. Jane was an extraordinary beauty, even
given the current circumstances. Her huge Marlo Thomas eyes,
though red and swollen at that moment, peeked out from under flaw-
lessly trimmed raven bangs. Those eyes seduced anyone who came
into Jane's presence. Furthermore, she had that perfect body for
which International hunted the world. She surely could have been a
Playmate.

I walked to my desk to put away the purse I had been clutching to
my chest since I came into this dreadful scene. Jane's predicament
brought on another memory. I had also lost a home to bankruptcy
two years after I moved to Los Angeles. I had always rented after
that. "Can you go to your mother's home too?"

"It won't be easy to go back, but I don't seem to have any other
out."

I thought about the situation, which seemed too close to my own:
no money, no husband, children to raise, and no child support. Any
single mother would be capable of the same thievery. What was I
thinking I had been capable. "How about I let you resign rather than
get fired, as I suspect Malloy will push for? That way you won't have
problems finding other work. Or maybe you can even get rehired at
another Playboy Club."

"The money's good here but. . ." Jane paused. "Honestly? I don't ever want to work for this organization again. I don't think management, except you of course, is any better than my husband." Jane stood. She pulled her hairpiece the rest of the way off. "I just wanted to be a good wife and mother." She gulped to stop from crying again.

We stared at each other with clear understanding. "You can make up whatever you want for an exit interview," Jane offered and blew her nose again. "It doesn't matter. I've lost everything. I can only start over in my hometown. Fond du Lac isn't too small." She walked to the door and turned to face me again. "Thanks. Wish me luck."

"Wait." I retrieved the card from the modeling agency. "Take this. Tell the agency I sent you." Jane needed that job more than I. Besides, I was already planning to leave Chicago, wasn't I?

Jane read the card. "Do you think I could do this?"

"Yes! You could model anywhere." I hugged Jane. "Good luck."

Once Jane left I went back to my desk and typed out the report. I knew I could easily be in the same mess as Jane. I needed to be careful. As I typed I thought about the other girls who stole from Playboy just as Jane said. One stood out more than most. One night while working the Gift Shop, Dinah threatened to quit because I held back a paycheck to pay her outstanding debt to Playboy. I agreed to give her the check if she stayed and made good on her debt. "Sure," Dinah said. "I'll cash it tomorrow and give you half. I'll pay the other half next check."

The next day Dinah had found a substitute to work for her, and she had flown to Baltimore to be with her wealthy boyfriend who had a son only two years younger than Dinah. I felt like a patsy that day, but not as much as when I discovered that the soon-to-be rich wife had stolen several items from the gift shop on her way out. Dinah never gave a formal resignation and never returned.

I again remembered my own thievery. I pulled out my purse and retrieved $17.50. I checked the hallway for any potential spies then I opened the petty cash and returned the loan vowing never, ever to do that again.

Feeling a heaviness lift from my chest, I returned to my desk. When I placed the finished report in the middle to review, I found a short note from Barry which I had missed. Typical of his behavior he sent a memo, which said:

"How would you like to get paid the same way you get Bunny Council minutes out?"

His sarcastic words ruffled me so much I would have quit on the spot if he had been standing there.

I wadded up the note and tossed it as hard as I could into the trash. "Only a day late," I yelled and kicked at the container. Had he ever thought of asking why? Had he ever thought to ask when he could expect the minutes? Had he forgotten how he reamed me out because every room operated short and wanted my attention there? Had he forgotten about the hours of interviews? Had he ever questioned his own deceit about my position with Playboy? I settled on one answer—someone obviously chewed his ass over an issue and he decided to take it out on me in one way or the other. "As always," I sighed, "shit rolls down hill."

Head against my chair, I rubbed my temples in small circular motions with the tips of my fingers. Why had I been more uptight than normal? Why did my head ache so? Of course, my damn period was due. I'd wished it would get there soon so everything would be viewed without the monthly edginess. I imagined Malloy telling the other Room Directors to avoid me because "she's on the curse." When would women be seen as equals to men? Or, in the very least, as more than commodities? No, how about more capable than men. Wishful thinking.

I had little further time for reflection. Bunnies poured in for inspection. One brought the Playboy camera and asked me to pose so she could practice. "Tonight will be my first night to do this," she said as she pointed the camera at me.

"Ok, but first let me fix my makeup." I pulled a small square bag from my purse and dumped the contents onto the desk. I rummaged through the assortment of eye shadow, mascara, rouge and lipstick, freshened up and then coaxed a brush through my hair. I'd have to leave it in the wild mass of frizzy curls. "Ready," I said, forcing a smile.

The Camera Bunny took several Polaroid shots. They improved with each pose. After about six, she handed the stack to me. "Thanks," the Bunny said and headed happily for her new assignment.

MOTHER RABBIT

I studied each. I decided the technical quality was adequate while the subject appeared tired and sad. The pictures told the truth.

Eleven

Masquerade

Bunny Mother's appearance and personality: Set the right exam-
ple for your Bunnies in both these areas. Stay lovely, bright, warm
and friendly. Reminder Memo to Bunny Mothers

Barry scurried into my office, followed by Judy Wax. Prepared to dislike the poet I had already drawn a ghoulish mental picture of the woman who unfairly stole my job. Instead, my first sight of Judy Wax intrigued me.

Before me stood a small, 5'4", soft-spoken, articulate woman who resembled Connie Stevens. Well dressed in classic, ladylike style, Judy was handsome, not pretty, and gave not a hint that she felt superior to anyone else. Yet while her dark hair flowed into a fashionable pageboy, her eyeglasses gave her a dash of intellectualism. Judy Wax epitomized what an editor should look like for a fashion magazine, but not *Playboy*. Still, pangs of envy filled me. I wanted the Bunny Director's job. The woman who pilfered it wrote poetry and hadn't had a job in fourteen years. She had a working husband, two children, nice life, money and most likely a mink coat. I wanted to trade places to see how it felt to live on the other side.

Judy offered her hand and said, "I've heard such good things about you. I look forward to working together."

I shook her hand and wanted to tell Mrs. Wax I hadn't heard anything about her and the jury was still out on whether I'd like working with her or not. Instead I smiled and said, "Thank you."

Barry ushered Judy out as fast as he'd brought her in, without either of us exchanging other courtesies or making future plans. "Bye, bye," I sang out at them as they withdrew. Time enough left with Playboy to get to know Judy. Time I hoped wouldn't be too painful.

Both Carl and Greg were sent home from school with possible strep throat infections. I left work to take them to the doctor and wondered what kind of impression that would make on Judy her first day. As the boys and I waited our turn at the crowded clinic, I read the daily inter-office memos and made notes for the First Page column. Though it became more difficult with each schedule, I made every effort to have a positive and educational message. I had no intention of taking out my own unhappiness at Playboy on the Bunnies.

After an hour wait, Doctor Sherwood saw Carl and Greg. While he examined them, he asked me if I worked and where. "Playboy, eh? I don't think I ever knew there was such a thing as a Bunny Mother."

In my opinion, the doctor wasted too much time on me rather than attending to the boys. He seemed overly impressed with the whole Playboy idea. "And to think, I've met the Bunny leader." The doctor chuckled.

I pressed forward. "Carl," I nodded to him, "often complains about his legs aching and Greg never gets through a winter without two or three ear aches. Is there anything we can do?"

"Carl is a tall boy, growing fast. The pain is probably the result of those spurts." He checked Carl's legs and ankles. "How old are you, son?"

"Fourteen."

"Tall for a boy your age." Doctor Sherwood cocked his head to the side. "Nearly six feet?"

Carl nodded.

"We'll keep an eye on it," The doctor assured. He then checked Greg's ears. "They look fine now. If he doesn't grow out of the problem, he may have to get some tests followed by corrective surgery. But that's too drastic for the time being." He gave each boy a penicillin shot in there behind. "There. That should get them over the crisis."

Although the boys' faces turned red from the pain delivered with the shots, neither shed a tear. It was obvious they weren't going to act like babies.

The doctor turned his attention again to me, each question about the Club more lascivious than the last. I stopped myself from giving him an outright rebuke when he told me there would be no charge for his services that day. "If you can arrange it though, I'd like to bring a few colleagues to Playboy for lunch."

"Sure." I batted my eyes in an exaggerated, coquettish manner. "Give me a call when you decide." I handed him my card. He wore a wedding band. Brown-shoes-white-socks night at the Club flashed into my head. I had to repress my urge to laugh.

Though I hated handouts, the timing had been perfect. I had my paycheck but once the bills were paid I wanted to take Carl and Greg shopping for a few needed clothes. That would deplete my funds fast. "Thank you, Doctor Sherwood, for being so kind," I said, genuinely sincere. "I look forward to seeing you at the Club."

Before putting the boys on a bus for home, I took them back to the Club for a quick dinner. Carl could hardly get the warm soup down his sore throat. Greg, not one to pass up a meal, forced down a steak. Knowing that the boys were contagious, I needed to get them out of the Club and home. I hated not having a car which meant they had to go by bus and possibly contaminate the other passengers, or worse yet they could be the victims of some terrible crime.

"Hurry home and get into bed. Keep your hand over your mouth if you cough or sneeze. Try not to breathe on other people," I lectured as I gathered their dishes and glasses to take directly to the dish-washer.

We walked to the bus stop together. I hugged each boy though Carl seemed embarrassed by the public show of affection. "I wish I could go with you," I said.

"Hurry up, lady," the bus driver shouted. "I ain't got all day."

"I'll leave early," I called to them as they stepped onto the bus. I stood on the corner until the bus drove out of sight. I should never have made such a promise I so rarely could keep.

Of course my plan to leave early was foiled. Daisy, fully dressed for the Showroom, dropped into the office with her five-year-old son. "Will you keep an eye on him until my boyfriend picks him up? My babysitter got sick."

Before I had a chance to answer, Daisy skipped out of the office with her manmade breasts bouncing like two perfect rounds of milky dough above her costume's bra. I made a note to have Daisy see the seamstress for yet another costume fitting.

"What's your name?" I asked the wide-eyed boy.

His answer came in the form of a howl, "I want my mommy." Followed by a lonesome wail that would have startled a wolf pack.

Barry, shirt sleeves rolled above his elbows, raced through the door. He had impeccable timing. "What the hell," he roared.

I pointed to the boy. "Daisy dropped him off because her sitter didn't show. Her boyfriend is due here in a few minutes." I hoped.

Barry's face turned an amazing crimson color. I didn't have any idea his usual angry flush could get even deeper. "I've had enough of this. Playboy isn't a day care center."

"What are the women supposed to do? Maybe we should have a children's center so we won't go short on the floor." I hoped such a suggestion—providing an option for the girls desperately needed for work—would diffuse the situation. It didn't.

"NO MORE KIDS IN HERE—EVER! INCLUDING YOURS." He lifted his glasses and wiped his forehead. "UNDERSTOOD?"

"Yes, sir," I answered like a recruit to a drill sergeant.

"Now get rid of him."

The little boy responded to Barry's outburst with an even louder moan and tears to go along.

Great father he made, I thought. "Does that go for Coco's, too?" I almost ducked behind my desk, afraid Barry would take a swing at me.

He didn't. Instead, Barry calmed down. "You look good today," he said.

I doubted I'd ever understand his often contradictory, almost schizophrenic manner. I'd worn a hat that day to hide my especially unruly curls, but it wasn't anything special. Barry seemed to only compliment me when he got cornered.

"Good night." He saluted with a finger to his forehead. "I've got to get home to babysit, myself." He started to leave. Instead he stopped and turned to face me. "Oh, yeah. I don't want any more Bunnies dropped off by the boyfriends or any other man in front of the Club. It spoils the keyholders' fantasies." Then he dashed away.

Attempting to distract the little boy whose name I still didn't know I gave him a pad and pen so he could draw. He took them. He dropped both in his lap unused and continued to sit sniffling until a half hour later when Bill Anderson, my landlord, appeared. "Where's the boy?"

"Mr. Anderson?" I hadn't really given him much notice before. His hair, always uncombed, seemed worse today. His clothes, though good quality, fit poorly as though someone had given them to him and Anderson couldn't be bothered to exchange them for the proper size.

"Yeah. I'm here to pick up Daisy's kid." He pointed at the now sullen-faced child huddled in the corner of the couch. "Come on, boy. I'm takin' ya home." His gruff tone brought back the few encounters I had with him. I couldn't recall any pleasantness about him.

The boy stood and walked out with Anderson. I still hadn't heard the child's name. So, after all the nasty things Anderson said about the girls, he still had one on the side. What could be the difference to him between a mistress and a whore, as he had called the Bunnies at one of our first meetings? On the other hand, what did Daisy see in him? Couldn't be his looks or personality. Money. The townhouse complex where I lived was only one of several complexes Anderson owned. It had to be money for the breast implants. The thought was delicious.

My heart ached for Daisy's little boy. Boys. I had to get home myself.

Carl and Greg had fallen sound asleep in their own beds. They had to be sick to succumb so early. Poor Fraulein practically brought her leash to me.

A light snow fell as I strolled with Fraulein who was donned in her newly purchased coat. It was the only way California-Fraulein would leave the warm house to fight Chicago's bone-chilling cold and bitter wind. On our way to the park, I passed several closed stores. Fraulein took her position between the buildings and me, a recent obsession. It didn't matter who stood near the walls. Fraulein nudged behind them as each person stepped forward to my embarrassed, "Excuse me. Excuse me." Any attempt to coerce Fraulein to walk away from the people standing along the buildings made her even more determined. She'd spread her legs out and plant all four feet solidly in place. No amount of effort could move her. So I had to endure this nightly trek if we were to walk in the park.

Once in the park, the snow fell faster. Though not much of a park when compared to the California beaches and Sierra Mountains, I found the square dotted with juniper bushes and oak trees a true refuge from the city's skyscrapers. I could hear the muffled rush of highway traffic and yet I felt at peace for at least those few moments Fraulein and I toured the area. I reminded myself that I needed to stop comparing Chicago with Los Angeles if I ever wanted to be less homesick.

As I marveled at how Fraulein could find enjoyment in every twig, I recalled the letter I had received from Clark the day before. I had to let him know he couldn't visit me around Christmas as he had asked. I based my decision on two reasons; I didn't want him there with Carl and Greg and I didn't know if I wanted to see him at all since nothing had changed. Besides the boys looked forward to their Aunt Tekkie's visit then.

As Fraulein and I strolled back to the house, the snowflakes felt refreshing against my skin. I lifted my face the way I had as a child and stuck my tongue out to catch the tiny morsels. Gazing skyward, I wondered when I had last seen the moon or stars as I had over the ocean. And forget sunsets. It seemed dark in mid-day when the sun went behind the many skyscrapers and deep into the gray sky.

So fatigued, I could hardly move one foot in front of the other. Moreover, my evening chores were hardly over. Because of the many interruptions that day, I'd have to finish the schedule to avoid Barry's wrath again. I also needed to keep up my cathartic ritual of writing in my journal. I had a lot to say tonight.

Back at the kitchen table, I placed the calendar on top of the pile of papers I had brought home. Thanksgiving was only a little over a week away. I hadn't even thought about a dinner. My eyes moved from the calendar to take in the cheerless kitchen. No way would my sons and I share a special dinner in this room. The linoleum floor curled and yellowed along the edges and was worn through to the plywood where all the previous tenants had stood at the sink.

I put a pot of coffee on and took milk from the refrigerator. The note I had left for the boys still hung on the door. The $10.00 to be used for a few groceries was gone. Had the boys bought those items before they went to bed? I checked. No bread, no potatoes, no new milk. I thought to wake Carl and ask him when he suddenly appeared in the kitchen.

"What are you doing out of bed?" I felt his forehead.

"I want some juice," Carl whispered.

I poured the juice and asked, "Did you see the note on the refrigerator?"

"Yeah, but you forgot to leave the money." He shrugged.

"No matter. You and Greg shouldn't be out in this weather with your throats as they are."

I rummaged through my memory and clearly saw myself place the money behind the note. The janitor! He had to have taken it. He'd come back that day to replace one more part in the furnace. How would I ever prove that? When would all the betrayal end? Even though, I certainly had lost all good feelings about my fellow man, I wouldn't let Carl see how distraught I had become.

At least I found good news in the day's mail. Angelo had finally sent a support payment. I now had a little extra money. So Carl and I made plans to shop on Saturday if he and Greg felt better. Carl finished the juice and shuffled off to bed.

The theft stripped the last ounce of my energy. I set the schedule aside. I'd deal with it in the morning before I left for Playboy. I picked up my journal and began writing.

Two hours passed before I closed the cover and went to bed.

When I arrived around noon I stopped by training first to make sure the Room Directors, the half on the agenda, had shown up. I also wanted to give them a refresher to correct several recurring problems.

Training turned out to be an infuriating waste of two hours. Every time I offered a suggestion, Coco, who shouldn't have been there, contradicted me. And what Coco told the Room Directors didn't come close to my expectations. When Coco got cornered for information, she'd defer to me, and then chat with persons nearest to her about personal issues through the whole answer. Coco made training as chaotic and confusing as she did everything else. Working with her certainly meant long difficult hours.

On the bright side, I walked into the session just as Tom took it upon himself to Dip. Though he didn't wear three-inch heels and a corset, he did carry a loaded tray. He swaggered to the table, dipped and slid. His legs spread close to a split before Carlie rescued him. The spectators' laughter could probably be heard as far away as Wrigley Field. It lightened the otherwise tense encounter between Bunnies and most of the Room Directors. Except for Chris Malloy. He leaned into a corner, arms crossed over his chest and scowling, mostly at Carlie.

I also noticed an odd mark like red fingers spread wide around Carlie's upper arm. I made a note to ask her about how that happened.

Once through the training session I did a quick check of the Club, which seemed busier than usual. Maybe a convention in town. Everything seemed under control until I noticed four Living Room Bunnies were wearing blue. I made an on-the-spot switch with the Bunnies in the Playroom, where two wore orange. Not quite a perfect solution but an improvement. How did that ever happen? I could hardly wait to hear the wrath of both Barry and the Room Directors.

No sooner had that issue been somewhat solved, when Tom, the Room Director, asked, "Will coffee ruin a mink?"

"What?"

Tom handed me the accident report. Apparently Bunny Charlene spilled hot coffee on a keyholder and his wife. I shrugged but had other concerns about Charlene. One night last week she had to be taken off shift because she couldn't stop crying about spending the weekend in jail for passing a stolen check, which her fiancé had given her to get her teeth fixed. Shortly after that she didn't show for work at all, for which I gave her demerits. Charlene's excuse for a no-show: she was babysitting her friend's child but her friend never picked him up and Charlene hadn't seen her since. As I had with Sally, I had to deal with Charlene before her situation got too out of hand.

After all that, I finally copied and distributed the schedule. It was then, with my desk somewhat cleared, that I found a note from Judy Wax, asking me to phone. I looked at the clock. Nearly 6:00 pm. I looked at the note. "As soon as you get in." I'd never checked the pile of messages on my desk. After my early departure yesterday, this might be the second strike against me. Looking at the message, all sorts of problems bounced around in my head. My eyes darted from the note to the phone and back to the note. Could Judy want to talk with me about the unfinished schedule? Maybe the lack of full-time Bunnies? No, maybe Judy would tell me to look for another job. Silly! Judy was my boss after all and could call me for many reasons.

I reviewed the hectic day in my mind, preparing an excuse for not returning Judy's call. I reached for the phone, but stopped to scratch my arm. Large welts, almost bloody, climbed my right forearm like a disorganized vine. Nerves. I dialed Judy's extension.

Nothing could have prepared me for what Judy said. "Coco reported that Lydia didn't show up for her shift."

"She probably had the wrong time," I offered. "I'm sure she'll be in for the 5:00 pm shift."

"Coco called the Mansion," Judy went on. "The girls said she wasn't there. Any idea where she could be?"

"As far as I know Lydia's not living in the dorm any longer. Coco knows that."

"She didn't tell me."

"If Lydia doesn't show up shortly for the next shift, I'll start calling around. Otherwise it's a no-show . . ."

"And her job," Judy added. "Her work record and mental stability are both questionable."

"Yes. I'll get on it." I wanted to ask Judy how she knew about all that so soon. "I'll call you right back."

I worried that Lydia had done something foolish again. I also wondered why Coco called the Mansion but I'd find out for myself. I needed to call the dorm anyway for a Reserve Girl to fill in for Lydia. The Bunny who answered said there was no time to talk because there had been an emergency. The anxious sounding Bunny hung up. I conjured up the image of Lydia sprawled across her bed. But that would be nonsense because she didn't live in the dorm any more.

I called back. The line was busy. I called A dorm, and sent a girl to the other dorm. Jasmine called back. Sounding panicked she reported, "The door's locked and I can't get in."

I tried the first number again and a strange woman answered who said she was the nurse. She too reported there was an emergency and hung up. I became frustrated and angry. Didn't I have enough authority to know what had happened? Fearing the worst, I needed to get to the bottom of all the secrecy.

I dialed Mrs. Bundy who explained that the ambulance had just taken Lydia away. "It doesn't look good. The best I could tell, the emergency team couldn't get a pulse."

"Why was she in the dorm to begin with?" I almost yelled the question.

"I'm not sure, except to end her life as a way to get back at me." Mrs. Bundy sounded sincerely grieved for the first time since I had met her.

"We don't know if Lydia's life is over. Plus I'm sure she only wanted to be where she had once felt so comfortable." I had hoped that would soothe any guilt Mrs. Bundy felt. "What else do you know?"

"Kathy found her face down on the floor." Mrs. Bundy's breathing sped up. "Her body was surrounded with empty bottles of sleeping pills, tranquilizers and nerve pills. She also slit her wrists."

"Oh my." I sighed.

"That stupid Kathy called the police for an ambulance. Do you know what that means?"

Any sympathy I had for this bitch evaporated. Lydia might be dead and Mrs. Bundy cared only that the police had become involved. "Mrs. Bundy, if she is dead, the police would be called any way."

"Not if we handled it the way we always do."

"What does that mean?" Fear sharpened my anger.

"Nothing. I've got to go get the blood off the floor before it stains." For more times in one day than I cared to count someone hung up on me.

I composed myself and called Judy.

"I already know," Judy murmured. "The hospital called to get next of kin information. Lydia died. The police will be round in the morning to investigate."

I lowered the receiver to its cradle. I rested my head in my hands and cried, "I failed Lydia just as I failed Mom and Toti. How many more?"

"Hey! What's up?" Coco's inappropriate mirth enraged me even more than Mrs. Bundy's callousness. None of those people had a lick of decency.

I lifted my head and glared.

"Ooooh, you better fix your face before Barry sees the mascara blotches." Coco plopped onto the couch tucking one leg under her. "I came by to tell you I'm leavin' early 'cause my sitter has an appointment."

"I didn't even know you were still at work." I didn't care how I sounded to this twit sitting opposite me.

"Yeah, I know. A lot goin' on today."

"Do you even have a clue about the seriousness of Lydia's condition?" I pushed to see if perhaps I had misread Coco. Perhaps she truly had no idea.

"Well, of course I do." Coco twisted a piece of her newly dyed blond hair. "But, get real. She wanted to do herself in for a long time. I don't have any sympathy for girl like that."

"It can't be because of your Catholic upbringing," I muttered.

"What?"

"Nothing. Listen, Coco, I'd love to sit and chat with you, but you need to relieve your sitter and," I dragged a pile of papers to the middle of my desk, "I have a stack of work to do."

"Right. See ya tomorrow." Coco jumped up and bounced out of the office.

"Bimbo," I said to her back.

I again woke up on the couch. I rushed to check the clock. "Damn!" I tore up the stairs. "Carl," I huffed out as loud as I could. I hadn't set the alarm. I pushed open the boys' bedroom door. Both were still asleep. "Damn!" I repeated.

I shook Carl. "What?" he groaned. He turned away.

"Get up, Carl. You're late again."

No response.

"CARL!" I screamed and shook him harder. Still, no response. I charged down the hall to the bathroom and soaked a washcloth in cold water. I rolled Carl onto his back and called out his name again. When he refused to wake up, I dripped cold water from the cloth onto his face.

Carl bolted straight up. "What?"

"Get dressed. You're late again for school and you know what that means." I threw underwear and socks at him. "I'll make a piece of toast for you. You'll have to eat it on the way."

Carl stretched as meticulously as a cat. He stood took off his pajamas, folded them and placed them on his pillow. He stepped into his underpants. He sat to put on his socks. Every movement was calculated and without hurry.

"Come on. Move it!" I had become more agitated by the second. I looked over at Greg. He was sleeping through the whole scene.

"I don't care if they kick me outta school." Carl stood again and slipped a shirt over his head and pulled up a pair of khakis. "I hate it there. I shoulda stayed with Aunt Marie."

Guilt overwhelmed me. Carl hadn't been happy with the move to Chicago since the first day. Maybe I should send them back to New York until I got back to L.A. "Look, Carl. If you hang in for a short time more, I'll try to get us back home."

Carl didn't comment. "I don't want anything to eat." He ambled from the room and I plopped onto Carl's bed. I could not remember feeling this defeated in a long time. Now I had to deal with Greg.

Greg's counselor had called me to the school a few days earlier to tell me that Greg's behavior had become intolerable. When it had been all sorted out, it was clear Greg was only showing his creative charisma. As I dripped the water over Greg's head to wake him, an even tougher job than with Carl, I compelled myself to speak about the school's concerns to him that morning.

"Let me alone," Greg moaned as though someone was torturing him. After he'd been tormented for several minutes he rolled over and popped his eyes open. "MOM."

"Get up, my sleeping prince. You're late for school."

"Ugh, school."

I fluffed Greg's hair. When it had recently grown to his shoulders the principal ordered him to have it cut. Greg did, but neither his teacher, nor the principal felt the trim met their standards and demanded in front of his classmates that Greg cut his hair even shorter. He came home in tears, embarrassed by the way the teacher ridiculed him. I gave the teacher hell for the way she treated him which probably aggravated the situation, just as it had in L.A.

"Come on sleepy head. Rise and shine." I had always thought schools should operate according to the individual's clock. Greg had always been and no doubt would continue to be a night owl. He performed better that way. But society demanded conformity, not individuality. I knew Greg could be difficult, but underneath that facade his feelings got hurt easily.

I sat on the edge of his bed. His drowsiness didn't hide the sadness I saw in his large sleepy eyes. "Mom, do I have to go to that school? I'd rather work full time at Newton's."

I rubbed Greg's back. "I know it's tough." I thought back to the recent session with Greg's teacher.

"Greg's very bright," the teacher had started. "He's a nonconformist. He flicks his big hair to the side in a big-guy manner, wears tight pants and Beatle Boots. To add to that, he's one of the two biggest boys in the room. The others look up to him for the wrong reasons, which makes the class hard to control." The teacher finished her litany with the fact Greg upset her by answering her rudely or not paying attention.

I found most of the teacher's concerns legitimate except the hair and clothes. Of course the teacher hadn't been willing to work with Greg's creative nature.

"Mom?" Greg asked. "What are you thinking about?"

"You know I spoke with your teacher the other day?"

Greg nodded.

"You're very bright and a leader, so," I tried to paraphrase the conversation in a way Greg would accept and feel better about himself, "You must be more careful what you do because the others will follow you."

Greg picked at a small hole in the bedspread I'd recently purchased at the Salvation Army Thrift Store.

"Also," I took hold of his hand before he could widen the rip, "because you are bright, the teacher is apt to get exasperated if you act out rather than learn. Teachers enjoy bright students, they take pride in them, but they don't like to see those students waste their brains. They want them to succeed." I leaned back against the headboard.

Greg withdrew his hand. He stared beyond me to the other side of the room. "I'll go back." He gave in. "But not today. I have an earache."

"If you keep using that excuse, no one will believe you when you actually are sick." I checked the clock. "No time to get there, now. But tomorrow you'd better be up and out the door early."

"Thanks, Mom. I promise."

I stood, but gazed at him for a few seconds. "And no working at Newton's today since you're sick."

Greg nodded. I left him snug in his bed, but couldn't be sure he'd keep his pledge. I'd call later to check on him. I had to get ready for work myself though I preferred Greg's choice.

We couldn't get back to California soon enough.

Chapter Twelve

Mingling

Mingling by any female employee with any patron or guest is not allowed and shall be cause for immediate dismissal. Bunnies may, however, briefly converse with patrons, provided that conversation is limited to polite formalities and information about The Playboy Club. A Bunny may not, under any circumstances, divulge personal information about herself or other Bunnies, e.g. what they do outside the Club, last name, phone numbers, addresses, etc. 520.2.8 Addition to Bunny Manual/1963

Just before Thanksgiving, Judy Wax personally brought me a copy of the Sunday TV magazine with a picture on the front page of a girl and a caption that read, "She's a Bunny and she loves it."

"Do you know her?" Judy handed the newspaper to me. "Turn to the article and other pictures inside."

"Yes," I answered. "But I don't know who authorized the article."

"It doesn't matter." Judy sat on the couch and patted the cushion. "You need to get this recovered." She crossed her legs with the grace of a dancer. I wondered if Judy's raven hair ever had a strand out of place and then I wondered if it was her natural color.

"Barry promised a whole remodeling. You can see how far that went." I circled my arm in front of me to show off the room, peeling paint still visible.

"Back to the girl in the news." Judy's calm voice commanded attention. "Does she still work here?"

"Yes, but not under that name. At least, here she calls herself Ellie." I had an idea what Judy would say next.

"The fellow, a friend, who gave me this article," Judy breathed a tired sigh, "told me the woman in the article is a well-known area call girl."

I recalled the cards I had found on the gift shop counter. Ellie also had continued to accumulate many demerits for ignoring my constant reminders about all the personal phone calls she received. Ellie took demerits in stride even when I told her she would be suspended and possibly terminated if she continued to thumb her nose at the rules. Ellie only smiled.

I laid the article aside. "It doesn't surprise me. Barry and International have been on the hunt for ages for a hooker in the Hutch. Until recently no one would have picked Ellie."

"What do you mean?" Judy rearranged the radiant royal blue scarf she wore around her neck. Her eyes projected the same brilliant color.

That day I looked better than usual in my newly purchased wig and emerald green wool suit—my own eyes reflecting its color. I always knew when I looked good. Men all the way to work did double takes and the Room Directors commented, "You look terrific." When I felt put together well, no other woman—including Judy—intimidated me.

"I've had to talk with Ellie about calling cards she left out in the gift shop." I withdrew a sample from the desk drawer to show Judy. "She's had numerous personal phone calls as well. Yet there has been no definitive evidence. Until now, of course."

Judy stood. "Too bad, because after this article ran, the police arrested her at the Gaslight. She apparently solicited at other area clubs besides Playboy. I'm afraid this will be very bad publicity for Playboy."

I envisioned a barrage of reporters and police circulating about the Club. "To tell you the truth I'm glad it's over, no matter the result. We hired Ellie with the best intentions. We can't follow all 70 girls around every minute of the day."

"Did you hire her?"

"She was one of several I screened for Barry and Keith to give final approval." I shrugged. "They liked her down-on-the-farm youthfulness."

"Yes, they would." Judy smiled. She seemed to find that male trait cute rather than offensive.

"At least I won't have to fire Ellie for Bunny Image," I scoffed. I loved the mockery it made of the corporation. "The police will take care of it like they did Bunny Linda when they caught her shoplifting," I went on. "Several girls who lived in the Mansion with Linda accused her of stealing from them, too."

Judy scowled at me. I guessed Judy didn't get the irony.

"Don't worry though. International didn't let me talk to the police with Linda so I'm sure they won't trust me to talk to them about Ellie." My acerbity started to feel good. "You know those guys really don't need us, except for the dirty work."

Judy brushed lint from her suit. "Do you think there are other Bunnies that are prostituting?"

Disappointed that Judy hadn't been snagged into my own ire, I answered with even more causticity. "How can any of us be sure? I do know that I get calls all the time."

"Calls?"

"For Bunnies. Men think I'm like a madam. One even asked me what kind of Bunny Mother I was when I turned him down. Just this morning I got a call from a man who wanted to rent a Bunny. For what, God only knows." I shook my head. "Boys will be boys."

"Yes." Judy nodded, but not with the same disdain I expressed.

Judy placed her hand on her chin and drifted into deep thought. I waited for what I sensed would be another major issue to consider. "I'm afraid," she repeated the phrase, "I'm afraid reporters and the police will delve into other rumors that the girls often get abortions." She slid her hands inside her jacket pockets and regarded me as though she had hoped I would shed light on her concern. Finally when I added nothing, she asked, "Are those rumors true?"

"Some girls have had abortions, yes," I answered without wavering.

"Well we can't have that." Judy waved her hand back and forth as though the breezy motion would rid Playboy, Inc. of the problem. "It's not right."

"What are you thinking? It often is the Bunny's only alternative."

"They should marry the father." Judy's mouth formed a defiant pucker.

"You mean the one who promised the girl he'd leave his wife for her? Or the guy, married or not, who works in management at International who's not supposed to be dating employees, but everyone turns a blind eye? Or maybe one of Hef's buddies?" My sentences came so quickly they blurred into one.

"There is birth control, although I feel the girls should abstain." Judy pulled her jacket down though it hadn't ridden up. "Do you know where the girls get the doctor's name?"

"You should ask Coco. The girls, including her, got abortions long before I arrived." My snide honesty made Judy cringe. "Coco not only was the Bunny Mother for a couple of years, but a Bunny before that." My anger erupted into uncontrolled information pouring from my mouth, faster and faster. "Coco's baby is the only one she's kept. So if you're looking for a scapegoat, I'm not it. I'm neither a madam nor do I run an abortion clinic." I fell back into my chair exhausted from my tirade.

Judy looked like a stone carving. When she did shift positions, she said, "Well, that was a mouthful." She took the article from my desk. "You don't like me very much do you?"

"I didn't think I would, but actually I do—as a person. Since I've been truthful so far, I'll go on. I find you too naive about the real world. You've been sheltered too long, which didn't prepare you for a management position here. The one I had been promised."

"Oh, I didn't know." Judy sounded and looked sincerely unaware.

"Barry makes a lot of promises, like redecorating my office." I sneered as I glanced around. "He also uses his management position to keep a Bunny on the side and give special privileges to his favorite girls. But you know about favoritism, don't you?"

"That's a low blow." Judy's face became a mix of hurt and angry lines.

Once again I had an overwhelming desire to quit right then. Instead my uncontrolled verbosity got the best of me. I stood to my full 5'9" height so I'd be more intimidating. "You and Playboy can't have it all."

I paced the threadbare carpet, warming to my subject. "You want a Bunny Mother to be fair, yet double-cross and squeal on everyone. I should be loyal to the General Manager, Barry, yet tell International everything that is going on. I should be someone to whom the Bunnies can tell anything in confidence—remember the good mother—yet tell you and Barry everything I've heard. And I should listen to the way the Room Directors, bartenders and the male managers talk behind the Bunnies' backs in the most disparaging way, but tell the girls it's not so." I was now yelling and pounding one fist into the palm of the other hand. "What all of you need is a two-timing, double-dealing female who does not expect respect from anyone but pretends to give it to everyone. She's over forty, has no children or grown children, is a widow, or divorced, or has a husband who travels so the Bunny Mother can give every breath of her life to Playboy, Inc."

Judy's mouth had hinged open like a ventriloquist's dummy. Her eyes formed huge perfect O's. I almost laughed at the sight. Instead I said with great pride, "That felt good." I strolled back to my desk. At that moment I felt powerful enough to tell off everyone. But I had to stay on this job until the boys finished out the semester and my nose was done. Meanwhile, I'd take as much from Playboy as I could.

Judy relaxed against the back of the couch. "Well, that was quite a production." She seemed flustered rather than angry. "Since we are having this chat, I'll take advantage and share with you Barry and Keith's concern."

"First of all, Judy," I emphasized each word, "I don't consider this a chat and it irks me even more that those two have a complaint."

Judy raised her hand as though trying to halt another harangue. "When I took over as the Bunny Director they told me you were too independent and failed to inform them about what was going on."

Had Judy not heard anything I had said? "I will try to play the little helpless female, but I may not succeed." I batted my eyelashes, a bad habit I now displayed when in similar conversations.

"I know you do everything you're supposed to do." Judy again sounded sincere. "But, you should tell them what they want to know. Women must give deference to men."

I could hardly believe what I heard. Yet now I had a clear understanding of why Judy got the Bunny Director's job and I hadn't. They all knew I disagreed with Judy's postulation. My independence and intelligence had become a threat.

Judy stood. "Thank you for your time."

I pictured Judy saying that very same thing after she and her editor husband made love, yet at the same time, I couldn't help but admire the woman's grace once again as she left my office. No matter how Judy felt about a woman's place in the world, she had class. She hadn't flustered easily and certainly hadn't raised her voice. Judy acted like a girl who had been trained in a finishing school.

Frustration aside, before I left for the day, I'd make sure I did a thorough check of the Bunnies in each room of the Club. I wanted no interruptions on Thanksgiving Day. But first I had to finish the paperwork Coco started. As usual Coco spent more time talking, mostly about herself, than getting her work done. Some Bunny Mother she'd make for the busy Chicago Club. At least International won't think Coco's too independent—just undependable.

Work completed, I freshened my makeup and went over the conversation I'd had with Coco that morning. Coco rambled on about her fourteen-year relationship with Harold, a married man, the father of Coco's child and two others with his wife. Harold was the cause of all Coco's abortions.

"Why do you stay with him?" I asked, though I really wanted Coco to get out of my office so I could get something accomplished for once.

"I met him when I was twenty-four. I was a Bunny." She reached into her purse and retrieved a picture of herself in costume.

I found it astounding that Coco carried the memento with her. I did have to admit, though the picture had been taken only four years before, Coco looked worlds younger. Was this what I would be like if I kept waiting for Clark to leave his wife? I handed the photo back.

"Our relationship," Coco continued, "was on-again, off-again. Harold once said he'd divorce his wife." She grew still, looking into the distance as if she'd gone in search of the rest of the story. Then she lowered her head and fingered the photo. "I told Harold not to."

Twice in the same conversation I was bowled over by an astounding revelation. "Why?"

"My father did that to my mother. She never recovered from the deceit and shame." She raised her head. She shrugged. "I accept things as they are. End of story."

My eyes stung around the sockets. For the first time I had sympathy for this immature, mixed-up woman living in a child's imagination while yet garnering enough courage to face reality.

Coco broke the awkward silence between us. "Want to hear a better story?"

I nodded so vigorously my wig slid to the side. I settled it back in place as I waited for the next chapter in Coco's life. I must get this wig refitted—but never mind. Not right now.

"Last night I got my third moving violation. I was racing home after getting my baby from the sitter. I didn't want Harold to give up waiting for me and leave. I see him so little." She scribbled some notes on the schedule as she chatted. "Anyway, I had to go to the bathroom so bad, I wet my pants while the officer wrote the ticket." Coco's laughter disappeared almost as fast as it came. "But I will lose my license."

At that moment a light bulb went off in my head, just like one in a cartoon. The Bunnies preferred Coco or at least they had, because she acted like one of them. She didn't behave like management and so she couldn't be a threat. Coco acted like a Bunny while I displayed the true skills of a supervisor, not a buddy. Yet my managerial skills, keeping work and personal lives separate, were also drawbacks. I had few friends and I was lonely.

As I put the final touches on Coco's paper work, I decided I still couldn't forgive Coco's wacky lifestyle. I also wouldn't accept Coco's excuses about unfinished business. Or let her skip out early after coming in late almost every day, expecting me to clean up any mess she left behind in the wake of her chatter and chaos. Matter of fact—I paused with my pen in the air—International deserved Coco.

After having been with Coco over the past several weeks, I had a clearer understanding why both the Bunnies and Room Directors told me during one council meeting, "You take everything in stride. You're so calm, but by the book—no nonsense."

I smiled to myself. They hadn't yet seen the obstinate, fearless side of me that Judy and Chris Malloy had. And Barry. Yet I knew I couldn't be more opposite from Coco if I tried.

"Well, Coco, you can have this job."

I shoved the paperwork into the out box. I could at least count on my assistant Brooke to type it up and distribute copies.

I had one last task to attend to—Stella from Payroll. After that I'd complete inspections and head home to spend a quiet Thanksgiving with my sons. Stella had called me earlier, between my dealings with Coco and Judy. Though Stella always exaggerated a problem, that day she sounded truly out of sorts, indicating she needed to see me in ten minutes. So I had dropped everything and walked to Payroll, only to find that Stella had gone to lunch. After wasting my morning with Coco, I could hardly contain my fury with Stella who seemed to enjoy toying with people's patience. I decided I wouldn't interrupt her while she watched her more important noon soap opera. Instead, I left a nasty note promising to return when I could squeeze her into my schedule.

Now I had to confront the witch. True to form, she greeted me by flapping the last payroll in my face.

"This is wrong."

Her upper arms swung along. Her smugness only highlighted her round cheeks and ill-proportioned features—small bird-like eyes and long narrow nose.

I browsed through the papers. Clearly Coco's doing. Not only had the sequence not been alphabetized as I always did, it was Coco's atrocious handwriting. Any sympathy I had felt for Coco earlier disappeared. "Why are you speaking with me when you know as well as I who did this?"

I threw the papers back at Stella I couldn't help think she looked like a sausage dressed in a too-small paisley casing.

"Coco's not here, and I damn well won't tell Barry his precious babe made an error. Or I should say errors." Stella gave me a challenging smile, overflowing with bravado.

"Errors?"

"Yeah, the dumb bitch paid Bunny Daisy twice. Someone shoulda caught the mistake." Her accusing look fell squarely on me. "If that's not bad enough, two pages are missing."

I had had enough for one day. "You probably blew your skinny nose on them." I stopped halfway to the door, but decided to brave Stella one more time. Meanwhile, she was sucking in so much air, she looked as though she might explode at any moment.

"Since you're too scared to talk with Coco, I'll do your dirty work," I announced. "But don't expect my kindness next time. Besides, why didn't you catch Daisy's double paycheck? Isn't that what you get paid for?"

For the first time since I had met her, the clerk was speechless. I smiled and waved to her over my shoulder. "Happy Thanksgiving." Though upset with Stella, I held more hostility toward Daisy for never reporting the double wages. Now I would have to deal with her and Coco.

I finally made it to the inspection only to get stopped. "Hey," Carlie called out. "I've got a strange but funny happening to tell you."

I needed a good laugh but I didn't want any more odd events for today. "Nothing too bad, I hope," I said as we stood side-by-side, Carlie perching. I caught Chris Malloy keeping an eye on us. I nodded to him. Malloy turned away.

"My apartment was robbed last night while I was sleeping," Carlie gushed out her revelation.

"What! That's horrible."

"Actually it's pretty hilarious. The crook took some money and my goldfish in their bowl and their food but not before he coated the walls with black hand prints." Carlie's uproarious laugh-talk attracted customers at the nearby four-top.

I put a finger to my mouth, but also giggled. "The burglar isn't too bright, is he?"

We chatted for a few more minutes before I moved on with Malloy's eyes following me until I left his floor.

On my final check in the Penthouse, I overheard a disturbing conversation between a keyholder and Nadine, who had just been announced as the Bunny of the Month. "Do you like to dance?" Nadine asked as she performed a perfect dip to place a beer on the table before the handsome gentleman.

"Yes, I do."

"So do I." Nadine emptied the ashtray by placing another on top, turning it upside down and emptying the filled one. She set the cleaned ashtray in the center of the table, again accompanied by a perfect dip. "I go every Wednesday to the Chez Paris."

"Odd. So do I." The keyholder displayed more teeth than Bobby Kennedy when he smiled.

I motioned to Nadine, who excused herself from the table. When she reached me she said, "Did I make a mistake?"

"Not any obvious one. But if you're playing some kind of game to get a date with that man, you're walking on thin ice."

Nadine took a step back. "We were just talking."

"Be sure that's all you're doing. I'd hate to have to terminate one of my best Bunnies."

Nadine smiled serenely. "Have a good Thanksgiving."

"You, too." I knew exactly what Nadine had been up to but I couldn't prove it. The girls had so many tricks up their sleeves, I could hardly keep up. I couldn't wait to get home.

Back in my office I tied up any loose ends to guarantee no phone calls the next day while my sons and I enjoyed a special holiday feast. As if to spite me, the telephone rang. Though I didn't want to delay my departure any more than I had, I must answer. Barry demanded my immediate presence in his office.

I said I would drop over in a few minutes on my way home. I recalled what I told Judy earlier. When I got there, Barry took his usual pose—feet spread apart and propped on his desk.

"What could be so urgent, Barry?"

He scratched his balls. Was it a nervous reaction or did he think the vulgarity could be seductive?

"My secretary told me that Malloy received $100 for three Bunnies he got for one of the regulars."

Please, not more bad news today I thought. "Who told your secretary?"

"The Bunnies." *Scratch.* "They went for Malloy thinking it was a date, as apparently he led them to believe." *Scratch.* "When they got to the so-called party, the girls discovered it was not just an informal social gathering." Barry stopped playing with his balls and lifted both hands in the air. "Haven't you explained to the Bunnies that dating keyholders is a clear violation of the rules?"

For the second time today, I had had enough and decided to let loose. My indignation boiled like a witch's brew. "Yes, I have gone over the rules regularly. But the girls know that they face retaliation and harassment if they don't do what YOU and the Room Directors want, no matter what the violation."

"Hold on. . ."

"No, you hold on. I've had about enough of the double-standard here. Plus I'm tired of cleaning up all the messes."

Barry dropped his feet to the floor. I stepped backward toward the exit. Fortunately he didn't leave his chair. Though I could have whopped his butt anyway if he tried something, I couldn't lose my job. What was getting into me? I must be watching too many movies.

"Ok, ok." Barry lit a cigar. "I'll talk with Malloy, but you need to say something to the Bunnies. Make them trust you enough to tell you how they're forced into situations they don't want to be in."

Barry either had forgotten he had been lumped in that group or he truly thought he covered his tracks. "How do you think I find out most things around here?" I asked. "From the Bunnies who trust me, and most of them do."

Barry contemplated his cigar while I wondered what more words of wisdom rambled around in his pea brain. "Thank you for coming over," he said without taking his eyes off the ember tip. "Oh, by the way—I've rehired Rajean and told her she would only have to work the nights she wants. Have a good Thanksgiving."

I left without returning the farewell. Again, Barry had gone behind my back. Again, he played favorites. Again, I would have to take the fall for his arrogance.

Carl, Greg and I ate Thanksgiving dinner at the Holiday Inn's revolving tower. The boys wore clothes I bought with my last support payment nearly three weeks ago. They looked sharp in their chinos, brown leather belts to match their shoes, and shirts with button-down collars. I doubted the principal at either school would complain about their new image—no more imitating the Beatles' black turtlenecks, tight black pants and hair cuts, at least until they got back to L.A. I spent much more than I had planned on the shopping spree and now this dinner, which would delay my rent payment by a week. My sons' needs outweighed the landlord's for the time being.

The Holiday Inn allowed us to enjoy a meal using china, crystal and utensils that matched. Just for this occasion, none of the Salvation Army dishes, jelly jar glasses and paper napkins that I served with at home on our chipped Formica table. We placed an elegant linen napkin on our laps and toasted with the water glasses just to hear them clink. And I couldn't be happier that none of the tableware had a black Big Bunny emblem embossed on them.

Though the food was delicious, none of us could summon a truly positive mood. Rather, we all spoke nostalgically about L.A. and how soon we could move back. Even surrounded by walls of windows that climbed several stories and provided a heart-stopping view, we couldn't forget the damp, cold, ubiquitous wind whipping our faces whenever we ventured outside. The icy air ushered in from Lake Michigan couldn't compare to the refreshing salty breezes of the Pacific. And the milky gray winter water that flowed along Chicago's North Shore only worsened our homesickness.

We listed our complaints about our current lives. "Neither Greg nor I have made any real friends," Carl started. "And my legs ache all the time from the dampness and cold."

"I haven't had any time to make friends either, and like you I don't like the schools here," I joined in.

"You know I hate school," Greg moaned. "It is too cold here. The skies are always gloomy."

We all agreed we missed our California friends. I thought about Playboy as we ate pumpkin pie. I loved most of the Bunnies, the seamstress, and most of the Room Directors, busboys and bartenders. Forget the management, though.

Two hours after we began dinner, and utterly stuffed, we pushed away from the table. The dinner took the last of my funds but I believed it had been worth getting out of our dreary townhouse. Plus no one had to cook or clean up.

At the entrance to the Holiday Inn a man passing me called out, "Aren't you the Bunny Mother?"

Startled by the sudden attention I could barely stammer, "Yes."

"I thought so. I've wanted to talk with you so many times at the Club but you're always busy."

"Yes. I hardly have time for myself." I found the man attractive, but in a cowboy rather than business-suit sort of way. On the other hand, his attire of camel cashmere coat, silk tie and azure shirt to match his eyes made a clear statement about his wealth. Taller than most men that I had met in Chicago, he posed a striking figure.

"Married?" he asked as he nodded to Carl and Greg.

"Divorced, but these are my sons." I felt uncomfortable with such a discussion in front of the boys.

The man took a business card from his wallet and gave it to me. "Maybe we could have a drink sometime at the Club or dinner elsewhere."

"Perhaps." I stuck the card in my coat pocket.

"Sorry to run off, but I'm meeting friends from out of town." His broad smile brought out inviting lines around his eyes. "Good-by, boys," he said to Carl and Greg and pushed through the door into the hotel lobby.

For the first time in months I felt an exciting tingle from my waist to my knees. I retrieved the card. *Lawrence Marconi, Consultant.* I looked forward to finding out more about Mr. Marconi.

The temperature was warm for that time of year and with it came sprinkles. No matter, the boys and I strolled along Michigan Avenue looking at the windows filled with elaborate Christmas decorations. I tried to provide my sons with as many fun activities as possible. Last weekend we had ventured back to the Museum of Science and Industry where we had been so absorbed, we spent three hours on only one floor. A row of Christmas trees decorated in the styles of several countries lined one wall. Underneath each tree, Merry Christmas had been written in the language of the country. It had been a lovely way to kick off the season.

I observed my sons' reflections in the windows they passed. Something coiled around my chest tighter and tighter as I thought about how unhappy the two boys had been. Nothing replaced the warmth of California's sun or the established friendships of many years. Life always comes down to making choices, I realized. Most of the time I knew what truly mattered, but I questioned if I always chose it. For instance, working for Playboy. My sons had suffered. I, not they, elected to make that move primarily for my benefit, though I had expected we'd be better off financially. That had not happened. How would my quitting Playboy affect them?

Chapter Thirteen

Holiday Spirits

You should all be aware that it costs about $300 to recruit, train and make productive one of our Bunnies. One of the main complaints by Bunnies who voluntarily leave our employ is that rules governing Room Directors, Shift Managers, bartenders and entertainers dating are not being enforced. The Bunnies complain about favoritism in scheduling, seating, etc. They complain about pressure from male members of the staff who want to date them and make them feel as though they are obligated to comply. Our procedures and policies are very clear! You are aware of them! They are to be enforced to the letter constantly! Interoffice memo to Room Directors and bartenders 1967

The Club's attendance increased daily as patrons got an early start to celebrating the holidays. I promised myself that Christmas in the Bonura home would be just as festive despite my longing to be as far from Chicago and Playboy, Inc. as possible. Though nearly evicted because of the late rental payment, I planned to postpone my next installment, too, if Angelo didn't send money in time for me to pick up the boys' gifts which had been held on lay-away. If he stuck with his past record, the usual payment and no presents would be all they could expect from Angelo. Already $40.00 in arrears, he couldn't be counted on for any help.

I waited for a bus, a ritual I dreaded more each day since the notorious Chicago winter had set in. To take my mind off the slush, the graying snow piled at the curb and the wind that made my blood turn to ice, I went over my agenda for the next couple of weeks. Though many employees and celebrities alike could hardly wait for the parties hosted by Hef at the Mansion, I'd have liked to find a solid excuse to miss them. If rumors had it right, those wild gatherings left little to the imagination and made *Playboy Magazine* appear tame.

The ride took far longer than usual because of icy streets. I doubted I would ever get used to a winter environment where brown twigs posed as trees and clouds looked like metal rather than the huge white cotton puffs of the California coast. I also doubted I'd ever get warm again.

I brushed the snow from my coat and entered the Playboy lobby ready to do battle one more day. John, one of the two newly hired Room Directors, asked me to join him for a quick cup of coffee in the lounge. I always enjoyed such offers because I got to know the men who looked after my Bunnies in my absence. As we sipped the steamy brew I complained about the weather.

"I'm used to it," John answered as he refilled our cups. "I was raised in the east."

A transfer from the New York Club, John came highly recommended and well educated. Lou, the other transfer, had been a different story. One Bunny who had also switched Clubs about a month earlier turned the shade of a bleached oatmeal sack when she saw Lou in Chicago. Her body trembled so wildly when she first saw him her tray of drinks nearly spilled to the floor. "He raped me," she whimpered. She went on to tell me that was why she moved away from New York.

The Bunny told an all-too-familiar story. She had spurned his unwanted advances, but Lou didn't understand or maybe didn't want to comprehend the meaning of "NO!" I asked why she hadn't reported the assault. She only replied with a bitter laugh. I would be on the alert with Lou, certainly.

While John and I talked, he revealed he had been so strapped for money he became indebted to a loan shark. He left New York hoping to get away from the crook. "At least until I can get my act together and save the money I owe him. Otherwise. . ." He shrugged.

I didn't want to think about the otherwise. I gave him my sympathy, and we parted. Room Directors were no better than the Bunnies at sticking to a budget, but neither was I. All of us lived from paycheck to paycheck. Now I felt even more depressed than I had standing at the bus stop.

The rash that plagued me and several Bunnies reappeared. I had gone to see Doctor Sherwood again. Like the first time, he didn't charge me for the session or the ointment which kept the nasty redness at bay. Doctor Sherwood apparently remained starry-eyed about treating the Bunny Mother. I secretly thanked the powers-that-be for the doctor's generosity at a time when I had little cash. Tonight he and his colleagues would be at the Club for dinner as he had asked me to arrange. Perhaps Brooke would have dinner with them. I would rather go home. On the other hand, I conceded that I looked exceptionally sharp that day and who knew, Doctor Sherwood might have a rich single friend who liked kids.

More Christmas gifts from the Bunnies had been piled on my desk. I logged each one so I could remember which girl gave which gift. To date I had received 24 including a Japanese lantern, 7 bottles of perfume, 2 perfume dispensers, scented drawer dividers, candles, 2 boxes of candy, a poinsettia, a robe, earrings, pins, a compact, and a sweater from Barry. I had already taken the sweater back to the store because it had a faded crease where it had been folded for so long. I gathered it probably had belonged to his wife who didn't like it enough to wear it. I got a nicer, more useful sweater in the exchange.

"Talk about bad weather." Brooke startled me. Brooke's nose and cheeks held a red glow from the winter air she brought in like a wind. The breeze reached out like chilled fingers and wrapped around me.

"Brrr." I shook.

"You look great," Brooke commented as she hung her coat and slipped off clear-plastic rubbers covering her shoes.

"Thanks." My pleasure turned to self-doubt when I wondered how I had looked other times.

"Got a date?" As always, Brooke was dressed to the nines, taking no mind of the expense.

"No, but I think you might." I decided Brooke could eat dinner with the doctors.

"Huh?"

"I've arranged for four doctors to have dinner in the V.I.P. Room. Do you mind joining them for a short time?"

Brooke thought for a moment. "I'd be delighted. It will be better than spending another evening with crazy Larry."

"Isn't he your new beau?" I asked as I shuffled through the papers in the in-box.

"Yeah, but all he wants to do is take off my clothes and chase me around the apartment." Brooke actually ran around the room. When she stopped she bowed and announced theatrically, as though to the audience in one of the showrooms, "Larry's gotta go. Thank you very much."

"Where do these guys come from?" I chuckled.

"I guess they think if you work for Playboy anything goes." Brooke took a stack of papers from my desk and plunged into her tasks for the day. "But there is a good side. Even though Larry lives in my apartment building, so do several other eligible men looking for dates. You should move there."

"And be chased naked around my apartment?" We laughed so hard I had to dab the tears from my eyes.

The phone rang. I rolled my eyes as I reached for it. "And the fun begins." I hadn't expected the person on the other end—a reporter from the Washington D.C. Evening Star who actually wanted to talk with Hugh Hefner and "none of his underlings." I explained that I could handle any concern, until I heard it. The reporter gave Hefner until Friday to call him back or he threatened, "I will write an editorial exposing him for the con man he is."

As the reporter went on with his tirade I had a hard time holding in my laughter. At one point I placed a hand over the mouthpiece. The reporter demanded his $25.00 membership fee back from 1960 when the Washington Club was supposed to open, which was the only reason he had become a member. At that point he shouted, "Hugh Hefner, that Tall Paul with a pipe in his mouth, will only build the Washington Club after the Hanoi Club—which will have Vietnamese girls as Bunnies." He ended his diatribe with this unintelligible statement, "I don't swing, so I won't ring."

I tried to soothe the man's ire by telling him he could use the facilities at the Baltimore Club. The reporter wanted nothing to do with that. He only wanted to talk to the Tall Paul or the editorial would run. When he hung up, I stared at Brooke for a few moments and then said, "What a screwball!" I repeated the phone conversation to Brooke for a good laugh. Then I called Hugh Hefner to tell him the possibility of bad press. He took the whole incident in stride and told me, "Publicity is publicity. All publicity is good." I tucked that piece of wisdom into my memory bank.

Everyone got into the holiday spirit, although I still wasn't looking forward to the parties and the rowdy celebrants at the Club. The boys and I however couldn't wait for Tekkie's visit while she was on break from U.C.L.A.

To my delight, Greg took it upon himself to wrap all the gifts of quality perfume supplied by International for the Bunnies' Christmas presents, a benevolent gesture that came close to being derailed when six bottles of perfume were stolen from my office before I could take them home for Greg to wrap. My mood had been brought down more when I got my $25.00 bonus, which was the same amount the Room Directors received. I had thought my position warranted more recognition, but I held my complaint to myself.

Carl and Greg picked out a tree at the Salvation Army for our house. I tried to persuade them that the aluminum tree fad had passed, but they would hear nothing of it. The glitzy tree reminded them of the one they had in California which made their first Christmas away from their real home more welcoming. The four-foot tree perched on a table in the center of the front window. Decorated in multi-colored, somewhat scratched ornaments Greg retrieved from a neighbor's trash, the silver limbs glowed in red and green as the electric color-wheel rotated behind. Once in place we admired our work and brought in the holiday with cocoa made the way my mother had done twenty years before. We went over plans for the highly anticipated arrival of Tekkie.

"It'll be just like home when she gets here," Carl said.

Each night closer to Christmas the keyholders and their guests became more riotous. Some members even had to be asked to leave the Club. I caught one keyholder pinching a Bunny's butt in plain view of Chris Malloy. When he did nothing about the unacceptable behavior, I approached him. "Why aren't you speaking to that man who just pinched Carlie's behind?"

"It's the holidays. They don't mean any harm." He leaned against one end of the bar with his hands relaxed to his side and his chin slightly raised. He surveyed his domain through half-closed eyes.

Carlie had reached the bar to give her order and overheard

Malloy's response. She rolled her eyes at me. She kept her mouth shut because she knew if she said one word, Malloy would retaliate in some way.

"So, there would be no problem if I went around the room and pinched every man's behind, including yours?" I challenged Malloy's explanation.

Malloy stood away from the bar, arms now crossed over his chest. "No, it does matter. That would be obscene."

"Mr. Malloy, if you don't handle this situation right this minute, I will. But let me be clear, I will embarrass you in the process." I never took my eyes off his as I leaned as close as I could toward him.

Without an answer, Malloy walked over to the male member, explained the situation and asked him to leave. The man stood, threw his key at Carlie and retreated.

"I guess he's giving up his membership," Carlie snickered to me.

"Who needs that kind of keyholder anyway?" I asked.

Yet none of these shenanigans would prepare me for either the Christmas Party at the Mansion or New Year's Eve in the Club.

Hugh Hefner hosted the annual party at the Mansion on the Friday before Christmas Day. At least at this gathering he greeted guests in a maroon dinner jacket with black satin lapels, rather than the usual silk pajamas. By the time I got to the festivities, party-goers packed every room (except Hef's private quarters) and the pool. The door guards must have had quite a time checking arrivals against their approved guest list.

I squeezed my way through the crowd to the main room only to find it filled with people either standing several deep, sitting on pillows against the walls or trying to dance by bobbing up and down in one place. I made it to a group I knew—Barry, Malloy, Judy and her husband, who surprised me with his good looks and quiet, polite charm. When Tom joined the group, he handed me a glass of champagne.

With champagne in hand I struggled through the crush and downstairs to the pool, hoping to get away from the smoke and pandemonium. As I arrived at the pool, a Bunny was swimming after her falsies that had escaped from her suit. I had to hold back my laughter as I watched a male swimmer retrieve them. Once the Good Samaritan placed the soggy foam rubber in her hand the Bunny made a fast exit while another asked me to loan her some eyelash glue. The rather tipsy girl held one lash in her hand while the other lay slightly askew on her lid.

When I got a closer look, the girl was Kelly, the Bunny who seemed to get away with everything until I suspended her for two weeks for an incident that happened a few nights earlier. Kelly had served a last round of drinks to a table of four. When finished she gave the $15 tab to the key holder. He gave her a twenty-dollar bill. When Kelly got to the bar, she realized she had made a mistake and that the tab had actually been $25. So Kelly took the tab back. She explained the mistake, but the member accused her of cheating him. Kelly tried to explain again. The member went into a tirade, which included calling her names. She swore back. The Room Director tried to quiet both down but it didn't work. The member left screaming. His guests followed. Meanwhile, other Room Directors hurried on the scene thinking there had to be a Bunny in distress. I had to suspend Kelly for swearing and losing her temper at a customer when she should have let the Room Director handle the problem. When I held the counseling session and suspended Kelly, the Bunny told me, "You should have heard what he called my mother."

"He doesn't know your mother," I answered.

Kelly had no response and left for two weeks.

Tonight I chose not to speak to the inebriated Kelly. Instead I went back to the main room. On the way up the stairs, a Club bartender told me his wallet was taken from his pants while he swam. I had no answer for that problem—with the hundreds of people in the Mansion it could have been anyone. Judging by the bartender's drunkenness, he could have also mislaid it.

Tom asked me to dance to a sour trio whose members had had too much to drink. What Tom and I did couldn't be categorized as true dancing since space only allowed us to pick up one foot at a time and remain in place rather than do the Frug as the music intended. Tom asked me if I knew Lou had raped a Bunny in New York. I told him I did but I didn't want to discuss such things at the party.

"You know it won't be the first or last time such a thing will happen," Tom said before we dropped the subject.

The music ended and I took leave of Tom without further comment. I searched for both Brooke and Carlie, but never found them.
After one more swing through the area I found a chair next to two
Bunnies. Someone handed me a second glass of champagne. I sipped
it though I had had nothing to eat yet. It didn't matter, since I overheard a server say they had run out of food and were waiting for
more. They hadn't run out of booze though. It flowed freely. A human mass swarmed each tray of alcohol delivered by a white jacketed
server and denuded it like locusts in a field.

Sitting in the corner, I had a better view of the activity. The room
was a kaleidoscope of red velvet, green silk, black satin and white se-
quins. Spilled food and drinks carpeted the floor. Every few minutes
someone broke a glass, and then an unsmiling butler waiting close at
hand would step in to sweep up the shards. Several partiers had
passed out, a few threw-up and one man even urinated in his slacks.
Sadly the nastiest in the horde worked at International or the magazine. On the other hand, the Bunnies were the best behaved, though
many had had too much to drink.

As soon as I set my empty champagne glass on a tray, someone
handed me another. After downing that glass, the room started to
whirl. Smoke mixed with red and green and swirled in a hazy eddy. I
couldn't steady my focus. Everything spun to the rhythm of the out-
of-tune trio. It was time to go home, and I'd better take a cab because
I had no way of navigating myself to the bus.

As soon as I got inside my townhouse, I fell onto the couch with
my coat half-off, and passed out. Greg had stayed up to watch a
movie and when it was over, he managed to get me to my bedroom. I
undressed to my slip but left all my makeup on, including my false
eyelashes.

I awakened at 9:30 the following morning with the worst hang-
over I could ever remember. I washed my face, dressed in slacks,
sweater and a hat that covered my hair and went to the Club. I gradu-
ally put on my makeup throughout the morning. I didn't care how I
looked because I had decided not to make any inspections that day. I
didn't want to face one more mishap.

Bunnies and Room Directors, one of whom was still smashed and
one who had less than four hours sleep, trickled in for their shifts.

The Bunny who had lost her falsies the night before called in to report the pool's chlorine had given her a serious rash. When Carlie appeared, I asked why she hadn't been at the party.

"If I want to get laid, I'll stand on a street corner and get paid." Then she broke down crying.

"What's wrong?" I got up so fast I knocked over my chair. The ache in my head banged back and forth like a steel ball.

"Oooh, Alyce. I don't know what to do." She sobbed harder. She blew her nose and folded herself into the couch.

"What's happened? You can tell me, you know that. I'll help as best I can." I rubbed small circles in the center of Carlie's back.

"I had planned to go to the party at least for a little while. But. . ." Carlie's wail made her whole body shudder.

"Take your time. Do you want something to drink?"

Carlie shook her and blew her nose again. If she had any makeup on before, it had all been washed away. Carlie took a deep shivering breath. "You know Chris Malloy is always on my back."

"Yes, I do and it doesn't make me happy," I said.

Carlie rested her head against the couch back. "He's been asking me out ever since I got here. I stick by the rules and won't go. He doesn't like being turned down so he's made trouble for me."

"Did he say something to you yesterday to stop you from going to the party?"

"You could say that." Carlie didn't elaborate.

I waited. In the background of the silent office, I heard the cheerful chatter of the Bunnies down the hall in the dressing room. I wondered if Carlie would say any more.

Carlie raised her head to look straight into my eyes. "He showed up at my apartment as I was getting ready for the party. Like a fool I let him in. I was trying to be nice." The sobbing began again. This time it came in loud, uncontrolled bursts. "He raped me." She collapsed onto me. "Then he threatened that if I told a soul he'd come back and hurt me."

I held her hard against my chest. I rubbed her back again. We stayed like that for over fifteen minutes. "Go home, Carlie. I'll take care of this." I pulled my distraught friend to her feet. "Do you need a ride?"

"No, I'll take a cab." She wiped her face with a tissue. "Thank you,

Alyce, for listening. I doubt you'll be able to do anything. I've already taken the giant leap and pressed charges."

"Are you sure you want to go through with this?" I knew the police and the general public commonly pinned blame on the woman in such an incident.

"Yes, I'm very sure. Even if my name is dragged through the mud. Someone has to stand up to these animals." Carlie's steely tone confirmed her determination.

"I'm still speaking to Barry on Monday about this." I paused. "That is if I have your permission."

"Of course, but it won't change my mind or make any difference to management's double standard."

"I have nothing to lose," I said. "I will demand that they fire the bastard or I'll go to the newspapers and see how much bad press Hef really thinks is good."

Carlie looked puzzled. "What?"

"Never mind. It's something he told me once and I'm certainly happy to test those waters." I hugged Carlie and watched as she walked, her shoulders slumped, down the hall and out of view. "Bastards! All of them," I said to the ugly room.

On Monday I didn't have a chance to report the rape to Barry. He waited in my office. At first he didn't notice me come in. He paced, hands entwined behind his back, and with each step he puffed a cigar he never removed from between his teeth. If he clenched the foul thing any tighter, he surely would have bitten it in two. When he realized I stood in the doorway, he stopped. "You're finally here."

I checked the time. "I'm not late."

"No. No. I need to talk with you." Barry puffed a few more times on the cigar. Smoke circled around his head. "So get settled and let's get down to it."

I hung my coat and sat at my desk. For the moment I put Carlie aside and prepared myself for what I thought Barry would tell me. My first thought was that I had to transfer. But to where? My hands trembled as a tingling spread into my chest. Barry didn't sit.

"I'm not going to beat around the bush," Barry said with such firmness I then thought I was about to be fired.

"Good."

"Carlie must be terminated. Do it for Bunny Image." Barry actually headed for the door.

"Hold on," I shouted.

Barry slid to a halt and turned to face me.

"Why," I asked standing my ground.

Barry didn't move one inch. "Carlie's a troublemaker."

I cocked my head to the side and raised one brow. I waited for Barry's explanation. When none came, I asked, "How is she a troublemaker? She happens to be my most dependable and capable Bunny."

Barry fidgeted with the buttons on his cashmere coat. "She went to the police. She claimed Mr. Malloy raped her."

"It's true." I stayed calm and firm.

"Even so," Barry dismissed Carlie's story with a wave of his hand, "she shouldn't go to the police. Bad publicity."

I rose, ready to take on the issue full force. "How would you handle the situation if you had been raped?"

"Never happen." He chuckled.

"This is not a laughing matter, Barry. What else should Carlie have done? Gone to you?"

"She should have told you. You're the Mother, for Christ sakes." Beads of sweat formed above his upper lip and along his hairline.

I offered a mocking smile. "Yes, I am a mother and she did tell me. But Chris Malloy should not only be prosecuted for his assault—I want him fired. Carlie stays."

"Impossible," Barry shouted. He patted his pockets, probably searching for another cigar. He only smoked when stressed. "The girl's not a team player."

"First of all, Barry," I inched toward him, "her name is Carlie, so use it. Second of all, what kind of team is this that expects a woman to succumb to any male's whim, whether it's harmful to her or not?" I took a deep breath. "Malloy goes or I'll go to the press. You don't want the world to know all this, do you?"

"That's blackmail." Barry wiped his face with a handkerchief.

"Call it what you want. Carlie stays. Malloy goes. And I don't care how you explain all of it to International."

Barry kept his mouth shut. He appeared to be rummaging through his mind for a come-back. Then he offered an absurd defense. "I had to fire John because he borrowed money from me and many other guys, but never paid us back. I can't afford to lose another Room Director."

"That sounds like a personal problem which has nothing to do with Carlie and Malloy." I couldn't wait for any reply. "I've heard you think I'm too independent. So my ultimatum shouldn't come as a shock. Right now I have nothing to lose and Playboy has. It's your choice, Barry."

Within two days Barry fired Malloy. He didn't take the termination well. Malloy told a few of his colleagues as he departed, "I'm gonna beat that bitch silly."

I didn't know to which "bitch" he referred—Carlie or me. Yet he must have been persuaded against the idea because it never happened. He disappeared with rape charges pending.

Lawrence Marconi called me a few days before New Year's and asked me out. I explained I had to work because of the large numbers of keyholders and their guests expected to celebrate at the Club. "Then I'll join you there on New Year's, if you don't mind," he said.

I conjured up his pleasing image. I could hear the charm in his voice. "Sure. That would be perfect." We made arrangements for him to get to the Club around 8:00 pm for dinner and the show.

Tekkie had arrived a few days before Christmas and had taken over the cooking, baking and caring for the boys and Fraulein. I relished the help, and the boys couldn't get enough of their much loved sister-aunt. She even helped Carl with a four-page paper on the Roman Empire. Together they spent hours in Chicago's main library. It would be hard to see her leave, not only because she had been such an aid, but she was so much fun for the boys.

Christmas day brought quiet pleasure to the four of us. We opened our gifts including the model car set I had promised Greg, a watch in need of repair from Clark to me, and matching slippers for Tekkie and me that Greg got at Newton's. After we ate breakfast, Tekkie and I prepared a turkey dinner while the boys painted their model toys. The dinner was as perfect as any we remembered and would provide scrumptious leftovers, often the best part. The slow-paced family day could have been better had the boys heard from their father.

The next day we happily planned to trek through Old Town but instead turned back after everyone got too cold waiting for the bus. So we went home to make a further dent in the leftovers, play cards and watch TV. For me those two days were so delicious I could taste them.

On December 27, Angelo sent $20.00. Four weeks late and $60.00 short.

Chapter Fourteen

Snow Days

Bunnies have been models, college coeds, actresses, dancers, stewardesses, teachers or secretaries. A Bunny—like the PLAYBOY Playmate—is the girl next door. She is the American romanticized myth . . . beautiful, desirable, and a nice fun-loving person. A Bunny is not a broad or a "hippie." She may be sexy, but fresh, healthy sexy—not cheap or lewd. A Bunny is chosen for 1) Beauty 2) Personality 3) Ability. "Be a Playboy Club Bunny" Booklet

I hung my coat, pulled off my boots and put on heels. No sooner had I completed that unpleasant task than Barry called me over to his office. I had to dress again in an outfit suited more to an Eskimo to walk the one block to his office at International. If he didn't have a good reason for my immediate appearance, I would have a most difficult time holding my temper in check.

Slopping through the slush and interminable snow, I reached Barry's office drenched and feeling like a drowned rat without a fur coat. Barry sat behind his desk, this time with both feet planted securely on the ground and not spread-eagle as he had in the past. He balanced on the edge of his chair. His eyes darted around the room, never settling on me.

"Sit." Barry motioned me to a chair. "This won't take long."

Barry's nervousness made me uneasy too. "It must be big to get me over here in such a rush." I'd hoped he would discount that, but he didn't. As I sat, water squished from my coat. I crossed my legs. The nylons stuck together. Even my girdle seemed damp.

"You know that International thinks you're top management material but you're too independent." Barry hardly glanced at me since he probably realized he was parroting my own words. "With that in mind, I've been asked if I want Coco back permanently."

The rush of startled adrenaline shot around in my body. I said nothing. I lowered my leg and crossed my ankles, legs bent to one side.

"I told them I'm faced with two good Bunny Mothers, but I wanted to keep you." He raised his eyes to look in my direction but above my head at the wall behind me.

I knew since Barry had difficulty making eye contact he hadn't told me the whole truth. "What else, Barry? Quit beating around the bush."

"Ok, ok." He lit a cigar. The cigar gave Barry the Al Capone thug look. He really should take up pipe smoking; it was more sophisticated. But then, the image of Hef and his pipe flashed before me.

"International explained that since Coco had already been promised her job back if she wanted, she had to get it. She won't go to New York or Miami so I had no choice."

I bet, I thought. "What are you saying Barry?"

"Coco will take over the Chicago Club. She wants to stay near her child's father." He paused then quickly added, "But not for a while yet."

I stood. "What does that mean for me? I don't want New York either." I didn't want to move my sons again.

"Have you thought about Miami? It's too late for the L.A. Club." His eyes formed large almost perfect circles as they finally locked onto me.

"L.A.? Why didn't anyone think to ask me if I'd like to take a job in my own town?" My voice became louder with each word.

Barry shrugged. "I didn't even know about the opening. A Los Angeles Bunny got the job." His features pleaded innocence.

I didn't believe him. We faced each other for several moments—I glared while Barry's eyes begged like a puppy's. "You really don't need a Bunny Mother since every step I take, you must check first. But I'll think about Miami. If I decide to take it, I won't move there until school ends." I also wanted to make sure my nose operation took place. I had an appointment with the doctor soon.

"Good. All managers' jobs are frozen for the time being anyway."

Typical Barry. He'd known that all along, but wanted me to sweat a little. The office held a silence deeper than any tomb. "Is that all?" I asked.

He nodded. I left him still looking like a child caught hitting the boy next door. I was positive Barry, not International, had chosen Coco because of the Malloy and Carlie incident. If I hadn't insisted Malloy lose his job over Carlie's rape, I no doubt wouldn't be moving to another Club. Paybacks could be hell. Yet there could have been no other decision for me.

Though hurt, I decided the move to Miami might be what I needed, even if temporary. What better way to see a new place than to have Playboy pay my way?

Back at my own office, I once again took off my now soaked boots and coat. I shook the coat like a rug and hung it. I slipped on my dry shoes and checked myself in an old cracked mirror near the door. "No more straight hair." I pulled a brush through my thoroughly frizzed red locks. As I sat at my desk, Carlie stomped into the office. Water saturated every inch of her clothing including the wool fedora, which sagged heavily over her face.

"How did you get so drenched?" I asked.

Carlie removed her boots and drained the water from them into a planter. "My cab had an accident. The traffic is so backed up due to the snow, which I doubt will ever stop, I couldn't find a bus. So I walked to work." Water from her wool coat dripped into large puddles on the floor and webbed out like creeks.

"That's five miles!" I shrieked.

"Don't I know that!" Carlie pointed to her red, swollen, seriously wet feet.

"You're a blessing." I smiled. "Already, six girls have called in because of the weather. And from what this storm looks like, we're in for a rough winter."

December 31 came so fast I had little time to get enough girls scheduled for the enormous crowd expected on each level of the Club. Seeing Tekkie off at the airport made the day less festive for the boys and me. Though I knew Barry might get ruffled, Carl and Greg came to the Club with me for lunch. Greg busied himself by taking down the Club's Christmas tree and packing the ornaments away.

Carl moped around, but finally watched a story on TV where a man's brother got killed. He astounded me when he said, "I know how he must feel never to see someone he loves again. That's the way I feel since Aunt Tekkie left."

When Greg finished his self-appointed task, I sent the two boys off and promised I'd get home as soon as possible. Carl and Greg planned to continue work on their car models, take Fraulein for a walk, watch TV and eat the special treat I prepared for them—ham, candied yams and corn. All that would be followed by Tekkie's famous fudge brownies.

Though I looked forward to my dinner with Lawrence Marconi, I hoped to have an early evening with few problems at the Club. I had taken more care in getting ready that day so I looked my absolute best without being overdressed or gaudy. I chose a royal blue chemise, matching shoes and pearl earrings. I took much effort to apply my makeup just the way Lucinda had taught me.

To my complete amazement, after some manipulation my hair had finally behaved. For once my bangs stayed straight while the rest flipped neatly at my shoulders. A further wonder—at the end of the day, the hairdo looked close to what it had when I left my house that morning.

Members started coming in great numbers around 9:00 pm. Those who arrived early got good seats, but soon only standing room was available. As each minute of heavy drinking ticked by, the partiers grew more unruly. Lawrence was a welcome sight when he showed at eight as planned. He and I had a cocktail in the Playmate Bar followed by a gourmet dinner in the V.I.P. Room before the crowd got too unbearable.

When we finished coffee and dessert I sent Lawrence on his way against his wishes about 11:30 pm so I could make a final check of all levels and go home. Once my inspection began I realized how fortunate my decision had been. I could barely find a Bunny because of the sea of drunks swaying not to the music, but to steady themselves.

Mona grabbed my arm as I passed. She pointed to a man who had just pulled up his pants after he pooped in the corner by the Piano Bar. "I guess he didn't want to lose his seat," I said, somehow beyond surprise now at the goings on in this Club.

Once my rounds had been completed at about five minutes before midnight, I took all the Bunnies off the floor and locked them in the Bunny Lounge. If I left them on the floor they probably would be mauled and who knew what else. I gave Rick, a Room Director, orders to not let them out until the Club closed for the night.

My Bunny Mother job finished for that eve, I headed home to do my real mother duties. I flagged a cab and hurried on my way. Carl and Greg had decorated the living room with streamers Greg got from the drug store. I made popcorn, which we all devoured including Fraulein. At 2:00 am we went to sleep and didn't wake up until ten the next morning.

Back at work after New Year's Day, I found out what happened when Rick freed the Bunnies. All the staff went to the Playmate Bar to get ripping drunk. By the time their binge finished, Bunnies had lost tails, ears, and shoes. Many got no-shows for their shifts following the impromptu gala. I didn't think I could live through another holiday season at the Club.

It seemed the partying hadn't ended that early on New Year's morning either. When Heidi came to work drunk I had Brenda take her place at the pool table—and I once more promised myself I'd never work in such a world as Playboy in the future.

I hardly had a chance to sit at my desk when Barry called, screaming that the Gift Shop receipts were short on New Year's Eve because I had put Sheila in there. "She made so many dumb mistakes. What's the matter with you?"

I decided it was high time I put my freshest New Year's resolution into action. "You're the one who fired a girl before I could train someone else. It's not easy finding someone with a brain who'd rather work the Gift Shop than the floor where she can earn more money. So I guess you're the stupid one."

Barry's heavy breathing sounded like the echo I heard when I held a sea shell to my ear. "Go to the 5 and 10 cent store. The money will look good to them," he huffed. "So try, honey."

Honey, indeed. Barry was so transparent. "I've been there," I said, "but there are still a few catches—like looking good in a costume. And you know, the next fired girl who threatens to go to the newspaper I'll send over to you." I slammed the phone down.

Within minutes Tom came into the office, yelling about going one

Bunny short.

"Talk to Barry," I screamed back, and it felt good.

"What?" Tom appeared genuinely dismayed.

"Barry keeps firing the Bunnies." I took Tom by the arm and led him out the door. "Maybe he has a solution." I smiled, batted my eyes and waved good-by.

Tom walked away shaking his head. "The whole place is crazy," he mumbled.

"My sentiments exactly," I whispered to myself.

Bunny inspection took far more time than usual because each one wanted to share with me her private version of what happened New Year's Eve. I pictured 70 pregnant Bunnies hopping around the Hutch in no time. To each new piece of the night's event I could only respond, "Oh my!"

The funniest story actually happened that morning. Nancie had an appointment with a gynecologist. She had to give a urine specimen and discovered no one had filled the toilet paper in the lady's room. "So after I peed, I grabbed some tissue from my purse and wiped."

"During the doctor's examination," she went on, "he asked me, 'Do you give green stamps?'"

The other Bunnies and I were puzzled. "What kind of question is that?" one girl asked.

"The doctor peeled a page of stamps from my vagina to show me," Nancie said. "I tried to explain to him—"

The Bunnies and I nearly fell over from laughing so hard.

"But I was so embarrassed!" Nancie could hardly speak for her own laughter. "Then he asked me where he should go to redeem them!"

Many yelled, "Stop, stop, my eyelashes will come off."

Mona then added her story. "I went out with a doctor once. When I got home after our date, I realized one earring and an eyelash were missing. Then I remembered he tried to spit something from his mouth. My eyelash. Don't know what became of the earring."

"Oh my," I said again. Everyone roared as I fanned them out of the room.

As soon as the Bunnies cleared my office, a delivery boy arrived with a box of red roses. The card read, "Thanks for a wonderful evening. Hope to see you soon." Lawrence Marconi had sent them.

I stuck my nose into the petals and inhaled. Clark hadn't even called to wish me a Happy New Year, and Lawrence had sent a gift. Maybe my relationship with Lawrence could be the one. So far he'd been nothing but a gentleman. For the first time in years I looked forward to dating a new man even if I didn't get that twitching sensation with him as I had with Clark.

Almost as though he knew when the flowers would be delivered, Lawrence called. I thanked him and we made arrangements to have a real date the following Friday when I finished work for the evening. I hung up feeling like a teenage girl going to my first prom.

The weather forecaster's prediction for more snow came true. In fact the snow never stopped. What I deemed overwhelming at 3 ½" in one snowfall a few days into the New Year began to seem a mere wisp of white fluff as January marched forward. I longed for that little bit of snow on the day I had to wait a half hour for a bus. As I stood shivering and getting wetter with each flake, a four-foot icicle fell from the twenty floor building behind me and missed impaling me by inches. If it had hit me, I had no doubt it would have killed me.

Maybe my life had been spared so I could enjoy an evening out with Lawrence. He picked me up at the Club, but we ate dinner at Eli's in a cozy dining room while we listened to the soft sounds of a piano coming from the separate bar area. Lawrence regaled me with compliments and said, "I was drawn to you the first time I saw you."

Flattered by talk I hadn't heard in such a long time, I felt willing to do almost anything to prolong the fairy tale evening. So I eagerly agreed to go to an intimate club similar to what I knew in L.A. as a lounge—small, packed, with good music and a tiny dance floor. For a split second I longed for Clark. Lawrence and I had a couple of drinks, a Rob Roy for me, which had become my favorite cocktail, and danced.

While twirling around the packed floor, Lawrence asked, "Why don't you take off your girdle so you can dance more freely? Then I'll take you to another place."

Though an odd request—after all, no upstanding woman would go without it—getting out of my long-line panty girdle brought the relief I knew the Bunnies felt each time they took off their costumes. Once removed, I stuffed the contraption into my purse. We then left the lounge arm in arm and giggling like school kids.

"I need to stop at my apartment," Lawrence said as he helped me into his Cadillac. "I'm going to change into something more comfortable for dancing, too."

We drove for a short time to a building within a block of my townhouse and went inside. That was when everything went from a blissful dream to a horrifying nightmare. Lawrence bolted the door and removed his jacket, then slipped off his shirt and unbuckled his belt. "Take off your clothes," he demanded as he reached for the buttons on my dress. I backed away. "I won't hurt you. I only want to see you naked then chase you around for a while."

The memory of Brooke's dance around my office flashed into my head. Impossible. Lawrence couldn't be the same guy, could he? "Look," I said, keeping a safe distance between us. "I don't know what made you think I was going to play this game, but I'm not."

Lawrence lunged for my arm. "You're a friend of Brooke's, aren't you?"

"Yes," I whispered. Lawrence. Larry. How could I have been so blind? But what did I know? I had never seen Larry, and Brooke hadn't dated him long. I had been so filled with anticipation about Lawrence, I hadn't considered how little I knew about him.

I grabbed my coat and rushed to the door. I fumbled with the lock, but I managed to get out before Lawrence—or Larry—realized what had happened. Though he had a fondness to wander around nude I felt confident he wouldn't chase me into the hall and out into the frigid winter night. I ran, slipping and sliding, the one block to the safety of my home. I could hardly wait to tell Brooke what had happened.

As I leaned against my own locked door, I said, "I guess he won't be the one." Fraulein approached me, wagging her tail in the most welcoming greeting. I scratched the dog's ears and vowed off men.

No sooner had I made that vow than I discovered the letter from Clark in the mail that had arrived that morning. He wanted to visit from January 23 to February 5. "But," he wrote, "I won't come to Chicago unless I know for certain you have no one else and that nothing has changed between us."

I tore the letter into tiny pieces and tossed it into the waste can. "How dare you ask me if I have someone else?" The confetti floated to the bottom of the container.

As I undressed for bed, a tiresome routine, sadness overwhelmed me. I didn't want Clark to see my townhouse furnished with Salvation Army goods, or find me in such a questionable emotional state, and I had yet to improve on my personal looks as planned. For all those reasons I didn't want him to visit. But most important of all, he hadn't left his wife.

Though exhausted, I wrote in my journal. I thought I'd write only a few lines. Instead I finished the last line over two hours later. I'd write Clark in the morning when my mind cleared out the anger and melancholy. I only wanted Clark to see my bright side, even though I would be telling him he couldn't visit.

In the midst of the never-ending snow, January at the Club was dead. Like the rest of Americans, most keyholders headed to gyms to take off the pounds gained over the holidays, rather than to bars or dinner clubs. So everyone had high expectations for business to pick up with the upcoming Housewares Show at McCormick Place which promised 60,000 attendees.

January 16 started with a bang, but not the one hoped for. Chicago awakened to the headlines that McCormick Place had burned to the ground. So the conference attendees packed their bags and went back home two days after they had arrived. Not only did this disaster have repercussions on Chicago's economy but the building left in ashes proved to be a tremendous emotional loss also. Business at the Club was poor as a result and many girls were taken off the schedule. For the first time since I had arrived in Chicago, the Playboy Club seemed like a dark, empty cave.

When three more inches of snow fell, I became even more resentful of nature's way of piling on the misery. But within a week the temperature soared to a record-breaking 65 degrees. When the sun shone, I dressed in lighter clothes as I had in L.A., and as I bussed to work, I recaptured my once normal high spirit. I had heard rumors about a January thaw, but hadn't dreamed it would turn out so beautiful.

The gorgeous day was short lived, however. By the time I left work for home, a gale force wind whipped pellets of rain against my face and nearly bent my umbrella in half. Tornado warnings had been issued and several ripped through Chicago's South Side, as well as through southern Illinois. I managed to get home safely and when I took Fraulein for her evening walk, everything had been transformed once again. The wind had subsided and the rain stopped. In their place came warmth, clear skies and a full moon. What a day! I longed for L.A.'s less moody climate.

Two days later, the real blizzard began. Thankful Greg had no school because it was Records Day, I wouldn't have to argue with him about leaving the house in such awful weather. Carl had a sinus headache from which he endlessly suffered in the relentless Chicago humidity and constant barometric changes. The blizzard allowed him to stay home without my feeling guilty, after he had been tardy and absent so often.

Once again I bundled into every item of winter clothing I had— boots, wool tweed coat, and black wool hat. By the time I had walked the one block to the bus stop, the fierce wind had begun to whip the snow around. Visibility dropped to zero. After waiting twenty minutes for the bus, I climbed aboard and squeezed into the crowd already standing in the aisle.

The snow didn't dampen the good humor of the regular travelers used to such winters, but two men from Florida hadn't prepared themselves for such weather. They begged to be let off at a corner in front of their hotel, not on the driver's everyday route. Other riders joined the Floridians, claiming if they had to walk back to their hotel, they could freeze. The driver never commented, but let them off at the normal stop one block further. As the two tourists exited the bus they waved and said, "We'll see you again in the summer."

I rode to my stop at Michigan and Walter. As I walked to the Club, the wet wind nearly knocked me over. I felt like those poor people I often saw on TV news when I lived in L.A. Back then I felt blessed to live in a more comfortable climate and never dreamed I'd be the one trekking in a blizzard with a temperature of 29 degrees.

Of course there was no end of problems at the Club. Several Bunnies called in to say their cars were stuck in driveways, so they'd called cabs but had no idea when the taxis would show. If the snow kept up, it wouldn't matter who showed for work since I doubted few keyholders would make it there unless they couldn't get home.

Bunny Carmen called to report what became a typical reason for not showing up for work. She had made it to the Dan Ryan Expressway but the traffic hardly moved because of a twenty-seven-car pile-up. So Carmen got off and tried taking side streets, but got stuck. Someone helped her out, only for the car to run out of gas. Carmen got a lift to a gas station and back to her car. Once she got going again, she couldn't get through because too many cars had gotten stuck and blocked the way. So she walked the short distance back to her home.

The Bunnies waiting for cabs started calling to say none had come. I doubted any taxis would be found. I gave every girl who made it in ten well-deserved merits. Mona reported to work late, but at least she made it. She told me, "In all the years I've lived here I've never seen anything like this. Cars and buses are every-which-way on Michigan Avenue." Her voice rose in a screech like the storm outside. "The wind blew me into the street. I could have died. Drivers weren't paying any attention to the traffic lights or even the one-way signs." When she finished, she was so out of breath she sat down.

Shortly after that, Barry telephoned to question me about why I'd included a relief Bunny Mother in my budget when he was forced to cut down on porters and busboys to meet International's budget cuts. Classic Barry—he never bothered to inquire about how everyone was enduring the blizzard.

I had already learned from the accounting office the Chicago Club had made a net profit of $250,000 in 1966 and that International held almost $2,000,000 of unused profits accumulated by the Club since it opened in 1960. Though I wondered why the money hadn't been used as it should, I kept my mouth shut. I offered another solution to Barry who it turned out actually had been concerned about weekend Bunny Mother coverage and not layoffs. "I'll talk with Brooke and work out a schedule to meet that need."

Barry seemed satisfied for the moment—which was good because Bunny Ann called to tell me if I left immediately we could catch a ride home with Tom. I dropped everything and fled out the door. At the Club entrance several cars lodged in a snow bank made it impossible for my ride to free itself. So I left Ann there and caught a ride with Rick whose car was parked on the other side of the street. Nancie and I plowed ankle deep through the drifts and climbed into his waiting vehicle. Rick maneuvered through the many stalled cars and drove down Outer Drive which looked more like a graveyard for unwanted automobiles. Abandoned vehicles clogged the highway making it almost impossible to get through. The wind blew so hard the car shook.

After several attempts to exit the highway, Rick settled on Fullerton Street, joining the long line of hopeful drivers already waiting. It took us a half hour to go three blocks. So when someone in front of us took a sudden left, Rick followed. Though creeping along at no more than ten miles per hour, Rick never stopped. While other cars skidded and swerved and often landed in snow banks, Rick plodded along in his Mustang with no snow tires. His good driving could be the only reason I finally reached my house two hours after I left the Club.

The following morning, January 27, the newscasters reported that Chicago received 25" of snow. It was the worst storm in the city's history. Businesses closed, schools canceled classes, abandoned cars littered the highways, buses didn't run, and people were stranded everywhere. Since Brooke's babysitter couldn't get to her house, Brooke wasn't going to work. So I knew I had no choice but to get dressed and trek in.

With no bus service, I had to walk six blocks to the El. I saw drifts higher than apartment doors and windows. When I reached Newton's Drug Store, I stopped to call the Club, but there were so many people in line waiting to use the phone and waiting for buses, I chose instead to tramp on. Navigating through drifts and abandoned buses and cars, I thought the city looked like what I imagined a war zone would be after the battle was over. Nothing moved. Just dead white silence.

Finally, I made it to the train. Then, once I got off, I had to walk another six blocks to the Club. Snow packed around my boots, spilling over the tops and forming icy pools around my feet. I sought relief and a hot cup of coffee in a shop around the corner from the Club. Bunny Brenda was sitting at the counter. She told me that the Club wouldn't be open until 5:00 pm. I bought a coffee cake for those who did show. Brenda decided to go back to the Club with me and type the schedule.

As expected the phone rang nonstop with Bunnies reporting they couldn't make it into the Club. Ann told me I'd been lucky to leave with Rick since her ride never got free of the drift until 9:00 pm. After that, several cars got stuck in front of them on Outer Drive and they had to dig them out before they could continue. They only traveled a short distance further before they got too stuck to move, so began to walk. A kind motorist picked them up and drove them to a restaurant. Then Ann parlayed another ride—only to get stuck again. Then a policeman gave them a lift, until that car got stuck, too. Ann gave up and finally walked the rest of the way to her apartment.

Thank goodness my own experience hadn't been quite so harrowing. Now I wondered how I would get home today. As predicted, few customers came to the Club so it would close at midnight. All through the day and evening, amazing stories filled each conversation. Brooke called to let me know that her entire apartment building was having a party to pass the time. I didn't appreciate her almost taunting attitude while I'd had to journey through a miserable mess to get to work. I held my tongue.

I joined Barry and several others for dinner, served by one Bunny who had hitchhiked to work and another who had managed to ride the El. By the time I left the Club, the snow and wind had stopped. I got the first train but it didn't stop at my exit so I had to walk about a mile to my house. I didn't mind though because the weather had one more surprise for me. It had turned nice.

The boys had just come in the door when I got there. They'd spent almost the whole day in and out of the snow. We were happy to be safe and together in our warm home. That euphoria ended, however, when I turned on the radio and discovered that the three astronauts, Virgil Grissom, Edward White and Roger Chaffee, had died that day from asphyxiation when a fire swept through the command module of Apollo I during a preflight test at Cape Kennedy. Apollo was due to take off in 25 days, but that would be postponed indefinitely. Carl, Greg and I talked about the tragedy for nearly a half hour. We would always remember the date: January 27, 1967.

Carl often surprised me. This time he'd had enough sense to get milk at the store since none would be delivered. "I heard all the stores were being raided and the food supplies would be scarce," he said. "That seemed to be bigger news than the Apollo." He seemed disillusioned by the self-centeredness of people. Though I often felt the same way, I tried to explain how individual survival overrode anything. Wasn't I faced with that myself?

The next morning my neighbors and others in the area formed block groups to remove snow from side streets and shovel out cars. Few said anything about Apollo. Most seemed only concerned about their own immediate needs.

On Monday the schools remained closed as the city-wide clean-up and digging out continued. I attempted to move back into routine gear as ordinary life resumed.

Chapter Fifteen

Count Down

Congratulations! You're about to embark on one of the most exciting experiences a Bunny or Playmate can have— making a personal appearance. Whether it's for a promotion, a contest, or a business meeting, a personal appearance puts you in the spotlight. If you are chosen to make such a personal appearance, it means PLAYBOY Magazine and the Playboy Clubs feel that you are truly representative of the feminine charm and beauty for which Playboy is noted. "Playboy Promotions and You" Brochure.

If January had been the month from hell, February started out quite ordinary. Bunny Patti had an abortion after she called her boyfriend in New York and a woman answered. Carol's lover broke the news that he wasn't going to divorce his wife to marry her. Playboy's modeling service booked more girls than usual for shows while others snuck off, against Playboy's rules, to moonlight at the Gaslight to make enough money for their bills. The IRS ruled not to allow Bunnies to write off make-up and hairpieces based on the government's claim that all women had those.

On the less usual side of life, many Bunnies who aspired to be actresses saw persistent efforts pay off. Bunnies Colleen and Elaine had their dreams come true when they packed up and left Playboy to honor Hollywood movie contracts. With each departure, I had a small celebration. Unfortunately many Bunnies drank too much at these events and came to work with serious hangovers.

An unexpected event occurred one morning after I got Carl and Greg off to school and went back to sleep because I was so exhausted. At about 11:00 am someone banged on the front door and awakened me. I thought it was the landlord dropping by to harass me about the boys playing too loudly in the courtyard or about Fraulein's barking. Mr. Anderson's complaints seemed to happen on a more regular basis as the months passed. Maybe he had had enough of overdue rent payments.

I threw on my bathrobe and slippers and shuffled, yawning and stretching, to the door. Before I had fully awakened, Lawrence Marconi pushed the door open. I blocked his entry. "What are you doing here?"

"I want to talk with you about Brooke." He actually whimpered like a hurt boy.

"Brooke?"

"Yeah. I know you talked to her about me and I want to know what she said." He put pressure on the door. I braced myself against it to keep him on the stoop.

"I don't know what you're talking about and I don't want to talk to you, now or ever. For that matter I don't want to see you anymore, either." I slammed the door in his face.

Though he skulked off, I feared I hadn't seen the end of Lawrence Marconi. Why had Brooke told Lawrence anything? I thought Brooke had ended it with him never to see him again. Had Brooke also become a person I couldn't trust, or had she felt too much shame to let me know she kept some sort of connection to Lawrence?

That night after everyone in the household had gone to bed, I heard strange noises—footsteps and then a clatter—outside my apartment. I looked out my bedroom window but saw nothing. The uncommon sounds persisted. I crept down the stairs in the dark and checked each door and window of the main level to make sure they had been locked. I pulled drapes slowly aside to search the courtyard. I saw no motion. After Lawrence's visit that morning, I suspected my imagination had run wild, picturing that the crazy man had come back to kill me. "I really have been watching too many movies," I thought and stumbled back up the stairs to bed.

I of course made it to work quite late. I didn't care. Coco should cover my absence. In the elevator, I reminded myself that Barry was concerned about there being too many Bunny Mothers and thought no more about my tardiness.

Barry was waiting in my office. He had come to work earlier than usual. "You should be making room inspections."

This didn't make sense. He knew I normally didn't make inspections until later in the day. To avoid any confrontation with him, though, I did as he requested. When I returned an hour later, I discovered the real reason he wanted me out of the office. He'd been talking with Coco behind my back. Coco reported that Barry ordered her to take Bonnie, his latest fling, off the Elevator and put her on the Door so she'd work later and not pester him.

"I guess he's tired of her now as he gets with all the others."

"You know Barry," Coco sang her reply.

"I wonder why he didn't tell me that himself." I never expected an answer and Coco didn't offer one. I assumed we both understood why. I had more integrity than either Barry or Coco.

The encounter with Lawrence paled in comparison to two February events at the Club—they concerned drugs and the union. Since my first day at the Club I had heard rumors (and not just from Mrs. Bundy) about drugs being used by many Playboy employees. I had already experienced such antics first hand with the Bunnies. I had often smelled marijuana in the Bunnies' dressing room or in an employee's car, but hadn't seen anyone smoking anything other than a cigarette. I had the smarts to understand people throughout the country used marijuana and other illegal substances. Playboy certainly hadn't cornered that market. Such drug usage only made the news more often than in the past so it made management more sensitive to possible local abuse.

When those rumors filtered to Barry from a key holder he went on the warpath. But naturally he wasn't about to do the dirty work. Instead, he ordered me to stay after 8:00 pm one night and search the Bunnies' lockers when the girls had either gone home or to their work-stations for the evening. So I painstakingly took everything from each locker. I went through every purse and every pocket. I felt every seam just like a drug enforcement officer. I found nothing. When I told Barry he seemed unhappy, rather than pleased.

The next day Barry's spirits rose, though, when he found out that Mrs. Bundy had done a search of the girls' rooms in the Mansion and discovered "peculiar looking needles" in Bunny Carrie's possessions.

Though Barry had never given me the idea he even knew the Bunny's name, he expressed his certainty that Carrie had to be the same one about whom the key holder gossiped. I wondered if that keyholder had it in for the Bunny because she'd rejected him.

It turned out Carrie had been arrested for three outstanding traffic tickets the very day Mrs. Bundy searched the dorms. This came as no surprise to me because Carrie once had to go to driving school or lose her temporary license—and she'd got the temporary after paying another Bunny $25.00 to go to the classes the first time. Carrie's record was a disaster, but then what could we expect from a girl who regularly got lost driving to Chicago from Indiana?"

When the police searched Carrie, they found drugs. Her lawyer stopped by my office to let me know that the Bunny would miss work because she was in jail. That arrest probably made Mrs. Bundy especially happy since Carrie was three months behind in her rent. Mrs. Bundy had delivered her ultimatum only a few days earlier: Carrie either paid the amount she owed at the end of that week or she'd have to move out.

"It looks like she found another place to live," Mrs. Bundy sneered when I reported Carrie's whereabouts.

Traffic violations and drugs weren't the only reasons Bunnies got arrested. One time a policeman hit on Adrian when he stopped her car. She swore at him and he arrested her for disorderly conduct. Mona, Adrian's passenger, bolted out of the car and swung at the officer. He arrested her for assault and battery. I took them off the schedule until the mess was straightened out but the two Bunnies never faced any disciplinary action for breaking Playboy rules.

The second major February event came when the Chicago Club employees voted in a union after a strike by the New York Club Bunnies. Such a move may have stopped unsupervised drug searches, but the Bunnies would discover being unionized wouldn't be what they had thought. Under the union the girls received $1.45 an hour and a guarantee of $68.00 for a forty-hour week. They no longer could arrange for their own replacements and they couldn't work over 40 hours a week or they'd have to be paid time and a half—and management wasn't about to see that happen too often. When the Bunnies reported for work, they were assured four hours pay. The girls received only two paid holidays and one week paid vacation which meant they couldn't take off on a whim as many of them had done in the past. They would be paid a bonus factor for all Playboy items they sold, such as mugs. They didn't have to pay bartender or busboy fees or have wages deducted for costume cleaning. Yet Bunnies had to produce under that system or leave. Scheduling was much stricter and far less flexible. Gone were the days when a girl could be taken off the schedule for a month because she wanted to go away with her boyfriend. She'd have to make do with the allotted week leave.

Perhaps the most punishing aspect of the union regulations came in the structuring of tips. A 15% charge was added to each key-holder's check as a gratuity and if he wished to pay more, he could in cash only. Keyholders received a monthly bill for all the charged items. That meant tips, the mainstay for every Bunny which in the past had given many as much as $300.00 in weekly earnings, be-came far less lucrative. Overall, Bunnies on average earned less.

I wondered if under this system Bunnies would be asked for fewer command performances without pay at Hef's parties or weekends with keyholders who were Hef's special friends. On those weekends the Bunnies were called companions. Neither practice would be a loss though the Bunnies persisted in thinking the right rich guy might come along. I doubted the companions were looking for a per-manent relationship especially when many had been overheard mak-ing fun of the girls. The companions had on one occasion during the movie at the Mansion made one girl stand in front of the projector with a banana in her mouth while a sex scene played. From what I deduced, command performances could often be humiliating and rarely rewarding. Yet if a girl refused, under the old system, she could be placed on the black list and eventually even terminated—for Bunny Image, that catch-all excuse. Hardly fair choices.

Some Chicago Bunnies, like the New York girls, didn't relish the union system. Many looked for new jobs rather than have the privi-lege of striking, something they never had under the old way. It took all my and management's wits to explain to the Bunnies that even though only a few Bunnies voted for the union, 51% of all Playboy employees wanted it. So all employees legally had to be in the union.

On a positive note, for the first time the Bunnies had a grievance procedure in place which meant no girl could be fired on a vague pretense like Bunny Image without just and documented cause. Yet some girls, those on management's favored list, didn't like that because the union rules lumped them with the other girls. It also meant Barry couldn't set the Bunnies' salaries as he had—according to his fancy, usually based on the girl's looks and how much she kissed his ass rather than on her seniority and performance.

The grievance process was tested almost immediately. For the second time in my experience a Bunny came to me with the story of a keyholder pinching her butt while the Room Director stood by and did nothing. That time the Bunny filed a grievance which sent all the Room Directors, to my pleasure, into a tailspin.

When Ed, the male union representative met with me over the grievance, I discovered he was scared to death of the Bunnies. He made a living as a bartender and to him the Bunnies came from a sophisticated place on the other side of the world from his own. I didn't let on the girls were hard-working stiffs just like him. Better he stayed in awe because then he wouldn't be difficult.

The best time in February came when I finally met with Doctor Cohen, the plastic surgeon. He told me outright, "You have a man's nose on a woman's face." He took pictures and showed me. "But you'll probably want to keep it when you see these."

The pictures were the best I had ever seen of me. They made me more glamorous than the ones the Camera Bunny took. "No. Despite how wonderful I look in these, I still see a big, ugly nose in the mirror each morning."

Doctor Cohen then showed me what he planned to do by sketching on one of the photos. "I'll lower the bridge and make the nose smaller all around, but not so small that it doesn't match your angular face."

I watched him draw the lines trying to imagine the real thing. The doctor said it would cost $500.00 but that I could put most of it on my insurance. I made the appointment for the operation on April 7, which my horoscope said would be a good time. A few days after my initial appointment I discovered I would only have to pay $150.00 because I had major medical insurance. Life seemed good.

It didn't take long for someone from Playboy to chill my spirits even more than the ten degree temperature outside. The first one to pop my balloon that day was Barry, who said, "I'm changing policy. The Bunny Mother will no longer have to do floor inspections. It will be solely the Room Directors' duty."

"You don't think I can do the job?" Barry's decision offended me.

"It's not that, but you have other duties." Barry paced and again didn't make eye contact with me. "Besides," he pushed his glasses to the top of his head, "they're in a better position to observe the Bunnies throughout their shifts."

"And harass them," I yelled. "You're doing this to protect the Room Directors because I've been on their case about how badly they treat the Bunnies. They tell Bunnies things like 'your mouth is as big as your ass' or 'you smell like a whore.' Is that part of the Room Directors' job description?" I didn't wait for a comment, but plowed ahead. "The Room Directors treat the Bunnies like," I took a deep breath to settle my indignation, "like they are nothing but a commodity."

"You're taking this all wrong."

"So tell me, how am I supposed to take it?" I circled around my desk to face Barry. He had to stop pacing.

"It's more efficient this way." He left the office without further explanation.

I understood why this had happened. I had been forced to hire Bunny Petra, the girlfriend of the costume designer and friend of management. Petra at 4'10" and 85 pounds hadn't exactly met Bunny Image. However, she used her connections to suit her every whim. She never let anyone forget that she knew people in high places.

Despite unionization Petra continued to schedule her own shifts and days and never as a reserve, so work didn't interfere with her personal life. I could do little with a Bunny who'd run to International and whine. Though other girls would have been fired for calling a member "jerk," I could only suspend Petra by Barry's direct orders. Such favoritism angered the other girls and lowered the over-all morale.

One day I finally could do something about Petra. When I made an inspection in the Living Room, I discovered Petra breaking one of the top written rules—she was sitting at a booth with a keyholder. I could hardly believe the blatant violation, which insulted other patrons because Petra was showing a preference for that customer.

At first I was miffed. Then I realized I had Petra. I walked over to the booth and looked straight at Petra who had made no attempt to cover up her error. "Petra, you're fired."

I whirled around and caught the delighted smiles of the other Bunnies and the Room Director. Petra scrambled after me. "You can't do this to me. I'll go to Barry."

I answered over my shoulder, "You do that." I knew that neither Barry nor International could let that violation slide. Not only had she broken a very important rule, but the Club could lose its liquor license for the mingling.

Now, after Barry's edict about room inspections, I reached for the phone to call Judy and give my resignation. Before I could dial, Tom burst into my office. It probably was a good thing. I hadn't made all the preparations I needed.

Brooke entered the office just in time to see Tom pick up the schedule and hear him ask, "There's a lotta changes. Are you getting medical excuses and tracking tardiness?"

"That's why I'm here, isn't it?" I didn't hide my sarcasm. "And it really isn't your concern. Your job is the floor. Or didn't Barry tell you that?"

"I need an extra girl in the Play Room tonight," Tom hissed.

"It's 7:30! Where do you think I'll find one this late? You should have known this early enough to let me find someone."

"Well, at least try, sweetheart," Tom ordered.

"My name is Mrs. Bonura to you, doll," I answered through lips so tight they hurt. The blood in my head pounded hard enough for me to hear it.

Tom simply ordered, "Another girl. Tonight."

When he left, Brooke, who had sat nearby in quiet amazement, said, "Well, I guess there'll be no more thank you gifts."

Neither Brooke nor I made an effort to find another Bunny. "Tom and the rest of the Room Directors can go to hell if they think I'm here for their beck and call and to take the fall for their errors," I said with as much venom in my voice as I had ever displayed. "They don't know who they're messing with."

No sooner did those words flow from my mouth than the phone rang. "Now what?" I picked up the phone.

Hef's head secretary called with a most important assignment, at least to the secretary. Hugh Hefner was ready for a Bunny to model an old promotion costume.

"Now?" I shrieked.

"Of course." The secretary's smug attitude irritated me. "We can't disappoint Mr. Hefner, can we?"

"We've been waiting for this to happen for five weeks, so what's the hurry now?

"Mr. Hefner is ready tonight."

"This Club could close down or go on strike and the most important thing for Hefner is to pull a girl off the floor to model an ancient costume." I caught Brooke nodding in agreement.

"We'll expect her soon then," Hef's secretary said and hung up.

I held the dead receiver in my hand. "Won't Tom be delighted when he's told he has to pull Trudi from the floor and send her over to the Mansion?" My mood soared with the delicious prospect.

"Tom won't yell at the boss, I bet," Brooke snickered. "After what I've seen today I have half a mind to take that job with the Board of Education."

"Oh no! Not yet. Don't abandon me." Brooke had told me earlier in the week about making a possible change. "I won't be here much longer and we can split this joint together." I called Tom to let him know Hef's orders. Half way through his harangue, I hung up.

Brooke's mouth had dropped open and stayed that way until I finished my call. "What are you talking about?" she stammered. "When are you going?"

While we waited for Trudi, I went over the whole Coco-Miami story.

"I'm not working for Coco," Brooke declared. "It's bad enough that this place operates by the seat of the pants. Throw in Coco and the whole Club will be in turmoil."

"Maybe management deserves just that." This thought delighted me.

"The girls won't like it and don't deserve it," Brooke rebutted.

"I thought the Bunnies preferred Coco." I started to straighten my desk in preparation to leave for the day.

"They say that when they're mad. They're just like children. But they know they need you." Brooke stood up. "You're organized. You go by the book as you should. That way everyone's treated the same.

All the girls know it'll be hell with Coco."

"That's good to hear. But," I shook my head, "I'm afraid it's too late."

Trudi's appearance stopped our conversation. Once the Bunny was dressed and headed for the Mansion, Brooke and I left for the evening without checking one room. I also hadn't mentioned Lawrence. I'd do that at a more appropriate time.

When we parted, Brooke announced, "I am pursuing the Board of Ed job. Maybe they won't hire me soon."

During my bus ride home I couldn't concentrate on my magazine. Running over and over in my mind was how much I hated to go back to that hell hole in the morning. Playboy to outsiders looked like a well-oiled, well-run machine, but on the inside anything good that did happen was all luck. Nothing would ever change until the words trust and respect entered into Playboy's vocabulary and treatment of its female employees. For that brief moment I looked forward to housework, laundry and helping my boys with homework, rather than fighting for a career in a world dominated by men.

I checked through the mail when I first entered the townhouse. Angelo sent a $40.00 support payment. Holding the check buoyed my spirits. I needed to deposit it right away and prayed the money got to the bank before any checks bounced, especially the rent payment.

Besides the check from Angelo, Clark returned my Valentine's card with a quarter to buy a nicer one. I didn't appreciate his immature dig. He did write a PS telling me it was 80 degrees in L.A. It was only 20 in Chicago and I hated thinking about the difference.

That night instead of writing in my journal, I updated my resumé and made a list of prospective California employers, many of whom had recently contacted me after I had put out feelers. Would I be rushing to another job if Playboy had kept its promise about my promotion to Bunny Director? Could I have made any difference as a Bunny Director? I doubted it.

Though parts of Chicago pleased me—Lake Michigan, the museums and the river—the weather was horrid. It was time to return to sun and warm days without unbearable humidity. I also wanted everything in order after I spent what I deemed a paid vacation in Miami. Though I would have to endure Florida's humidity, I'd at least see the sun again.

Thrilled that February was a short month, I prepared for a busy March. Fortunately I had less than a month until my operation and six months until I gave notice, unless of course management got rid of me sooner. But sadly, as the weeks moved on, Lawrence became more worrisome.

During the first week in March, he called me every day. Usually I avoided the calls, but on the few occasions I had no choice he demanded to see me. "I've already explained to you I have another beau and I know nothing about Brooke's relationship with you. Now stop calling me."

Two days later he appeared at my townhouse. Just before that Carl had answered the phone. He didn't recognize Lawrence's voice at first. Once Carl did identify Lawrence, he gave the caller a pre-planned message, "My mother's not here."

Lawrence asked when I was expected back. Carl told him in about an hour. Not long after, the doorbell rang. Thank heaven, Greg answered the door. At only eleven years old his muscular build actually seemed more powerful than Lawrence's slight body.

"Can your mother at least come to the door?" Lawrence begged.

I shouted from upstairs, "NO!"

Lawrence yelled back, "Then when will you be available?"

To get rid of him for the moment and gather my thoughts, I answered, "Friday."

Greg slammed the door.

That didn't work. Lawrence waited for me outside the Club Friday night and followed me to the bus. I walked as fast as I could without answering Lawrence's plaintive: "Why won't you talk to me?"

"Why won't you have dinner with me so we can discuss this whole thing?" He grabbed at my arm, but my fast pace foiled his attempt. "I don't date Brooke anymore."

I remembered the calls Lawrence had made to Carlie. He must have believed no one knew. How stupid! When Carlie rejected his invitations, he called either Brooke or me, but we of course never took him up on his offers.

Luckily the crowded streets prevented Lawrence from any possible physical contact. I boarded the bus, leaving him at the curb. My heart raced to the point of making me dizzy. A good man noticed my distress and offered me his seat in the otherwise standing room only transportation. I laid my head back, closed my eyes and envisioned once again Lawrence's intent to harm me. My body trembled with such force it shook the seat. Without looking I knew everyone was staring at me. I was scared but had no idea who to turn to for help or advice.

That night sleep wouldn't come. Every sound—gate opening and closing, doors slamming, creaks, footsteps—raised the possibility of Lawrence spying on me from a dark alley. I couldn't continue to live like that. I had to confront him one last time.

Chapter Sixteen

Trading Places

PLAYBOY ORANGE HAS GONE TO WAR: If the Rabbit flags flying over Clubs are not as orangey as usual, it's because the nylon regularly used for the banners is being made up into parachutes to drop food and supplies over Viet Nam. The Playboy Paper, September 1967

As the Viet Nam War raged on, Playboy wanted to support the troops in some way. The corporation often donated to causes such as children's foundations or provided Bunny entertainment for a fund-raiser. Soldiers' needs rated high on Hugh Hefner's list.

In that same spirit, one March day I accompanied several Bunnies to the nearby Great Lakes Naval Hospital. The Bunnies entertained the ambulatory veterans and had bedside visits with those who couldn't be moved. Though wounded, the young soldiers never stopped smiling the whole time. They did however regret that the Bunnies didn't come in their ears and tails. Rather they wore the standard and quite appropriate Playboy promotional outfit. It had been recently approved by Hugh Hefner and consisted of a chemise with an above-the-knee white skirt and black bodice, a full length matching coat with the colors reversed, a black with white accent pill-box hat and black pumps.

Though the Bunnies put on their most optimistic faces while at the hospital, the girls and I couldn't hold back our sadness when we got back to the meager comfort of my office.

"I had no idea. They are just boys," Ingrid said. She couldn't have been any older than the wounded men she visited.

"Some of them have no legs," a tearful Sadie commented. "I can't imagine having no legs."

"How about that eighteen-year-old whose head was wired together," Joanne added. "What a bummer."

"Yeah, but we saw so many who I don't think will make it." Sadie wiped her eyes. "They're too battered and could hardly breathe. And most of them couldn't be more than twenty, could they?"

"It really makes you realize there's a war going on," Ingrid murmured.

"It's so futile," Mona added. "What are we doing in that godforsaken place any way?"

The room fell silent. The only sounds were the girls sniffling and blowing their noses. The depression could be felt like a heavy wet blanket spread over all of us.

Sadie perked up. "I'm going to Viet Nam on a Playboy promotional trip. The money's good and I can help in some small way."

"What about your kid?" Mona asked.

"My mother said she'd take care of him." Sadie's voice trailed off. "I can use the extra money. It's more meaningful than playing baseball for the additional cash."

"Or getting totally nude and shaving our body so some guy could paint us in red and white stripes like a barber pole for a lay-out in the VIP Magazine," Ramona huffed. "We got paid a hundred bucks for that gig, and everyone said there was no harm since the guy painting us didn't dig girls."

"Yeah," Joanne shouted out. "That's right. I remember, 'cause they told us no one would recognize us with all that paint. But I knew better." She shook her finger as though scolding the others. "My boyfriend then was a doctor and he would have known about it 'cause my crotch would have been shaved. So I didn't do the shoot."

"How 'bout going on the radio like I did and telling the world the quality of our keyholders has gone downhill." Mona giggled. "Man, have I had hell to pay for that slip-up."

Everyone laughed and nodded in agreement.

"I'm sure glad I got a chance to kick those stewardess' asses though," Ramona boasted.

I remembered that day with pleasure, too. Five Bunnies went on a

TV game show pilot called *Play Ball*. They played against TWA stewardesses selected from a computer search to ensure the brightest appeared. All had assumed the "dumb" Bunnies would lose miserably. Instead the Bunnies shut-out the stewardesses 8 to 0. I won, too, when International praised my choice of contestants—an Asian, a Black, a redhead, a blond and a brunette.

I surveyed the girls, all sitting in silence staring at the floor. Where had their thoughts run off to?

Joanne broke the unnerving stillness. "I need to do something like going to Nam."

"Yeah you do, girl," Sadie agreed.

"What do you mean?" I asked.

"It's no secret that Sue has named me in her divorce suit because I dated her husband for a while." Joanne sounded as though she was already on the witness stand.

"What were you thinking anyway?" Mona asked.

"He told me they had separated," Joanne whined.

"And you believed him?" Mona pressed.

"No matter, I could use the bucks. I need to get away," Joanne said as a way to close the subject.

As I listened to the girls' banter, I thought of Joanne's complicated situation. She was one of eight children raised on oatmeal and potatoes by a struggling divorced mother. Joanne herself became the single mother of three before she was twenty years old. She still searched for Mr. Right without facing the reality that few men would take on a ready-made family. As one of the older Bunnies, Joanne neared the time she would be terminated for Image. She'd probably go the way of most former Bunnies—work at the Gaslight. For Joanne, that might be a good thing. The strain of her life was taking its toll in her face, which her hard-lived years had begun to line like a road map. I empathized with Joanne. Life was tough for most of us, including me.

Sadie turned to me and brought the conversation back to her. "What will I earn?"

My mind had wandered off in a dreadful direction when Sadie asked. I could only picture Sadie coming home in a body bag like so many young men shown on the news.

"Alyce? Did you hear me?" Sadie asked. "What will I earn doing this, besides good feelings?"

"Let's see." I pulled out a pay schedule from a file.

"You're too damn organized." Sadie chuckled.

"First of all, Sadie was picked by International which in itself is special." I smiled at Sadie. "You'll be gone twenty days with all expenses paid. In addition you'll earn about $150.00 a week."

"Not bad for a girl from the South Side." Sadie danced around the room.

"What will you wear?" Ingrid asked.

"I'll travel in what we got on. I've been told to take a couple of costumes and our shorts outfits." Sadie shrugged. "Just like here."

After I finished ticking off those figures and the Viet Nam promotional had been examined from all angles, the girls wandered off one by one, to their dressing room. Some put on their street clothes while others readied themselves for their normal shifts.

Ingrid, one of the newly hired V.I.P. Room Bunnies, stayed.

"Is there something else you want to talk about?" I asked.

She nodded. "Management doesn't care that a war is going on unless they can get some publicity." Ingrid's Swedish accent became more noticeable as she talked.

"I think most people are troubled by the war. But," I walked to the couch and sat next to Ingrid, "they feel helpless so they need to find a way to forget it. To let life go on with some normalcy."

Ingrid took off the pillbox hat and twirled it in her hand. She didn't make any attempt to leave. She also didn't speak.

I studied the gorgeous natural blonde next to me. Though not overly busty, her proportions fit her tall slender frame, which she maneuvered with the grace of a ballerina. Ingrid had not a single arrogant fiber. Given time, she could probably get every man in Chicago to fall in love with her.

Ingrid broke her silence. "I need to tell you something, but no one else can know."

"Ok," I said, praying Ingrid didn't need an abortion. I had grown tired of being the go-between for so many girls. Even though I had been ordered not to provide the illegal abortion information, I still did, especially after Toti's suicide. I had to help these girls, law or no law. Saving the girls' lives seemed more important.

"Barry came to my apartment uninvited. Though I was able to put him off then, he calls me all the time. He always seems to be wherever I work, watching me."

"Has he tried anything?" Barry did have the power to get what he wanted from the girls when he wanted it, but I hoped he'd honor Ingrid's refusals.

"No. I try to avoid him and mind my own business, but I can't put him off forever. I'm afraid I'll lose my job."

I wanted to assure Ingrid that couldn't happen now there was a union. But I knew anything was possible when it came to Playboy management. I had opened my mouth to give Ingrid some sort of consoling words when Brooke popped in.

Ingrid hastened away. "Did I interrupt?" Brooke asked as she grabbed something from a file and headed for the door.

"No. It's ok. We all got a little depressed after our visit to the Naval hospital."

"Yeah, I bet," Brooke murmured.

When Brooke left I enjoyed a few moments of silence in my empty office. Then Barry called. "Why have you only scheduled three girls in the Penthouse?" he screamed. I held the receiver away from me, but could still hear him.

"That was your decision as of three weeks ago," I answered when I replaced the phone against my ear. I wanted to laugh.

"Are you sure?" Barry's tone was still combative.

I dug through the schedules and pulled out the "First Page." I read the part to Barry where he ordered that change.

Barry didn't acknowledge his error. "Put four girls there now and open the V.I.P. Room with two." He hung up.

I yanked Marlee from V.I.P. Though she met the language requirement for the room, I always made Marlee, born to Arabic parents, the last to be scheduled for V.I.P. because she spoke Arabic with a New England—her birth place—accent. Once the substitutions had been made, I waited for the Room Directors to call with their complaints.

The moment I thought that, Rick called. "Where's that fourth Bunny?"

"She's on her way." Once Marlee got on the floor, he'd call back about the choice.

"Is she walking or crawling?" I noted Rick's frustration, but could only laugh at his question.

I surely wouldn't ever miss Barry's wishy-washy management style. Before he went off the deep end again, I wanted to tell him about the shamrock stick-ons. But he hung up too fast. When he noticed the Bunnies weren't wearing any on their shoulders for the St. Patrick's Day celebration, he'd call back. Yet would he understand that the glue gave them a rash? Every time International dreamed up some promotional idea like the shamrocks, the Jamaican straw hats and the Mardi Gras beads, the girls seemed bound to suffer some nasty side effect.

One thing for certain, it was never boring at the Chicago Club. Quite to the contrary, I rarely had a moment to even go to the bathroom. Yet who would ever have thought I would be even remotely connected to President Kennedy's assassination?

One Friday late in March, Detective Head of the Chicago Police Department appeared at my office door. Even before he introduced himself, I found him quite handsome, young and well built, perhaps a weight lifter. He showed his badge and told me that he had been temporarily assigned to the F.B.I. He also let me know he had been one of President Kennedy's bodyguards when Kennedy visited Chicago.

What Bunny had gotten in trouble this time? I immediately settled on Joan who had called asking for her last paycheck to be wired to her in San Juan. Joan had gambled away all her money and couldn't get home.

It wasn't about Joan, though. Detective Head showed me a newspaper article with a picture of a man and asked if I had ever seen him in the Club. "He looks vaguely familiar, but I can't be sure," I answered. Though the detective attempted to cover the headline, I could read the man's name: Gordon Novel. The name rang a bell but at that moment I didn't know why.

"Well, Mrs. Bonura," Detective Head explained, "he's probably one of the most wanted men in America."

My heart beat increased. "What has he done?"

"He was the former Assistant District Attorney in New Orleans. Jim Garrison, the District Attorney there, wants Novel as a material witness in the plot to kill President Kennedy." He paused.

"But why are you here?" I asked. How could the Club be implicated in this?

"The New Orleans Police told me Gordon Novel had been seeing a Chicago Bunny."

"Two Chicago Bunnies worked in New Orleans, but one is no longer employed with Playboy. The other, Ramona, lives at the Mansion and is on today's schedule," I said, and then took the detective over to the key room to see if the wanted man had ever been at the Chicago Club.

Don in the Key Room recognized Novel right away. Though the records showed Novel had never been at the Chicago Club, International reported he had a key which had been canceled a year before.

Back in my office, I had Bunny Ramona pulled from the floor to talk with Detective Head. According to Ramona, Gordon Novel dated and at one time had been engaged to the Chicago Bunny Abby Mulligan.

"My God," I said. "I terminated her yesterday for not returning from her leave of absence and for not calling in."

Ramona reported that a man had called the Mansion a couple of weeks earlier, claiming that Abby's parents had said she had gone back to Chicago, but no one had heard from or seen her.

Detective Head thanked us and left. Ramona returned to the floor. I thought the whole issue had been put to rest until a couple of weeks later when a reporter from the United Press telephoned to ask if we still had a Bunny working at the Chicago Club by the name of Abby Mulligan. I told him no. As he probed further, the reporter asked for a picture of Abby. I again said, "No," and asked why he wanted it. The reporter told me that Gordon Novel had been arrested in a suburb of Columbus, Ohio, where he had apparently gone in pursuit of Abby. The newspapers wanted to run the Bunny's picture.

A week after that call, Barry sent me copies of two articles about Gordon Novel's arrest and his connection to Abby Mulligan. The newspaper reported that the new charge filed against Novel accused him of conspiring to commit simple burglary of a munitions dump in Houma, about 40 miles southwest of New Orleans.

Relieved by the news that the police had found their fugitive, I finally could put the situation behind me. Though my involvement had been minimal, the strain of an F.B.I. probe into Kennedy's assassination stretched my nerves to the max. I knew once the F.B.I.'s goal had been set, they could take down anyone. No matter how irrational my feelings, I feared my name would be left in some Bureau file forever to haunt me.

Carlie stopped in for inspection. "You look prettier than ever," I commented.

"Less stress, more sleep will do wonders." Carlie twirled. "You should try it."

"Yeah?" I snickered. "In my next life." There was a positive transformation in Carlie since Chris Malloy had been terminated and left Chicago.

"My word, this office is like a refrigerator," Carlie complained as she rubbed the chill from her bare arms.

I pointed to the radiator torn from the wall. Several pieces of pipe lay nearby. "Barry promised remodeling. You can see how far it's gone."

"But that radiator has been out for weeks," Carlie grumbled. "Aren't you freezing?"

"Off and on. I have a little electric heater under my desk." I moved my legs away for Carlie to see.

"Geesh!" Carlie said as she walked toward the door. She stopped and turned. "Oh, I forgot. Some guy by the name of John Caruso asked about you."

I rummaged through my memory. "I don't recall the name. He's not another cop, is he?"

"No. He's a keyholder and seemed very interested in you. He saw you making inspections when you were still doing them." Carlie walked out the door, waving over her shoulder. "Ta! Ta!"

In light of my encounters with Lawrence Marconi, I cautioned myself about getting involved with another admirer. Fortunately I hadn't heard from Lawrence in a while, but I kept a look-out, half expecting the pest to pop up at every corner.

Then there was the last letter from Clark in which he wrote, "You're ruining me because I can't get you out of my mind." It left me unmoved. He didn't seem to feel bad enough yet to leave his wife for me.

As soon as Carlie left, Patti came in. I let her know that she had to be suspended for two weeks because of her perpetual tardiness and caustic attitude with the members.

"My horoscope predicted this loss of money," she mumbled. "But I can't give up my earnings because I've gotta pay my sitter no matter what. I guaranteed her even though her lateness has me in this pickle."

"Perhaps she'll like the break also. You may both need the rest, and you can have some quality time with your daughter."

Patti was unwilling to accept any reasoning. "I'm gointa file a grievance. Then we'll see what'll happen when the union gets a hold of this. It's all favoritism." She glared at me. "I'll be back as soon as I talk with Barry. I know he's behind this whole business."

"Talking to Barry might not be such a good idea," I warned. "But when you calm down, do come back to finish our talk."

Patti didn't answer. She stormed out the door.

I agreed with Patti. There was some favoritism because the Bunnies who dated management never got bad reports. But such antics could also work in the opposite way. I had heard of a keyholder who bribed Room Directors to get one Bunny fired because he wanted her all for himself. Sometimes it was difficult to sort out who did what and for what reason.

About a half hour later Barry crashed into my office yelling, "When a Bunny is suspended she should leave the building. That includes Patti."

"She and I still have some talking to do. I told her to come back after she saw you." I laid down the stack of memos I had foolishly thought I'd get read.

"Be sure she's out of here before the dinner rush." Barry started out the door, but popped back in. "It's really cold in here."

I pointed to the radiator without looking up from the memos I had gone back to.

"Umm," he said and left.

Patti did return and through my persuasiveness, agreed she had difficulty being kind to some customers. "Especially when I've had little sleep. My daughter Terry has been sick off and on all winter and has kept me up."

"So maybe a break will be good, as I said earlier. God knows we all can use one." I smiled.

"Yeah." Patti tore the grievance form in half and tossed it into the waste basket. "I know I have to work on getting here on time, too. I'll make sure the sitter comes a half hour sooner or tell her she's fired."

Barry stopped me on my out for the evening. I explained what started out as a grievance ended with Patti accepting her suspension. "She'll probably return with a better attitude," I said, almost as a challenge.

Barry looked at his feet. "Good job," he murmured. He looked at me and said, "Have a nice evening."

I couldn't understand why Barry had such a difficult time accepting others' successes or admitting he sometimes over-reacted. Oh, well. Soon there will be no more Barry.

The whole male thing from Barry to Clark and every guy in between put me in a foul mood. Again I swore off men for the time being. In less than a week I would enter the hospital for the nose operation. Even with the anticipated pain, a quiet recovery and lots of rest seemed the perfect remedy for my unhappy state of mind. Leaving the boys on their own during my hospital stay would be the only drawback. But first I would celebrate an old-fashioned Easter with Carl and Greg in a couple of days.

After the boys found their Easter baskets which took surprisingly long for boys their ages, they made me breakfast and served me in bed. That too came as a surprise because I hadn't expected the special care and because the food had been well thought out and prepared. They brought me a pot of coffee, orange juice, a cheese omelet, a toasted English muffin with strawberry jam and a sticky bun from a local bakery.

Even though the weather turned cool and cloudy and it drizzled most of the day, the boys and Fraulein played outside for hours. Regardless of the holiday, there were still chores to do, including the wash. As I walked to the laundry, I kept a sharp look-out at the high rise on the corner to be sure I didn't run into Lawrence. I hadn't heard from him since his last call about a week before when I told him if he didn't quit bothering me I'd have to contact my friend Detective Head. After I blurted that out, I thought that actually, it wouldn't be such a bad plan. But Lawrence hadn't been seen or heard from since.

Despite having to do the laundry, and that the boys and dog getting filthy, I had a pleasant day. No rush, no phone calls, no Barry, no Lawrence, no abortions. Our little family ended the day munching on Easter treats and playing cards. As usual, Angelo never called or sent a card to his sons. I made up for that by giving each boy a foot-high chocolate bunny I said Angelo told me to buy. Both boys seemed delighted but their faint air of suspicion nearly broke my heart.

Chapter Seventeen

Absence Makes the Heart Grow Fonder

VIET CONG BULLET FOILED BY PLAYBOY : *Already a devoted fan of PLAYBOY,* Sp/4 *Donald Lasillo now owes his life to it. Last February Donald was badly injured by an enemy land mine, but dragged himself back into fire to help a wounded comrade. He was hit again, and this time it would have been through his heart, but for a copy of PLAYBOY he tucked in his shirt. Donald is recuperating now, probably reading an unmarred copy of his favorite magazine.* The Playboy Paper 1967

The Viet Nam War escalated to such a point Washington canceled Playboy's promotional tour. A disappointed Sadie had already packed and made all the arrangements necessary for the trip. Now I had to squeeze her back into the schedule. When I broke the news, Sadie said, "That's ok. I was born in Italy. My Mom is Italian, my Dad is American, but I don't know if I can prove my citizenship."

Though peeved at this late revelation, I also felt sympathy. So many of the girls found themselves in similar situations where their military fathers had met and married women in Europe while stationed there.

In a few days, April 7 to be exact, I would enter the hospital. Before I could take the two week leave from the Club, I had to find a temporary Bunny Mother. I asked Judy. Though in my opinion she still hadn't developed the finesse needed to be a top manager, she treated everyone fairly, came to work each day on time and finished her work without complaint. While Judy could be naive about a woman's role in the world, she treated me with dignity—a distinct improvement over Shar.

The only other person I felt could be up for the job was Carlie and she didn't want to be a Bunny Mother even on a temporary basis. "I'll help Judy any way I can, but I prefer being a Bunny," Carlie said. With both Carlie and Judy's help the Bunnies and the Club would be in good hands and I could have my operation without too much worry.

On the other hand, Carl and Greg would be on their own. Although I would only be in the hospital over a long weekend, I left them enough food for a week. I also gave them some money for emergencies. Greg of course would no doubt eat most meals without charge and spend every free moment at Newton's Drug Store. I planned to call the boys on Friday and Monday mornings to get them up for school and then again in the evenings to make sure they met their curfew. Both Carl and Greg had already shown their responsibility with Fraulein's care so I didn't have to worry about her.

On April 7, I took the bus to Michael Reese Hospital to begin what I hoped would be a life-altering experience. Shortly after I registered and settled into a room, John Caruso telephoned. He apparently had asked for me at the Club. When he discovered I had gone to the hospital, he asked the Playboy receptionist to patch him through. I politely declined his request to visit. What was with this guy? We had never actually met. What had I done to warrant such attention?

The attending physician and nurse showed such interest in my work they nearly forgot to give me a sleeping pill to ensure a good night's rest. "We've never met a Bunny Mother before," the nurse gushed.

Did I over-react or had the doctor examined me far too closely for just a nose job? Perhaps he got carried away with his own curiosity about the Playboy Mystique. When the doctor and nurse finally left the room, I called Carl and Greg. Fortunately both were at home, but while talking to them I was almost overcome by drowsiness. Was this how it felt to be stoned? As soon as I hung up the phone, I fell right to sleep.

The nurse shook me awake at 6:00 am to take a shower, but gave me no food before the operation. I called Carl at 6:30 to get him and Greg up for school. No problems there. The nurse returned with a penicillin shot and another sleeping pill and once again to wheel me to the operating room.

Though groggy, I remained awake through the whole procedure, so I heard everyone talk about me being a Bunny Mother. Then one nurse put tubes up my nose and sprayed something through them. The doctor began scraping my nose. I kept talking while Doctor Cohen scraped, and every so often he told me to "shut up." During the hour-long operation I went in and out of delirium. I felt no pain, but the doctor's handy-work became an irritating discomfort.

The procedure at last completed, the nurse wheeled me back to my room, where she prepared an ice pack and told me to keep it over my eyes but not on my nose. When I dosed, the pack fell to the floor and woke me up. I replaced the pack, dosed again, and again the pack fell. That went on for the rest of the morning. As drowsy as I still was, the experience seemed like a very strange dream.

By mid-afternoon I returned to a normal mental state and telephoned Clark, but his partner said he would be gone for an hour. Judy called. She told me that all the Bunnies had asked about me and didn't understand why I needed a nose job. I chuckled to myself. They probably thought I needed clothes more.

I called the boys, but didn't get an answer. That concerned me. I'd try again later. No sooner had I hung up the phone than John Caruso called to check on me. "Did you get the flowers I sent?" he asked.

"No, not yet, but thank you for thinking of me." I wanted to interrogate this persistent man who had never seen me face-to-face. Lawrence Marconi flashed into my mind. Ice flowed through my veins.

I fell asleep before calling the boys again and didn't wake up until the next morning. I felt miserable. My head seemed stuffed with cotton and filled with pain. I couldn't drink enough water to get rid of my dry mouth. My breakfast consisted of watered-down orange juice and a congealed gray mound plopped in the middle of an ash-colored puddle that turned out to be oatmeal—I guessed. Before I'd finished the unbearable meal, a nurse appeared and wheeled me to the treatment room. There, Doctor Cohen removed the lower bandages and squeezed my nose. I gasped at the pain.

"The swelling is moderate," the doctor announced with pride.

Moderate! How does one define that term? My eyes were swollen almost shut and black and blue like my swollen lips and jaw. I thanked all the gods that my swelling had been described as *moderate.*

"You'll need to stay here until Monday," the doctor directed.

I nodded. At that moment I couldn't imagine ever going home.

As the day wore on I felt better. John Caruso's bouquet of multi-colored tulips arrived. I also reached Carl who said he would hang out around the house. As I predicted, Greg was working at the drug store.

"Where were you two last night when I called?" I asked.

"Out in the park playing ball. We got back at nine like you told us."

I decided not to press further. I wanted to let Carl know I trusted him. "You have my phone number here, so be sure to call if you need anything, ok?"

"Ok, Mom."

"I'll see you Monday afternoon when you get home from school." I reached to scratch my nose but stopped with my hand mid-air as I remembered the doctor's orders.

"We miss you." Carl sounded wistful.

"It's only a couple of days."

Soon after we said good-by, the phone rang. My hospital room seemed as busy as the office. John Caruso called from the airport to see if I got the flowers yet and to tell me he knew about a few possible Bunny applicants. I again asked myself what was with this guy. Perhaps he had several women on a string with the promise to get them a job as a Bunny and planned to use me for his contact.

I ate my liquid lunch of apple sauce, Jell-o, chicken broth and milk, glad I could neither smell nor taste any of it. When I finished, Judy called with several questions and to let me know that Carmen had been in a car accident. "I'm not sure I can do this job," Judy whined.

Her remark made me feel worthwhile for the first time in many months. In my opinion Judy needed that stint as a Bunny Mother to fully understand the complex job.

Rest wouldn't come easily. As soon as I completed that call, two doctors dropped by to examine me. They also wanted to talk. One told me about a patient who had hemorrhaged after a similar operation, a complication which Doctor Cohen had told me never happened. It turned out the patient was a Bunny who did something too strenuous too soon. She went to bed with a man! I could only ask, "In that condition? What man would want to?"

Neither doctor answered.

Sunday morning after I ate a breakfast I couldn't taste, I took a sponge bath in the restroom. Worn out, I slept until lunch arrived. The roast beef and mashed potatoes with gravy looked good, but I still couldn't taste or smell it. I ate it any way. Everything seemed to hum along until Greg called. "Last night Carl, Fraulein and I were sitting on the stoop," he started with such rapid-fire speed I suspected bad news.

"Fraulein took off after a poodle. Its owners complained to the landlord. Mr. Anderson came over and wanted to talk with you." Greg paused.

"And, what happened?" I sounded like I had a severe cold.

"We told him you had to work late."

"Good!"

"But. . ." Greg stopped.

"But what?"

"He told us to tell you that either Fraulein goes or we move." Greg started to cry. "Fraulein didn't do anything."

I sighed loudly. "It isn't the first time she's been in trouble. Just as soon as you and your brother take your eyes off her she's off into something." I thought I sounded too angry so I added, "Fraulein's used to having her own yard and less confinement."

"Will we have to move?"

"Not if you and Carl stay out of trouble while I'm not at home. And not just when I'm in the hospital, but when I'm working, too." I wished that I also had Carl on the line. Greg shouldn't have to carry the whole burden. "Where's Carl?"

"Right here."

"Put him on." When Carl took over the phone I reiterated everything I had said to Greg. "You're older and need to be the head of the household while I'm not there. It's just until tomorrow."

"OK," Carl whispered.

I had barely replaced the receiver when Judy telephoned. "I'm already in trouble," she announced. "Sorry. How are you doing today?"

"Fine," I answered, forcing the frustration from my voice as much as I could. "But what's the problem?"

"I need your help with this damn schedule."

That was the first time I had ever heard "Lady" Judy swear. "Can't Coco help you? She's a seasoned employee with Bunny Mother skills, remember?"

"Well, she's so inconsistent." Judy stumbled over her words. "Besides, she took the vacation day you two agreed for her."

"I never would agree to let her take a day off when I'm in the hospital." How typical of Coco to take advantage of the situation, especially when my absence meant Coco might have to do a full day's work.

"I really didn't think you had," Judy said. "But I didn't want to bother you when you first came out of the operation. No matter. Things go more smoothly when she's not around."

After about a half hour of working the schedule we said good-by. "The Bunnies aren't the only ones who can't wait for you to get back," Judy said at the end of the conversation.

Soothed with gratification at Judy's remark, I slept for a couple of hours until 5:30 when Greg called again. "Carl fell on some glass in the park and cut the palm of his hand open," he reported.

"What?" My shout reverberated through my whole face as though a thousand needles had stuck me all at one moment.

"We took him over to Mrs. Truman's house. She called a taxi because she said Carl needed stitches." As Greg talked he sounded more anxious. "She came with us."

"Taxi? Where are you now?"

"In Michael Reese."

I got a floor pass and walked for an eternity through one pavilion after another to the emergency room. Carl and Greg waited in the lobby. A blood-soaked towel covered Carl's hand. Greg nearly cried when he saw my face. He told me he couldn't decide who looked worse —his brother or his mother.

After waiting nearly an hour, Carl finally saw a doctor who cleaned the jagged wound. When he finished suturing the lightning-shaped cut, the doctor gave Carl tetanus and penicillin shots. Only then did I figure out I needed my check-book to pay the bill. So I trekked back through all those pavilions to my room for the book. While there I asked the nurse to check with my doctor about releasing me that night so I could go home with Carl.

After I made the long trip to return to Carl, I found a police officer at his side. My heart dropped like an out-of-control elevator. What could have happened to bring Chicago's finest to the ER? Within minutes I calmed down as the officer explained it was routine because the accident occurred in a city park. The hospital had to call in the incident. I couldn't help wonder whose house was being robbed while that officer took down the information about Carl's relatively minor injury.

Mrs. Truman said she'd wait in the ER with the boys until I found out if I could go home. Before I left to make yet another trek to my own hospital floor, Mrs. Truman chastised me for leaving the boys home alone "while you have some cosmetic surgery."

"I have a deviated septum which made the surgery necessary," I responded. As I paid the $16.00 for Carl's bill, I thought that Mrs. Truman had no right to be so arrogant. She too was a divorced mother of two. Her son was Carl's good friend, but also the boy who seemed to bring on trouble. He'd run away several times, especially after police questioned him about neighborhood break-ins. Besides that, Mrs. Truman's eighteen-year-old daughter had married at sixteen because she got pregnant. Something about glass houses and throwing stones crossed my mind.

On my third trip to my room, I felt dizzy and extremely tired. I needed the additional night in the hospital, but Carl needed me more. What a mess!

According to the nurse, the doctor said I could leave but she wanted me to eat something first. "My sons are waiting for me. I'm tired and my son is in pain. We need to go now."

"Eat first," the nurse ordered as she slid a tray toward me.

I obliged. I grabbed a few bites. I pushed the lukewarm food down with forced swallows. I had no appetite. Once I ate about a third, the nurse let me pack and dress. Before I could get on the way with the boys, though, I had to go to the cashier to pay the portion of my own bill not covered by insurance, which totaled $84.00.

The ER still teemed with injured people. Though Carl and I both felt miserable on the cab ride home, we were all happy to be away from the horrors of the medical center. As soon as we got home at 8:30 pm, I fell into bed and didn't get up until 9:30 the following morning.

Carl stayed home from school because of his hand and Greg stayed to help. I sent Greg after groceries with a signed personal check and a note. Greg returned with everything on the list and became the nurse and cook. He seemed to enjoy the adult tasks. It was a relief to be home with the boys.

A couple of hours into the day, however, Mr. Anderson called about Fraulein, threatening me with the eviction. But I had a powerful response in reserve. I reminded him about Daisy. "If I have any more grief from you, Anderson, I'll tell your wife you're dating one of my Bunnies and taking care of her son to boot."

"You wouldn't," he shouted.

"Try me," I yelled back.

"Keep that animal under control," Anderson said and hung up.

I decided to weed through the mail. I found a standard get-well card from Clark. He hadn't called or sent flowers—just that everyday card. I threw it into the trash.

On the one-week anniversary of my operation, I took a cab to Doctor Cohen's office. I arrived an uncharacteristic half-hour early and chalked it up to anxiety. As the doctor began to cut away the bandages, he buzzed for a nurse. When no one came, he opened the door and screamed into the hall, "When I buzz, I want someone right away, especially if I'm in room one." His uncommon anger made me even more uneasy.

Each step of the procedure brought increased discomfort. I felt only a little pain when the doctor took off the cast and a little worse when he took the packing out of my nostrils. But when he removed the stitches, it smarted something wicked. After that the nurse used a special solution to wash off the adhesive, which also really hurt. I thought perhaps the nurse was taking out her embarrassment on me for the doctor's earlier scolding.

Though my face still stung from Doctor Cohen's work, it was heaven to breathe again. Even with some mucous blocking the passage, I could smell so I probably would be able to taste food. However I couldn't wear glasses, blow my nose, wash my hair or pluck my eyebrows. But despite the swelling and bruising, I could already notice an improvement.

While I rode home in a taxi, rain fell in torrents causing a blinding shield. The wind increased with each mile. By the time I got to the townhouse, tornado warnings had been posted and one had already taken the roof off a building on the South Side. My desire to go back to L.A. intensified. Even Florida looked better every minute.

The two weeks I had off from work flew by too fast. The dread of going back built each day closer to my return. Before I braved that first day, I had to make another visit to Doctor Cohen. "You're ready to put warm compresses on your nose and massage it with cold cream," the doctor announced as he demonstrated. "You're doing splendidly."

Along with his pleasure at my recovery and the excellent outcome of the operation, he said, "Don't be surprised if I show up at the Playboy Club with a few of my colleagues." I recalled Doctor Sherwood's same remark.

Suddenly I was completely irritated with these doctors and their voyeurism. At that moment all I could think was that they apparently saw me as only a titillating commodity, the same as they considered the Bunnies. They were just like the men who viewed the Playboy women as no better than whores. My post-operative ire grew. I'd love to see any doctor in a corset and three-inch heels toting a ten-pound tray, without a nurse to attend to their every demand. Where were the men who respected women for their brains?

I left the office in a huff, most likely inexplicable to Doctor Cohen.

From the moment I had my first contact at the office, though, my mood began to rise. Every Bunny I met threw her arms around me and said, "I'm so glad you're back. You have no idea what a mess it's been."

Of course they all added, "Your nose looks great. Even without makeup, you look younger. You'll be the prettiest girl here."

My self-esteem grew with every encounter. Even the Room Directors seemed thrilled to have me back in the Hutch. Tony, the bartender commented, "I like your new hair style."

I had to giggle. My hair was completely tucked under a hat. "It's not my hair." I pointed to the cloche. "It's my nose."

Even Coco couldn't hold back her appreciation. "You're the best Bunny Mother," she said. "You're always so calm and so organized. I don't know how you do it. You should be the one to stay here, not me."

"It's not in the stars," I said and ended the conversation. I felt sorry for Coco. She was over her head and she knew it.

The final victory came when Barry raced into my office at his usual high speed and charged me. He circled both arms around me and gushed, "I never thought I'd say this, but I really missed you."

"Well, get used to it, because you know I'll be gone for good in a few months." But I glowed inside at the pleasure of Barry's first-ever admission that he needed me.

Barry's smile fell into a frown. "I'll at least have you around 'til then."

I couldn't decide if I was happier because everyone missed me or because I obviously looked so good. I also was charmed by the bouquet of fifteen dark red, long-stem American Beauty roses sent to the office with a card signed by all the Bunnies that said, "Welcome Back."

But then Bunny Gail told me she hadn't wanted to get the roses. "You need clothes more." That put a dent in my feeling good about myself.

John Caruso called from Albany, New York, to welcome me back. He kept me on the phone for a half hour. Flowers or not, I didn't want to talk to him. Trying to figure out a gracious way to stop him from calling. I agreed to meet in mid-May when he returned to Chicago. Perhaps that would satisfy him for now. By then I would be able to wear makeup. Still John wanted to talk. How many phone calls would I have to endure until our meeting?

Fortunately, I could end the call when three long-haired local college boys came to my office for an interview Barry scheduled with a Bunny. Well into the session the questions started getting out of hand, which made the Bunny nervous.

"Don't you think Hefner's philosophy is harmful?" one asked, but didn't wait for an answer. "I mean, it could be detrimental when other people who don't understand it try to adopt it. You dig?" The boys ran out of tape. The Bunny excused herself and I showed the boys to the door.

"Sorry about the tape. We'll be back to finish." The leader smiled broadly.

"You'll have to clear it again with Mr. Fleishman," I instructed and closed the door on them. I would get to Barry first to let him know the boys' agenda was not in keeping with Playboy's. I doubted I'd see the hippie trio a second time.

Secretary's Week brought a heavy lunch crowd. Each woman received a rose from the Door Bunny. I questioned the assumption that all women coming to the Club would be secretaries. As I watched the steady parade of well-dressed women accompanied by dapper men, I also wondered why any secretary would choose the Playboy Club for her reward. The boss must care little about his secretary's feelings. Instead, his own ego got in the way. Apparently the boss in some warped way must have felt his employee would be impressed with the fact he had a membership to a club built to feed male fantasies.

Then I caught myself and checked my own negative attitude. Though I was drifting further and further into disillusionment about a woman's role, I had less than six months left to put up with this environment. Better times lay ahead. Soon I would be back in control in a more suitable L. A. business climate. I already had many offers, including one from my former boss who told me my replacement hadn't worked out. He wanted to place me in an even better and higher-paying job. I decided to take everything slowly and not jump at the first offer. I had updated my resumé and soon would start circulating it. My expectations soared for life after Playboy. Now, I would never take a job whose main objective was selling sexuality.

By the end of the month, I felt as though I had never left. I actually wished I could be back in the hospital. I'd enjoy the rest. But April wouldn't let go before two last surprises. The first came when the Russian Cosmonaut died in space. I anguished over any loss of life and only wanted success in all scientific endeavors. Although the blow to the space program filled the news, imagine my amazement when not one person at Playboy mentioned the tragedy. It seemed as though the accident had never happened. Baseball garnered more chatter than a downed space craft.

Abby Mulligan's appearance at the Club came as the second astounding event. She showed up in the Penthouse with my heating oil supplier, of all people—the same guy who had claimed he fixed my furnace only to have forgotten to deliver fuel.

I talked with Abby for a while. Both of us avoided speaking about Gordon Novel's connection to JFK. Abby told me she had been working in Cincinnati where all fired Chicago Bunnies worked if they stayed with Playboy. She planned to move back to Columbus. Abby admitted she didn't love Novel and broke up with him, but she kept the engagement ring. She also confessed she came to Chicago to get away from all the reporters. To me, Abby looked tired and older. Yet she still had a way of enhancing all her best qualities, especially her huge brown eyes. Although she'd been through a lot, Abby deserved better than the oil man. Didn't we all?

When I got back to my office, I found a poem written by John Caruso in my mail. Could any man continue that kind of attention over the long haul? I had mixed feelings about him. I was both exasperated by his constant attention and flattered that he could care that much.

May finally brought warm weather—and more tornadoes. This time the storms devastated close-by areas, one as near as five miles away. Not only did the tornadoes bring havoc to property but one twister killed 20 people and another killed 32. Bunnies came in late due to the bad weather while the Club filled with members wishing to wait out the storm.

I could not face another day of such weather, but living through Chicago's cold winter which set a record for snowfall—68"—had to have been worse. I would never get the chill out of my bones. Surely California's rare earthquakes and tremors had to be a far less threatening concern. Besides, even in those conditions, the sun shone.

One sun-filled day many Room Directors and Bunnies set aside their differences and went horseback riding before the Club opened. I had a concern that the ranch where they rode belonged to Bill Flabio, an entertainer and rumored member of the Mafia. When the Bunnies reported for work that day, several told me that a very beautiful former Bunny rode with them and that she was the girlfriend of Big Frank, the head of the Chicago Mafia.

"Fortunately for you," I admonished, "Big Frank wasn't there. I don't think you should be running around with the likes of him."

The Bunnies rolled their eyes. One said, "It wouldn't be the first time. Those guys come in all the time and most are looking for a girl."

"Just be careful," I said. Between the FBI and the Mafia, my head spun. What next?

Chapter Eighteen

Moving On

He wore an all-green Regency double-breasted suit; she, a cream satin mini-gown and flowers in her hair. For their star-spangled nuptial reception, actress Sharon Tate and film director Roman Polanski chose the Playboy Club of London. V I P THE PLAYBOY CLUB MAGAZINE

Eleven more weeks were left until I planned to give my formal resignation. I crossed each day off the calendar like a prisoner scratching a day's passing on a cell wall. Finally one day, to celebrate the diminishing time at Playboy, I wore all my makeup, something I hadn't done since my operation. For the first time in my life I felt gorgeous. Although the job still required false eyelashes, I needed less makeup with my reconstructed nose. My hair, which had grown beyond my shoulders now seemed a more lustrous red and fell down one side of my face adding glamour to my overall appearance. A newly hired Room Director couldn't take his eyes off me and kept repeating how beautiful and sexy I looked. Coco agreed. Many Bunnies chimed in, "Your hair looks great that way."

Finally, I had to confess, "It's my new nose." I myself could hardly believe the change in my looks. The agony of the whole ordeal, including my nearly ten months at Playboy, had been more than worth it. For the first few days I had been back to work, even Barry treated me as though he had never seen or worked with me before. I caught him scrutinizing my every move. Instead of barking out commands, Barry gave sensitive requests. For instance, one day he entered my office after an uncommon knock and asked, "Do you have time to go over the schedule? If not, I could come back."

He wasn't the only person who acted that way. Several girls offered to help me get the schedule out, run the Bunny training, and work when needed without a fuss. All the positive attention amazed and bewildered me because my skills and personality hadn't varied. Difficult as it appeared to believe, my nose made the difference. I didn't fool myself though. Once the newness wore off, the routine would set back in and I would once more be exhausted from working eighty hours a week. "Give me a 9 to 5, five-day-a-week job like I had before," I said to myself at the end of my first week back at the Club.

I knew all good things must come to an end, and they did. First, Angelo hadn't sent child support in over a month. I had counted on that money to help pay the rent. It astounded me that even after 10 years Angelo never seemed to think the boys were his duty. To him divorce must have meant he no longer had to be a father. Further, I only could collect one-week sick pay. The boys and I had survived the rest of my time off work on what little I had saved. As a result I only paid a third of the rent for that month. Though Mr. Anderson hadn't dared to confront me, his wife did.

"Whatdaya mean sendin' only a third of your rent?" Mrs. Anderson asked. I imagined her alcohol-induced red cheeks puffed with each word.

"You're already in trouble with them wild kids of yours and that dog." I heard Mrs. Anderson take a drag on a cigarette. "You shoulda got somebody to watch them hooligans while you were at work."

I had always suspected Mrs. Anderson and not her husband wore the pants in that family. I politely explained my circumstances. "I'm sure I'll be able to make this right before the end of the month. As far as my sons, they have never been in any trouble. They're just energetic like any healthy boys." I offered no defense for Fraulein's wanderings.

"Make it right? I don't care 'bout your child support problems, or your hospital bills, or no excuse you wanna hand out 'bout your boys. I run a business."

That got my goat. "What kind of business do you run when you won't pay for the repairs as noted in the lease?"

"What're you talkin' 'bout?" I noted a quieting in Mrs. Anderson's voice.

"I had no heat because the man from the oil company couldn't fill the tank until a pump had been repaired. He wouldn't repair it without full payment up front of $32.26 to be exact." I tapped a pen against my desk in rapid, angry strokes. "And the filter had never been cleaned as you had said. So the oil man charged extra to clean that as well."

I only heard a schwishing sound of air passing that the telephone made when no one talked. "Mrs. Anderson, are you still there?"

"Yeah. I'll check with my husband 'bout why the repairs haven't been done. Meanwhile send me the receipts and I'll deduct 'em from your rent. I still want you and the boys out of the apartment." She hung up without saying good-by or hearing my answer.

I suspected Mr. Anderson had told his wife the repairs had been completed. He most likely took the money set aside for the oil supplier and spent it on his paramour. The thought of the hell he would have to pay for his stupidity tickled me. Clark had already explained that without a formal eviction notice from either Anderson, I couldn't be forced to move. I planned to stay in the townhouse until the boys went to New York and I went to Miami.

By the end of my second week back from leave, I discovered the Club had fallen short of their expected profits, even though it still endured as number one in earnings. The shortfall meant that my office remodel would be delayed again; the non-working radiator still lay in disarray. It also meant several busboys and porters had to be laid off. The Club couldn't get cleaned properly, not that my office and the Bunnies' dressing room ever had. The decorating didn't matter to me since I wouldn't be around to enjoy it, yet I had concerns about the cleanliness of the Club proper. Although dim lighting hid most offenses, how would the members react to the unsanitary conditions? I believed Barry would somehow find a way to blame me for the whole situation. He often looked for a scapegoat. Of course International's offices, Barry's included, were spic and span.

The final straw came when Barry told me that I, and not Coco, would train a new Bunny Mother for the Toronto Club. My first encounter with Heather went poorly. I chalked it up to having my period when in reality I just didn't want the added burden. Plus I hated sounding more like a man who used a woman's cycle as the reason for any mood change—and that added to my irritation.

Within days my attitude reformed. I liked Heather who was fresh from the Peace Corps. She had a sharp mind, dressed well, spoke intelligently and picked up the Bunny Mother's tasks quickly. Within a week she had become more of an assistant for me than any of the others except Brooke.

A pleasant though brief event occurred in the third week. My former boss and mentor, Gil Roswell, visited while on a business trip to Chicago. I wished he had been more complimentary about my looks. After all, I had gone through so much to create them. But my office upstaged my new nose. Once Gil saw the tiny, poorly maintained space, he only had one thing to say, "Get out of here, right now."

Gil's shocked reaction only added fuel to my own ambitions. He gave me a few new ideas of places to send my resumé. "Of course you can always use me as a reference," he added. "But don't forget your college degree. You need to get that."

I confided that I had submitted applications to several colleges as he had encouraged months earlier. Although I had more than enough credits for a bachelor's degree, those units had been spread out over several years. All those universities wanted me to go back almost to my freshman year, which would mean starting over. "So I did what you also suggested. I applied for an MBA at Pepperdine University's Graduate School of Business. At first the Dean of Admissions denied my request."

"Yes," Gil interrupted. "I think you told me this. When you told me the circumstances, I thought you sounded terribly depressed."

"Yes. I probably did." I paused as I mentally reviewed that earlier conversation. I pushed those thoughts aside and brightened with news of what had just occurred. "Well, you'll never guess what happened?"

"What?" Gil asked as he brushed a chair clean before he sat.

"Pepperdine accepted all my college credits and I have been admitted into the MBA program. That school administration is so understanding."

A smile slowly filled Gil's face. "My call to the chancellor didn't hurt either."

"What?" I screeched. My mouth must have extended as wide open as it could. I quickly pressed my lips together and covered them with a hand.

Gil shrugged. "You know I believe you are more than capable. What harm could there be in one phone call?" Gil stood. "Let's see this Club and get some of that food you've bragged about."

I raced toward Gil and gave him a hard hug. "Thank you. I won't disappoint you."

"I know that you won't," he nodded at the office. "If you get out of here. But you have your feet in two-worlds—entertainment and business. You must choose one. I think you've made the right decision."

After the energizing day spent with Gil, I could hardly wait to find a normal office job and get on the road to completing my goals. I dreamed of one day owning a business where I'd be the boss. I'd hire women and men based on their abilities and not on how attractive they were.

The end of the school year drew closer. Angelo called to finalize Carl and Greg's summer visit. From our few words, I suspected Angelo and his new wife had separated again because he had made arrangements for Carl and Greg to stay with their Aunt Marie. Secretly, that pleased me.

Before we closed the conversation I asked about the support payment now five weeks in arrears.

"I thought since I'll have them all summer I already paid enough," Angelo explained.

"No, that's not the agreement. You won't send money to me while they're with you, but you're still obligated to pay for the time with me."

"Umm," Angelo replied. "So you're sending the boys here after you vacation with them. Right?" Angelo didn't make another comment about child support. Instead he asked, "Where're ya goin?"

"We haven't decided." I didn't want Angelo to know anything about what the future held for the boys and me, including my temporary move to Miami and return to California. Who knew what he'd do, especially if he no longer lived with his spouse?

"Greg told me about your nose."

I didn't acknowledge the comment. I feared Angelo thought I didn't need any money from him if I could get such an operation.

"You're beautiful enough the way you are," he added.

Angelo had long since lost the ability to charm me. I diverted the conversation to Greg's test scores. Perhaps he'd forget about my makeover and show more interest in the boys. "I have good news about Greg," I started.

"Yeah?"

"His state school test scores gave him a 6.6 grade average in English and a 7.7 for math. He may skip a grade." I sounded excited.

"It's better than skipping school like he often does." Angelo showed his usual sarcasm. He didn't have an ounce of fatherly love.

"He's bored."

"Well, I always thought Carl and Greg were smart, but being bored is just an excuse." Angelo discredited my explanation. "And besides Carl is too shy."

Had Angelo deliberately wanted to be mean or had he forgotten Carl and Greg were on the extension? I quickly said, "Carl needs to gain more self-assurance." Which you, moron, helped destroy, I told myself. "And Greg needs to be challenged."

"Maybe." Angelo sounded dubious.

I heard a click. Carl had probably hung up.

Afterwards, I told Greg not to worry about what his father said. "He often blurts out things he doesn't mean. Do you understand?"

Greg shrugged, "Sure. What's the big deal?" He turned his attention to a TV program.

Carl, on the other hand, stole away to his room and went to bed. I followed. I sat near him and asked, "How are you doing, handsome?"

"Ok, but sometimes Dad can be so . . ." He let the words trail off.

"I know. But we're ok, right?"

"Yeah, we're ok."

I ruffled his hair and kissed his forehead. "It won't be long before we get back to L.A."

"Yeah, I can't wait." Carl perked up.

"Me, either." I left the room and mumbled to myself again, "Me, either."

Nearly a month later, I was still doing the count-down. "Only 63 more days—nine weeks—before I give my month's notice," I talked to myself with the calendar in my hand. "Unless Playboy wants me to leave sooner."

This thought brought back Heather's comment earlier that day. She had decided not to go to Toronto. She didn't want to be a Bunny Mother. "It's tough work with no gratitude," Heather said. "You're the only reason I stayed. But now I'm going to be a travel agent. That way I get paid while I travel and I won't have to work so many hours."

Heather's decision saddened me. Yet I knew when I met her she wouldn't last. None of the good girls did.

Unfortunately, I still had to put up with Coco, who left me high and dry that afternoon as usual. I had to step in to conduct training at the last minute because she had to get home to her sick child.

"What about my son?" I asked. "He's getting stitches taken out today. I should be with him." Greg had fallen in the park this time, rather than Carl. Broken glass cut his leg below his knee.

"Sorry. I didn't know," Coco sounded genuinely concerned, for a split second. "But I do have seniority, and your son is much older than my baby. He can take care of himself."

If Coco hadn't fled out the door so fast, I would have scratched her eyes out. Instead I picked up a pad and pencil and sketched out a budget. I figured out that if Tekkie lived with me in California and if I earned the same salary I did at Playboy, I could afford a lovely house with a cleaning woman once a week. With someone doing the house-work Tekkie and I would be free to pursue other things, like sewing, repairing, creating. And school. I couldn't wait.

I laid the pad aside and stared at the brick wall out the window. "What a lovely dream." I sighed, then straightened up. "But it is pos-sible."

I had all the bills caught up, except the rent, for the first time since becoming a single mother. The rent would be taken care of in a week with or without Angelo's support payment. "Nothing will spoil this." I turned back to the figures on the paper. "I won't let it."

May sped by but not without Barry making my life miserable. As predicted his enchantment with the makeover had worn off.

I had barely put one foot into the Club's lobby one morning late in the month when a Room Director said Barry wanted me in his office ASAP. "Now what?" I turned and trotted down the block. Only two days before the big holiday weekend that kicked off summer and the heat already made my shoes stick to the pavement.

International's air-conditioned offices allowed me to regain my composure before I spoke to Barry. As I entered his office, Barry shouted, "The Club will open Sunday and Monday of Memorial Day weekend." He stubbed out his cigar.

"What? You told me otherwise." I towered over his desk. "That's only a few days away. How will I get Bunnies to work after I told them they had the time off?" I yelled. I didn't care how I sounded. I had had it with this jerk. "They're probably packed and on their way out of town as we speak."

Barry stood. "I don't care how you do it, but find someone." He walked toward the door as he so often had in the past to escape further discussion.

And just as I had done before, I blocked his stride toward the exit. "No members will be here. You know how slow that weekend is at the Club."

"Yeah, well." He shrugged in dismissal. My opinion carried no weight with him. "I've decided to try something new."

"Let's get down to the real truth. Who're you angry with?" My voice rose higher than I thought possible.

Barry retreated behind his desk. "You're stubborn and insubordinate."

"And you don't know what you're doing."

Barry's face turned the color of the brightest red apple. "Just do as I say or. . ."

"Or what? You'll fire me?" I turned and walked to the door. "I'll find Bunnies. But we'll run short and International won't make any money."

I fled back to the sanctuary of my own office. After several telephone calls, I filled a skeleton schedule. One Bunny complained that she had to work Level A in the bar. "Coco never put showroom girls on level A."

"You must be very happy then that Coco will be your Bunny Mother again." I even sounded snide to myself. I wondered how I sounded to the Bunny.

"Not really. You're a better Bunny Mother than Coco. But I've always been a Showroom Bunny," she whined. "I won't make as much money in the bar."

I knew that to be true even on regular weekends. "Everyone must take her turn in both places," I explained. "Otherwise how would I ever get Bunnies trained for the showroom?"

Neither of us said anything for a few moments. I could hear the Bunny's heavy breathing. Was she trying to come up with an answer?

"Well, no matter, I don't like it one bit." The Bunny hung up and I prayed she'd show up for work.

Once finished with the schedule I laughed and cried at the same time over the absurdity of the whole situation. Only the phone's ring stopped me from becoming totally hysterical. The receptionist reported that John Caruso was in the bar and asked to see me.

"Tell him I'll be right down." Finally I would meet the elusive and attentive Mr. John Caruso. Today he presented a welcome break.

I checked myself in the mirror. I looked great, even if I said so myself. With a premonition something good would happen that day, I had taken special care in choosing an outfit. I could hardly contain my excitement over meeting John. Suddenly my day, so filled with roller coaster emotions, seemed more than I could bear. I sat back down in my chair and lifted the phone to call the receptionist. I intended to postpone my meeting with John. When the operator didn't answer, I hung up. I walked to the door and stopped. "You're just nervous because you're afraid he won't like you," I told the woman looking at me in the mirror. Boy, she sure had a great nose. I had to laugh.

A few minutes later I found myself hesitating at the threshold to the bar. I surveyed the room. The dim lighting made it impossible to properly size up the clientele. I did however catch a nearby Bunny chewing gum and forgetting to place napkins on the four-top. I also thought the Bunny didn't dip. I'd have to speak to her later. Perhaps the Bunny's carelessness indicated how the girls would pay Playboy back for ruining their weekend plans.

Rick, the Room Director, came over. "Mr. Caruso is over there." He pointed to a table nestled in the corner.

I approached with caution. I could hardly make the figure out. When I reached the table, the man stood. "Alyce?"

I nodded.

"John Caruso." He shook my hand and then pulled out a chair.

So stunned by the man, I practically fell into the chair. John Caruso looked like a well-dressed, plump Soupy Sales. By the time we finished our drinks, I had discovered a charming, articulate man who I also suspected was married. So much for my knight in shining armor.

I begged off a dinner invitation. "I've got a ton of work to do before I go home to my sons. Perhaps another time." We said good-by and I knew there would never be another time.

Suddenly I missed Clark all over again.

June blew into Chicago with such meanness I began to think Illinois only had one kind of weather—nasty. Late spring brought unending rains, 4 ½ inches of which poured in one day. On that day I got to work late because the bus driver threatened to drive only a few blocks more, about a mile short of my destination, because he was on overtime and wanted to go home. I didn't believe him until he pulled to the curb, shut down the bus and left.

The other riders and I sat in dismayed silence, watching the driver disappear into streams of water blown horizontal by the wind. Finally, one man hopped off, shouting, "I'll call the bus company." He ran into a drug store, holding a newspaper over his head to protect himself. When he returned, the soaked newspaper now draped over his forehead, he told the waiting group that the company would send another driver. Within a half-hour a driver arrived and my trip resumed.

Fortunately I made it to the Club entrance without floating away in what seemed like a rush of water from a burst dam. When I pushed open the door, I found a lake inside. Level A was flooded. I took off my shoes and waded through ankle deep water to the stairs. Water squeezed from my stockings with each upward step.

Barry was waiting in my office. He paced as usual and puffed at a cigar. Step, step, puff, puff. The whole room filled with rancid smoke. I wished the window opened, even with the threat of rain.

"A Level's closed," Barry barked at me as though I had created the horrific weather.

"I assumed so," I answered but wanted to say, "No shit!"

"Can't do anything until the damn rain stops." Barry chomped down so hard on his cigar, it amazed me he didn't bite clean through it. I'd had that thought before. Another reason to leave Playboy—time for some fresh thinking.

I took off my trench coat and shook it. Beads of water flew around the room and pelted Barry. "Will the rain stop?"

"Don't be so sarcastic." Barry puffed again and again. Great billowing circles floated from his mouth. He looked like a mythical creature rising from a fire pit.

"I'm not sarcastic. But after living through the worst winter in Chicago's history, I can't believe this is normal. Is it?" As I opened my umbrella to dry, I recalled the day I had bought it just weeks into to my job with Playboy. I had been so hopeful then.

"NO!" Barry shouted and startled me. "We've got some guy coming from maintenance to get the water out of A Level. He'll also get a floor fan to help dry the carpet. We'll open tomorrow."

The next afternoon I got to the Club about 5:00 pm just as the rain began again. It had stopped for a few hours during the night, but at that moment heaven let loose all its fury as though punishing Chicago. When I walked through the A Level area, the carpet squished under my feet, forcing tiny bubbles to rise to the top. The whole place smelled like an ancient sunken ship.

The musty smell followed me all the way upstairs, making my nose itch and run, and stinging my eyes. When I reached my office, I called Barry. "You can't open A Level." My voice sounded harsh and determined.

"Those are the orders from International," Barry responded. "There's nothing else to do but obey them."

"But it's unsanitary and the service area is practically floating away." I argued. I imagined the Bunnies' satin shoes soaked in rancid liquid.

"It stays open," Barry yelled. "End of conversation." The line went dead.

A Level opened as planned and hummed with drenched patrons. By 7:30 pm another inch of water seeped into the bar. A Level closed.

The rain brought one good thing. I had no problem filling the schedule because A Level stayed shut. It suffered severe damage from the water and had to be completely torn apart. The area smelled like sewage and looked like a picture of a bombed village in Viet

Nam. Unfortunately anyone entering the Club had to pass by the devastation. So much for the well-publicized titillating welcome members expected.

In the midst of that surrealistic week, Barry decided to gather all the Bunnies to go over the Dip. "They're just not Dipping," he blurted to me one day. "Besides they need the hours with A Level down and the Playroom closed for the summer."

I couldn't convince Barry that the Bunny Dip wasn't always necessary. As I reached for the receiver to call the Bunnies in for the training I screamed, "Get me out of this place!" Then I checked the hall to see if anyone heard me.

Neither the rain nor short funds stopped management from scheduling Bunnies for costly promotional appearances. One day the Bunnies assigned to such an event returned smashed. When the girls had left for their appearance earlier, they looked like the fantasy Hef described as every man's dream. The Bunnies returned in a far less appealing state—hair pieces in hand, eyelashes askew, stained bust lines and glazed eyes. They carried unopened Champagne bottles into the Club. None could work a normal shift, nor should they have.

If that hadn't been enough for one month, I had to spend precious hours to accommodate another last minute decision from International. Management decided to celebrate the Toronto Club in Chicago as they had Jamaica. That meant I searched the country for Mounted Police jackets and hats for the Bunnies to wear. The closest warehouse that handled such an item was in Philadelphia. In order to get the jackets to the Club in time they had to be sent special delivery, which of course meant far more money than expected.

"I'd rather have busboys," I told Judy as we unpacked the boxes of jackets in varied shades of faded red.

Judy shook one free. She turned it around and around. She held it at arms' length to examine. "Needs cleaning," she said in her usual quiet and direct tone.

I pulled another from the box. "If these two are any indication of what the others look like, they all will need to be cleaned and altered." I couldn't believe all this work and money for a one week event. What could management be thinking? They must be steeped in daydreams in their ivory tower.

Judy stopped unpacking. The glint in her eyes made me suspicious. Then a beguiling smile filled her face. She plopped a crushed Mounted Police hat on her head.

"What's up?" I asked.

"You're going to laugh." Judy tossed a jacket onto a pile on the couch and grabbed another from the container.

"I can use a good laugh right about now." I waited for Judy to spill out what seemed so amusing.

"Barry wants to recoup some of the cost for these Canadian outfits. He suggested we sell the old white promotional shirts at $3.50 to the Bunnies." Judy's smile grew larger.

"What? Those old things are dingy gray with age and ugly to boot. Besides, most have the Bunny head on them so Hef would never allow it." I laughed. As she shook her head she said, "The Bunnies wouldn't take them if you gave them away."

We spent the next several minutes laughing over the absurdity of the whole idea. Judy had to remove her glasses to wipe her eyes. We both wanted to know on what planet Barry lived and how he could actually believe anyone would want those old rags except for cleaning.

Judy sobered. "You know, I never realized how tough your job really is until I filled in for you while you were in the hospital." She laid a jacket in her lap. "I don't know how you do it."

"Sometimes I don't either," I answered.

We unpacked the rest of the jackets in silence.

Chapter Nineteen

Parting Words

To my beloved Bunnies: It is with deep regret that I announce that I am leaving the Chicago Playboy Club. I will miss you all very much and thank you with all my heart for making my job enjoyable. If you don't hate me too much for letting you down this way, I would love to hear from you occasionally and will certainly write to you. Love, Alyce

The first week in July I shared a wonderful holiday with Carl and Greg in Montreal at the World's Fair. After leaving the O'Hare Airport, we had to change planes in Toronto, but had no problem getting through Customs for our first time. The agent only asked about our citizenship, how long we would be in Canada and what we planned to do during our stay. We didn't even have to show a birth certificate.

I stopped first at the money exchange, then the ladies' room. When I met up with Carl and Greg outside the men's room, I realized I had left my tote in the bathroom. I frantically searched the area but came up with nothing so I reported it. What a sad way to start the trip, especially because the boys' new sweaters had been packed in that tote. Within five minutes of submitting the report to loss and found, though, I was paged. Some honest person had turned it in. Everything inside remained as I had packed it. To celebrate, the boys and I went to the coffee shop for sundaes.

Soon we boarded another plane, and shortly after we finished eating dinner, we landed in Montreal. Our tiring day wouldn't close without more frustration. The cab driver gave me a little grief—when he dropped us off at the hotel, the driver put my suitcase on the curb in front of me. I had hardly any room to get out of the cab, fell over the suitcase, broke my purse and bruised my knee.

Mrs. Sullivan, the innkeeper, turned out to be more pleasant than her fellow French-Canadian. She showed us to a comfortable but old-fashioned room, papered in huge pink roses against a pale green background. The large dark wood of the oversized furniture made the room seem heavy and crowded. A faint odor of cigarettes and lavender permeated the chintz bedspread, its floral pattern competing with the walls. We shared the bath with five other rooms. The whole place seemed more like European accommodations than Canadian. No matter, the room and bath were clean and reasonable.

Mrs. Sullivan handed me the key and asked in a French accent, "Are you a model?"

I smiled, "No. But thank you for the compliment."

"You certainly look like one."

I decided Mrs. Sullivan's observation made a nice ending to a long and sometimes difficult day. The boys and I were too exhausted to give much attention to our preparations for bed. So, once in our pajamas, we promptly fell asleep.

We packed in as much as humanly possible into the next three days. Nearly everyone in Montreal spoke French. Every so often we'd hear other languages representing countries from around the world, which no doubt had to do with the World's Fair. It all added to the educational experience for the boys. We truly felt we were in a foreign land.

After breakfast the first full day in Canada, we took the Metro, Montreal's new subway system. Unlike New York City's grungy subways with which I had been familiar, Montreal's was clean and beautifully decorated. Once we disembarked on Isle St. Helene, we spent the entire day at the crowded fairgrounds. Eager to try everything, we ate something new—Belgian waffles—which with their topping of whipped cream and fresh strawberries seemed more like dessert and made an interesting departure from the American variety. In late afternoon we headed for the amusement section and rode a flume and a mini-rail around Ile-Notre-Dame and Isle St. Helene. Greg won a walkie-talkie set at one of the many games both boys played.

We had been so involved with all the events, the park closed before we could eat dinner. So we grabbed a bite at an all-night diner near our hotel. Happy, but weary, we finally got to bed at 3:30 am.

The next two delightful sun-filled days went the same as the first. The highlight came when Queen Elizabeth and Prince Phillip took a mini-rail ride and passed within ten feet of us. We all agreed that the Queen looked lovely and the Prince elegant. Carl made only one other comment about the royal couple. "I never believed they were real." He watched in awe as they passed. "I thought they were made up like Santa Claus."

On the fourth day we left Montreal. The boys wore their new Expo sweatshirts, while I of course dressed to the nines, including a suit, hat, and gloves. After we had a quick light lunch, I had to face reality—my sons would soon leave for Syracuse for the summer.

A half hour later, Carl and Greg boarded their airplane, a Convair 440, bound for Syracuse and Angelo. I shivered as I watched the plane taxi down the tarmac, leaving me alone and sad. Though I would see them in a few weeks when I visited New York before going to Miami, it gave me no solace at this lonely moment. My melancholy worsened with each minute of the three hours I had to wait for my own plane back to Chicago and my dreaded job. My spirits lifted slightly when I calculated that I had only a little over two months to go before I could move back to L.A.

On July 7, 1967 I turned thirty-four-years-old. I had been with Playboy for one year. Despite the fact that Carl and Greg summered in another state, I wanted my birthday to be full of joy rather than the usual work frustration. I also wanted to suppress my nagging thoughts about my aging body.

A card from Clark awaited me and immediately fulfilled part of my wish. He sent a $50.00 bill. Any birthday greeting from Clark surprised me. He had been disappointed and angry when I told him he couldn't visit because I was taking Carl and Greg to Montreal. "He still cares," I thought as I tucked the money into my wallet.

No sooner had I secured the funds than Coco called. She needed me in her office right away. Coco sounded furious and anxious. I couldn't begin to come up with a reason for Coco's disgruntled state.

Bracing myself for a confrontation, I checked myself in the mirror and trudged down the hall. I pushed open Coco's door and stopped cold. Several Bunnies stood with Coco, singing "Happy Birthday." When they finished their off-key rendition, Carlie handed me a card signed by all the girls. In the envelope I found $175.00. Coco led me to a chocolate cake with 34 candles aglow on top. For once no one mentioned tight Bunny costumes—we all devoured generous helpings of the chocolate confection and drank Kool-aid as we chatted and giggled like teenagers at a sleep-over. Overwhelmed by their show of affection, I could hardly focus on the conversation. I had no idea any of them cared that much. Why had I not noticed the girls' respect for me before now? I had to force the cake past the lump in my throat. My heart filled with both the joy I had wished for earlier and sadness because I had to leave this happy Hutch for a new one.

"Who knew my birthday?" My voice choked on each word.

"I did," Gail confessed. "I did your numerology a couple of months ago, remember?"

"You sneak." I shook a finger at Gail. "This is the best birthday. Thank you. The money will come in handy to make up for what I spent on my trip with my sons before I shipped them off to New York."

"Some of it better be spent on you," Coco said. "Maybe false nails, or something."

Typical of Coco's insensitivity, the comment almost made me laugh. Coco meant well but her words usually got skewed on the way out of her mouth. Besides, I did think my nails could use some help. On many occasions I hid my hands because my nails appeared ill-kept and as ragged as a mechanic's. I just might try the false ones.

"You know we're all sorry to see you go." Carlie wrapped her arms around me.

I checked Coco's reaction. None. Had Coco not heard that comment or did she choose to ignore it? No matter. It made me feel good even though Carlie was probably biased as my ally and friend.

"I hate to break this up. There's work to do," Coco directed.

"True enough," I agreed but wondered if Coco didn't want to hear any more positive things about me. As each girl left, she hugged me and wished me a happy birthday.

One girl whispered, "We never appreciate someone until we lose them."

I couldn't hold back my tears any longer. Now I'd have to redo my makeup, but for a good reason. I finally felt valued.

Back in my office, I found two-dozen long stemmed red roses in a vase on my desk from John Caruso. Apparently, he wouldn't give up easily. I feared he might even follow me to Miami and beyond.

My day turned out to be so full I could hardly cram everything into it. It wouldn't be over once I got home. I arrived at the townhouse around 9:00 pm and found a card from Carl and Greg. They hadn't forgotten me either. I made a sandwich to eat while I spent a lonely night packing. Fraulein paced and sniffed in the boys' room. "You'll see Carl and Greg soon, girl." I scratched her ears. "I miss them too."

Some things don't change, like Barry's indecisiveness and two-faced personality. And the miseries of the smoldering Chicago July. Despite the heat and Barry, though, I had two pleasant, yet bittersweet experiences during my last week of work there.

The first came when I had drinks with Heather and Carlie. Heather had already left Playboy for her travel agent job and it showed. I envied her stress-free face, absent of the frown lines and wrinkled forehead I had seen in my own.

On the other hand, Carlie intended to stay at Playboy as long as possible. She had been saving every penny she could and had a sizeable bank account. Already she had gone to real estate school for her license and was selling part time, planning to use the money to open her own company. "No more uncaring bosses for me," Carlie announced. "You're the only exception."

"My goal exactly," I agreed.

The three of us clinked our drink glasses.

Heather turned serious. "Why haven't you ever gotten married again, Alyce?"

"You're one to ask. I don't see a ring on your finger." I took a sip of my Rob Roy, set the glass down and stirred the swizzle stick around and around as I thought about my answer. "Actually I've had six proposals over the past ten years since I've been divorced. I came within two weeks of getting married to one of the guys. But . . ."

The others sipped their drinks and didn't press me further. I believed they probably already knew the only man at the moment for me was Clark. Or maybe they realized after one lousy marriage, making that commitment again would be tough. No one wanted to go through such a terrifying life again.

"Well," I ended the silence. "I'm sorry to be the one to break up this happy party, but I've got to finish packing. I leave the day after tomorrow."

"We know," Carlie whimpered. "It doesn't make us happy."

"You will keep in touch then, right?" I asked.

"Of course," both of my friends answered together.

We left the bar. Once on the street, we hugged and cried. For that moment, I didn't want to leave Chicago.

My desire to stay at the Chicago Playboy Club ended the very next day when I met with Barry and Judy for what I hoped would be the last time, at least for Barry. We met in Barry's office, the turf on which he most likely felt the safest.

Barry spoke first. "I had to transfer you because Coco came back." He rocked back on his heels and pushed his glasses to the top of his head. "There also have been personality clashes between you and a couple of Room Directors. And you've made your mistakes."

"Who hasn't screwed up from time to time?" I asked. "YOU?"

Barry opened his mouth, but Judy came to his rescue instead. "International believes you are an asset to the organization."

"Is that why I'm being transferred to Miami with a cut in salary? Because I'm an asset?" I glowered at Judy who as always showed no sign of being ruffled. "I'd hate to be a liability."

"Judy is your biggest rooter," Barry shouted. "So don't jump on her."

"Forgive me, but I'd rather have enemies if my rooters are so grateful they send me away. Besides." I looked at each one for a few seconds as though challenging them, "I've learned not to believe everything I'm told."

Barry clenched his teeth so tightly I could see a pulsing on each side of his jaw. Judy again tried to salvage the conversation and asked me in her soft, controlled tone, "When have I ever misled you? I'd really like to know."

Before I answered, Barry stepped away from his desk and bravely faced me. "I may have given you that impression, especially when you first got here."

I almost fell over from his unusual honesty. "Since we are laying everything on the table, let me confess to you," I said with conviction. No need to hide my feelings now. "I never intended to make Playboy a career. I only planned to stay two years, which is longer than most of your Bunny Mothers."

"That's not true," Judy objected in a surprising screech.

After I ticked off the Bunny Mothers from around the country who lasted only six months or less, Barry said, "She's right. We have a high turnover."

Judy slumped in dejection.

I continued. "After six months I too decided I would leave. If the transfer from Miami hadn't changed the schedule, I'd planned to give notice the end of September and return to L.A. in October. I belong there. I'm happy Coco will fill in for me. It makes my departure easier." I choked back tears, while my nose tingled and the lump in my throat grew to the size of a fist. So many emotions raced through me—hurt, betrayal, anger and aloneness. "My friends," I forced out, "thought I would last only those six months, but I actually made my initial decision to leave after three. Neither my sons nor I have been happy in Chicago. The weather isn't the only thing that's cold and miserable in this town."

A stunned Barry moved his mouth as though trying to form words. He raised a closed hand into the air. He appeared to want to make a fist and pound something. Instead he lowered his hand to his chin and said nothing.

"You needn't worry about my future. I already have a job waiting for me and I'm going on to college for my MBA." I didn't have a job yet. I'd only talked with several potential and interested employers, but Barry and Judy didn't need to know that.

"Well, I still would like you to go to Miami, because I think you are a good Bunny Mother," Barry said as he retreated to his desk, sat down and lit a cigar. "God knows they can use the help."

I walked to the front of the desk and looked into Barry's eyes. "I'll only go to see Miami. I will give no guarantee how long I'll stay, but not beyond October 2."

"Fair enough," Judy said. Barry jerked his head up. He pursed his lips and scrunched his forehead in anger. Judy confronted him with an equally belligerent look. Neither spoke.

"Good. I'll continue as planned then. I'm leaving day after tomorrow to visit my sons in Syracuse for a couple of days. Then I'll head south." I left the office, feeling quite pleased to get all that off my chest. Although my two supervisors said nothing, a few minutes later Judy caught up with me and invited me to join her for dinner. "My treat," Judy said. "And not at Playboy."

I hesitated until Judy begged, "Please."

"OK. Tomorrow," I agreed.

That evening Clark called. When I told him about Miami, he said, "I'm not surprised. But when are you coming home—for good?"

"I'm not sure." I hoped I sounded convincing. "It depends on how much I like Miami."

Clark seemed disappointed. I steeled myself not to care. I needed to do what was best for me from now on.

All the next day, Bunnies and Room Directors stopped by my office to say good-by. Coco stayed conspicuously out of sight. I packed up my personal items. I did no work. Yet the day sped by. I soon found myself with Judy eating a farewell dinner at the same steakhouse where Lawrence Marconi and I had gone so many months earlier. The thought of his stalking made me even more ready to depart from Chicago.

Judy and I shared the second bittersweet event that day during an evening which started with pleasantries during cocktails. I half-listened to Judy. I instead kept thinking about Carl and Greg. I'd see them the next day. I'd have to call for directions to Marie's farm when I got a rental car at the airport.

A comment from Judy brought me back to the present. "I'm so grateful I have had you as a Bunny Mother."

The waitress brought salads. I picked up my fork and stared at Judy. I expected a "but" to follow. When that didn't happen I simply answered, "Thank you."

"You did a superb job training Heather even if she decided not to become a Bunny Mother. And you never complained to me or gossiped about others."

"Where would that have gotten me but into a deeper hole?" I took a bite of salad. "I might have been shipped off to Miami sooner."

"You certainly worked under deplorable conditions." Judy patted my hand, an emotional display I'd not seen before. "I wouldn't fault you for voicing your concerns."

I felt uncomfortable and took another bite of salad as a way to withdraw my hand. "The Bunnies adore you," Judy said as she too ate.

"Not all of them."

"No, not all of them. In any job there are a few whom we can't win over—no one can." Judy said as if to dismiss the sarcasm I had shown in my own answer.

"You had a wonderful rapport with the girls, except for a couple, "Judy continued. "But those girls wouldn't like anyone."

"Ummm." My comment was all I could muster for the moment. I wanted to know what Judy's ulterior motive could be. I had let my anger with Playboy control my feelings to the point that I didn't trust Judy's niceness. Perhaps she had no fear of being honest now that I would be gone.

We spent the rest of the meal discussing families, goals and mundane topics like fashion trends. I had an early flight the next morning, which allowed me to keep the evening short. We promised to write and keep in touch. By the end of the evening I felt I had missed an opportunity to have Judy as a closer and needed friend. With some regret, I remembered my indignation toward her when we first met. Although I believed Judy would never have gotten the Bunny Director's job if it hadn't been for her husband, I had changed my mind about her ability. I now saw her as a capable manager, if not dynamic.

In the restaurant lobby I bumped into Coco and Shar. I didn't know they had been such chums. I was surprised to find that I no longer cared.

I carefully inspected Shar. For once I felt better looking and better dressed than Shar and Coco put together. I had really dolled up for my last day at the Club and it paid off when Shar nearly stumbled over her own feet drinking in my glamorous new appearance. Once again I congratulated myself for going through the agony of the nose job. I also had more confidence, which no doubt showed and perhaps even startled Shar.

"Well, well, fancy what the cat dragged in," I said to the two I now recognized as untrustworthy conspirators. I would be happy to be far away from such cutthroat women.

"Hhhello," Shar stuttered.

Coco just smiled sheepishly.

"You look great," Shar commented.

"Yes, I do," I said and left. I could feel Shar and Coco's eyes following me. I wanted to skip.

New York's oppressive summer humidity wrapped itself around me the next day. My hair became more unruly with each minute of the ride to the farm, although I had again made sure I looked better than normal in case Angelo might also be there. I didn't want to confront him, but if I had to, I wanted to look so good he'd regret every mean thing he ever did to me. How silly! I knew that would never happen.

As I approached the farm, I spotted the boys waiting on the front porch. Had they already grown? As soon as they noticed the car pull up the dirt driveway, the two jumped up and burst across the lawn. They ran alongside the car until I parked. Huge smiles filled their faces, which were tanned from working the land with their uncle Paul. Their hair had been shorn once again into brush cuts.

On the way to the farm I had decided that the boys and my sister would visit Miami just before Carl and Greg returned to L.A. and school. It would be a family vacation in a town none of them had seen before. I would take full advantage of this odd relocation to a place I had never planned to go.

I circled my arms around both boys, who nearly knocked me to the ground by their exuberance. I vowed that our future together would always be as happy as that moment. Once back in L.A. we would not be separated again.

Spring 1980

In the spring of 1980 Tekkie and I sipped coffee in the sun-filled breakfast nook of my newly purchased house a block off Melrose in Los Angeles. As we basked in California's warmth, I reflected on my time at Playboy. "I often wonder—if I had been sent to the Miami Club right from the start, would I have stayed and become a Floridian?"

Tekkie shrugged. "Who cares? You've been so successful since you moved back. California suits you, especially the lack of humidity."

"What?"

"Your hair." Tekkie chuckled as she pointed to my curls, which were tamer in the nearly desert climate.

I looked out the window to the back yard filled with avocado and lemon trees. Not only had my hair improved, but I had regained my natural glow, which I credited to the mild California weather. Plus my view was far better than the brick wall outside my Chicago office.

On the other hand, I remembered fondly how the Miami Club had turned out to be a world of difference from Chicago. It ran well and I worked my desired eight-hour day. Most days went by so slowly and without any problems, I became bored and questioned a need for a

Bunny Mother at all.

"I attended Playboy's first Bunny Mother Conference while at Miami." I spoke softly. I looked away from the rich yellows and greens of the abundant trees to my sister. "The most significant memory of that event is Hugh Hefner. He made a typical appearance—long enough to take a PR picture surrounded by the Bunny Mothers. Once the shoot had finished, he fled. I doubt he knew any of our names or where we worked, and he probably didn't care."

I went to the coffee pot and filled a cup. Holding the cup with both hands I mused. "You know, Tekkie, all the Miami employees including the Bunnies loved their work. Most members were regular customers who became our friends. During the week Playboy employees hosted the customers. On the weekends, the roles reversed. Customers opened their homes and yachts to us. All the Miami employees also appeared to respect each other which left little space for the sort of cutthroat competition I witnessed in Chicago. Even the entertainment joined the happy family."

I sat at the table covered in a brightly colored floral cloth. "Every time I went into the Playmate Bar, the trio played "Girl Talk," one of my favorite tunes in those days. Each time they played it to a different tempo—jazz, samba, rock." I smiled, thinking about those delightful moments so different from Chicago.

"I guess the only drawback was my cut in salary. But even that wouldn't have made my life unpleasant since Miami had a lower cost of living than Chicago."

Tekkie shook her head. "No. Another drawback was the miserable humidity." Tekkie apparently wouldn't soon forget her college vacation in Miami's heat.

In all honesty none of that mattered any longer. After graduating from Pepperdine University with an MBA I became exactly what I'd dreamed—a successful business woman and business owner. I knew then I had made the correct decision. Yet I had struggled to arrive at that conclusion. A critical feature of my dilemma had become clear midway through my employment with Playboy when Gil Roswell had told me, "You have your feet in two-worlds—entertainment and business. You must choose one."

When I first arrived at Playboy, I didn't have the insight to think beyond my immediate needs—to get away from Clark, make more money to provide for my family, and achieve the Bunny Director's position, which would mean even more money and visibility. I hadn't planned further. Playboy showed me that I must choose a business career. And Playboy also showed me that such a career would not be possible in that male-oriented enterprise. I had to leave the Hutch to move forward with my dreams. Ironically, subsequently most of my clients came from the entertainment field.

The passing years eased the hurt I had felt while at the Chicago Playboy Club, especially since my resolve to leave opened up so many other opportunities. My personal success erased any resentment toward Playboy's management.

"More important," I said, "Carl and Greg wanted to be here. They needed a stable environment, which I'm now able to provide."

"Not to say you look more rested." Tekkie held her cup up for a refill. I grabbed the pot and poured.

"Do you ever miss Playboy?" she asked. "After all, it did have glamour."

I hesitated and then answered, "No. I never miss working for Playboy. But I regret losing contact with the many Bunny Mothers and Bunnies who turned into friends."

Not all the Playboy women I had met went on to happy lives. Although several became as successful as I had, most slipped into oblivion, never landing that Hollywood contract or marrying Mr. Wealthy Right.

"Do you remember Judy Wax?" I asked.

"Vaguely."

"The other day I got the shock of my life. In fact it was the most devastating news since I left the Hutch." My gaze rested on a picture just above my sister's head. "She and her husband, Sheldon, the Playboy Magazine Editor, died in a plane crash."

Tears filled my eyes as I recounted how I heard the news. I was listening to the radio while picking up the boys' clutter, and was so stunned by the report I collapsed onto the couch to listen. Judy and Sheldon left Chicago O'Hare on May 25, 1979 on American Flight 191 bound for Los Angeles. Judy's book, *Starting in the Middle*, had been released and they were on their way to a book conference. Shortly after takeoff the port side engine fell from the wing. Hardly 400 feet off the ground and less than a minute after takeoff, Flight 191 crashed and burst into flames. All 271 passengers and crew died.

I wiped away a tear and added, "In Judy's book she talked about her fear of flying. She died too young." I hung my head and whispered, "I wish I had kept in touch with her."

Tekkie placed her hand on top of mine. "We all let too many of our friends get away."

As we sat each with our own thoughts, I remembered a day years earlier. I'd perused a week's worth of the L.A. Times and discovered an obituary about Bobbie, Hugh Hefner's former girlfriend, executive assistant and confidant. The article reported that Bobbie, age 34, committed suicide by a drug overdose in Chicago on January 1, 1975.

As I read further, I was shocked by what had happened to Bobbie. In March 1974 Bobbie had been indicted on drug charges based on her relationship with a known and prosecuted drug dealer. While in custody, F.B.I. agents pressured her to give information about drug use in the Playboy world, specifically Hugh Hefner.

After reading about Bobbie, I wondered if the sadness created for those caught up in the Playboy fantasy world would ever end. The only one who appeared truly unscathed was Hugh Hefner.

We stayed like that for several moments. Tekkie broke the silence and asked, "Whatever happened to Carlie? I liked her."

"So did I." I patted Tekkie's hand. "She fulfilled her dreams and became successful in real estate. She now owns several properties." I gazed out the window again. "But she never married."

Several days after my conversation with Tekkie, I stopped at my credit union. To my amazement Priscilla, a former Chicago Bunny, and Nikko, a Room Director also from Chicago, stood just in front of me in line.

"Priscilla?" I asked.

Priscilla turned and let out a loud screech, which drew everyone's attention. "Alyce!" she screamed again, and hugged me.

Once our transactions were finished, we went for coffee and caught up on each other's lives. I discovered Priscilla and Nikko had an affair. While the two were employed with Playboy, Priscilla left her scoundrel husband for Nikko, but when Barry discovered the affair, he fired them both. Nikko's wealthy Greek family cut him out of his inheritance when they found out about Priscilla. The two eventually got into trouble for passing bad checks.

My heart went out to them as they told me what had become of them. I had always liked them both, and it saddened me to see how the years had taken a toll on their lives and looks. Once a handsome couple, they now looked haggard and much older than their true thirty-five years.

"We live from paycheck to paycheck," Priscilla said and shrugged. "Not what we had expected."

After they parted I reminded myself that I, too, could have become involved with many Room Directors, had I and they not left for better jobs. Just like the Bunnies and Bunny Mothers, the good ones always left.

The last Playboy Club closed in 1988, in Lansing, Michigan, and shortly afterwards, Coco called. I had not heard from her since I left Miami. We met for dinner. Now mature women we were able to reminisce as friends, rather than as the adversaries we had been forced to become because of Playboy's management style. Though Coco was still perky and pretty, I found it astounding and sobering that she had stayed with Playboy, never married and had only one child. Yet she seemed satisfied.

While we chatted, I realized we were similar when it came to relationships. I hadn't married again. Clark and I were no longer lovers. Rather, we'd become life-long friends.

During that dinner Coco mentioned that Hef was hosting a party at his L.A. Mansion, which had become his home after he vacated the Chicago estate. Playboy, Inc. no longer meant Clubs. The corporation concentrated on the magazine, videos and T.V. show.

"No," I answered. "I really don't want to go."

"Neither do I." Coco's response surprised me, but so had her sudden appearance.

We parted ways that evening, knowing we had made amends. We went our separate ways, each content in the life we chose.

Yet I briefly wondered if I should have gone to the party, because I had learned as a business woman that you never burn bridges. More to the point, though, my conversation with Coco brought on some inner reflection. I was right to be proud of what I had accomplished.

I had sorted my life out and met goals I had set the year I took the Bunny Mother job—personal stability, a solid income, career mobility. I was a respected business woman, and although still attractive, I was pursued for my brains.

How satisfying.

About the Author

Tekla Dennison Miller, www.teklamiller.com is a former Michigan warden of a men's maximum security and a women's multi level prisons. She is also the author of two novels: *Life Sentences* and *Inevitable Sentences* and two memoirs: *The Warden Wore Pink* and *A Bowl of Cherries*. She is a national speaker on criminal justice and women's issues. Alyce Bonura, the Mother Rabbit, is the principal owner of Bonura Plus, Inc. www.ambtaxpros.com a tax consulting business that specializes in entertainment taxes and located in southern California.

Made in the USA
Lexington, KY
03 September 2014